The Impact
of Oil
on a Developing Country

The IMPACT
of OIL
on a DEVELOPING COUNTRY

The Case of Nigeria

AUGUSTINE A. IKEIN

Foreword by Letha A. See

New York
Westport, Connecticut
London

Copyright Acknowledgment

Tables A.7a, A.7b, A.8, and A.9 are from *International Petroleum Encyclopedia*, vol. 21 (Tulsa, OK: Penwell, 1988). Used with permission of the publisher.

Library of Congress Cataloging-in-Publication Data

Ikein, Augustine.
    The impact of oil on a developing country : the case of Nigeria / Augustine Ikein ; foreword by Letha A. See.
        p.   cm.
    Includes bibliographical references.
    ISBN 0-275-93364-4 (alk. paper)
    1. Petroleum industry and trade—Nigeria. 2. Nigeria—Economic policy. 3. Nigeria—Social policy.   I. Title.
HD9577.N52I38   1990
338.2'7282'09669—dc20   90-31185

British Library Cataloguing in Publication Data is available.

Library of Congress Catalog Card Number: 90-31185
ISBN: 0-275-93364-4

First published in 1990

Praeger Publishers, One Madison Avenue, New York, NY 10010
An imprint of Greenwood Publishing Group, Inc.

Printed in the United States of America

The paper used in this book complies with the Permanent Paper Standard issued by the National Information Standards Organization (Z39.48-1984).

10 9 8 7 6 5 4 3 2 1

To my father, mother, and uncle, who toiled so hard for my education. (They are all called back to be with the Lord in His Celestial City Where Peace Reigns. . . .)

Chief Asangwua Ikein

Madam Bomo-Pregha Ikein (nee Sokoromo)

Luke A. Sokoromo; and

to the victims of mineral exploration and exploitation around the world.

God, Grant me the serenity to accept the things I cannot change, the courage to change the things I can, and the wisdom to know the difference.

Contents

Tables

Figures

Foreword

Professor Ikein's timely book, *The Impact of Oil on a Developing Country: The Case of Nigeria,* is being published at just the right time — a time of increasingly complex relationships between the oil producing and consuming countries, with each seeking to optimize its interests and minimize its costs in both the international oil trade and in politics.

An added dimension is seen in the role of transnational corporations located in the host countries and in their link to the international economic and political order, particularly in the movement of strategic resources from producers to consumers around the world. The activities of these transnational corporations have strong economic and political influence on the host communities. Worst of all, these corporations often appear to give little or no attention to the human costs of their mineral exploration in the third world.

The book is readable and laudable — the work of a brilliant researcher who possesses a great deal of integrity and who has unleashed hard facts and expresses them clearly and accurately. Professor Ikein uses rigorous statistical analyses in his work to tease out significant trends in the socioeconomic development and growth pattern of a developing country.

He has utilized an integrative approach in providing an insightful perspective on the behavior of the oil companies and the producer states, and the concomitant effect on the lives of the inhabitants of the mineral producing areas.

Previous studies on the subject have been concerned primarily with trends in production, markets, revenues, and economic growth, which are no doubt helpful to the oil companies and to the producer government. So far, however, inadequate attention has been directed toward determining the impact on the mineral producing areas in the third world, particularly the impact on the welfare of the indigenous population. Dr. Ikein has taken a multidimensional approach and moved beyond the obvious in helping one to understand the linkage between the performance of the oil industry and the pattern of Nigeria's economic growth and development, as well as the implications of this for the oil producing areas. He has also extended his analyses beyond Nigeria to draw attention to the many similarities and differences among impacts of extractive economies (with specific exemplars) around the world.

It is worth adding here comments on this exemplary work on Nigeria from respected scholars on the subject and the area.

Nicholas Balabkins (Lehigh University, Pennsylvania) writes, "Dr. Ikein has written a book about the Nigerian economy, driven by one product, its high-quality oil. He also details the unintended economic, social, and political consequences of such a mono-crop economy. It is an epistemologically broad-based inquiry, which will delight and inspire all who seek wisdom and enlightenment about Nigeria and other sovereign countries of Africa."

E. Wayne Nafziger (Kansas State University) commented, "At independence in 1960, few observers anticipated that the story of Nigeria's economic development would be so linked to oil. During the euphoria of the oil boom in 1975, Nigeria's planners stated 'there will be no savings and foreign exchange constraint during the Third Plan [1975-80] and beyond.' One year later, in response to the overheated economy by demands for new programs and higher wages, Nigeria's Head of State Olusegun Obasanjo pointed out the petroleum revenue was not a cure-all.

'Though this country has great potential, she is not yet a rich nation. . . . Our resources from oil are not enough to satisfy the yearnings, aspirations, and genuine needs of our people, development, and social services.' By 1989 Nigeria's economic descent had been so protracted that the World Bank classified Nigeria, for the first time, as a low-income country along with Togo, Uganda, Pakistan, Yemen, and the like. A top Nigerian economic official indicated that striking it rich on oil in the 1970s was 'like a man who wins a lottery and builds a castle. He can't maintain it, and then has to borrow to move out.'

Professor Ikein explains Nigeria's sluggishness in terms of poor economic management during the oil boom of the 1970s and the oil glut of the 1980s. His approach integrates economics, politics, history, and geography, but views Nigeria and other extractive economies as part of an international system. Oil plays a central part in federal regional strength in the civil war, revenue allocation, public management, transnational corporations, technology transfer, the development of indigenous skills, the neglect of agricultural exports, and the social costs borne by producing areas. Dr. A. A. Ikein's analysis has implications not only for the future of Nigeria but also for other extractive third world economies."

One readily senses that Professor Ikein assumes a balanced posture, with no personal animus involved in his analyses of the impending problems and solutions. However, he is straightforward and direct in his assertion that the oil companies and the government have an obligation to effect better stewardship for the host communities. This fine scholar is willing to seek truth and to call attention to apparent inequity while remaining true to the scholarly objective.

Letha A. (Lee) See
Associate Professor
University of Georgia, Athens

Preface

The introduction of a new technology in a developing country to stimulate the engine of growth calls for change, either for better or for worse. The impact of the oil industry on a developing country such as Nigeria is no exception; it has created positive externalities, or derived benefits, along with negative externalities, or social costs, to the Nigerian society.

An examination of previous studies on the Nigerian oil industry shows that there has been too much emphasis on the economic significance of oil, to the extent that the human consequences, coupled with social costs to the host communities, are ignored, distorted, or simply forgotten. Apparently, resource development and economic progress are not synonymous with the overall social and economic development of the producing areas. Hence, the study here presented proposes to provide a comprehensive and fair analysis of the impact of the oil industry on the oil producing areas over a period of nearly thirty-two years (from the beginning of its historical development to its growth through years of boom and burst), with a prognosis for the future.

In this study, the author employs a multidimensional approach in exploring the relationship between the performance of the oil industry and the pattern of Nigeria's national and regional development, and its implication for the oil producing areas. The subject matter is presented in such a way as to characterize both the political and economic transformation of the country as well as its concomitant development strategies.

Chapter 1 discusses the historical development of the oil industry in Nigeria, which has links with the country's once celebrated palm oil trade. The palm oil trade was crucial in influencing British interest in annexing the territory once named the "oil protectorate" during the European scramble for Africa in the nineteenth century; the same area (the Niger Delta) harbors most of Nigeria's oil industry today.

Nigeria was established as a prospective oil country in the 1950's. Since then, however, the bulk of its oil activities has been contracted to foreign oil firms. Chapter 1 provides considerable background information on the behavior of the oil companies in partnership with the host government and examines the impact of the oil industry on the indigenous population in the oil producing areas with references to ecological factors such as education, health, housing, power, roads, water, and pollution. These factors are thought to most influence the well-being of the inhabitants and are also the government's chief concerns in development. The author presupposes that when a country profits from its natural resources, the quality of life of its citizenry will also improve. The truth of this relationship will be examined in further detail.

Chapter 2 discusses Nigeria as a developing country, with specific analyses of its geography, people, important minerals, and the producing areas where the minerals are located. It also discusses the political transition of the country from its colonial status to independence, along with an analysis of the country's mixed economic system. There is an in-depth analysis of both civil and military administration with special emphasis on the relationship between oil, politics, and development. Chapter 2 also reviews development planning theory and development planning projects that have taken place in Nigeria since 1946. Furthermore, there is a discussion of the role of oil in national and regional development, particularly with respect to the distribution of infrastructural facilities in the country and the condition of the social service delivery system in general, with specific reference to the condition of social services provided in the oil producing areas.

Chapter 3 examines selected studies of extractive industries in both developed and developing countries. It attempts to determine similarities and/or differences among the impacts of extractive economies around the world. Additionally, the writer discusses several substantive studies on oil impact assessment and the models applied by previous researchers on the subject. The author concludes that the impact of extractive economies on developed countries is different from their impact on developing countries (or third world characters existing as an enclave in developed countries).

Chapter 4 reviews substantive studies of the Nigerian oil industry, including the problems of oil spillage incidents and human and ecological problems, and stresses the need to establish a comprehensive mitigation policy.

Chapter 5 contains this book's statement of purpose, a formal exposition of impact assessment methodology, the method of data collection, the model applied, the research design, the hypotheses tested, and the method of analysis. The study sought to test the relationship between the impact of oil production and selected ecological factors or social indicators in Nigeria. The author assumed that changes in the socioeconomic development between oil producing areas and non-oil producing areas would be significantly different. An analysis of variance was employed to determine relative impact levels. It was shown that the spillover benefits to non-oil producing areas in terms of the development of the selected social indicators were statistically more significant than those to oil producing areas.

While the study was unable to refute the main proposition that there is a correlation between the trend of oil production and changes in social and economic activities in Nigeria, there was a correlation found between the trend of oil production and increased social costs to the producing areas. The statistical analysis of the study indicated that the nonproducing areas (states) gained more socioeconomic benefits from oil resource than did the oil producing areas (states). The source of imbalance could be linked to the federal government's distributional pattern of social and economic infrastructures in the country. The imbalance could also be attributed to structural inequities inherent in federal revenue-sharing formulae. This imbalance is not the fault of the nonproducing areas, but rather the result of an ineffective national distribution policy, which requires revision in order to meet its objectives of a balanced economy and equal benefits for all. Chapter 6 shows that the mere existence of an extractive industry to boost export receipts for the producer government in the third world does not necessarily cause balanced development in that area.

Chapter 7 discusses recommendations for the development of oil producing areas. It proposes specific steps that the government and the oil firms should take to minimize the social cost to oil producing areas and outlines the relevant community development planning that should take place in the mineral areas.

Chapter 8 makes a prognostic analysis of the future of oil and the mineral producing areas. The discussion in this chapter draws the reader's attention to the dependent nature of the Nigerian oil industry, which is influenced by international trade and geopolitics and is particularly susceptible to the erratic behavior of oil producing and consuming countries. The author analyzes the behavior patterns of oil consumer nations and of oil producing nations (OPEC and non-OPEC), and explains how their relationship in the international market can influence, directly or indirectly, the behavior and performance of the Nigerian oil industry. Also included is considerable discussion of future oil production, pricing, and revenue projections for Nigeria, extended to cover the fate of oil producing areas in the post-oil era.

Finally, the author relates systems theory to Nigeria's unique combination of elements. He supports the view that a decay in part will ultimately affect the rest of society if the negative externalities associated with oil activities remain unabated. The author has also employed an ecclesiastical (Islamic and Christian) view of systems theory to explain the need to care for the mineral producing areas through socially responsible behavior that balances economic interest with human ecology.

Acknowledgments

This work would not have come to fruition without the support and guidance of my family, friends, and colleagues in academia. First, a special gratitude to all previous researchers who have either stimulated my thoughts or given permission for me to use their work on the subject. Then, I wish especially to thank the members of my family: Adiledi, Abadere, Bara Sokoromo (Barbara Soky), Stella Ikein, Timi, Abidi A. Ikein, Bomo-Pregha, and Esweni Ikein, and the rest of the Ikeins and Sokoromos, whose continuing forbearance and patience during my studies encouraged me to achieve my educational goals.

My deepest appreciation goes to Dr. Letha See, Dr. M. Darlington, Dr. Lyle, Dr. Murty, Dr. Attah, and Dr. C. O. Alfred-Ockiya for their invaluable guidance. They have stimulated my thoughts without imposing their own views. I am greatly indebted to them for their constructive criticism and continual encouragement during the entire preparation of this work.

Additionally, a very special thanks goes to the staff of Atlanta University Library, to my typist, Mrs. Meredith Whiteman Lewis, for her secretarial assistance during manuscript preparation, and to Candace Krongold for her editorial work and final manuscript preparation. Also, my appreciation goes to Dr. Juanita Clarke for the contribution of her time and editorial input, and to the library staff of the Nigerian National Petroleum Corporation (in Lagos and Port Harcourt), the Nigerian Institute of International Affairs, the Federal Office of Statistics, Lagos, Nigeria, Talladega College, Alabama, and Praeger Publishers in New York for their assistance and cooperation in bringing this work to fruition. Also, I wish to express my deep appreciation to the following persons, for they have been particularly generous where I am concerned: Dr. Ibiba Sasime, the late Madam Lily Asangwa, Ezelle and Ethel Spann, Rufus M. Kpun, F. K. Tebepina, Walter Asangwua, Charles Sokoromo, Madam Ekpe Kpe Gai, Ati Abagwo, Victor Ikoloms, Chief Wozi, Mrs. Dorcas Sokoromo, G. M. Odumgba, Steve Orudiakumo, Fred Ogola, Isaac Oyebade, Dr. E. Ogoun, Tobi Egba, Adebayo Anjorin, R. Abah, Bountin Akpuruku, the late Chief Abasi, and the late J. T. Sokoromo.

Finally, it is said that one should always remember those who have helped them along the way. For this reason, I would like to personally remember these people: Edna Green, H. E. Dickson, Professor U. Akeh, Asuquo Ekpo, O. Jacobs, O. Odaji, O. Ben-Walson, Dr. A. A. Iruka, Dr. W. Awadzi, and the late Elvorah. I wish to pay a special tribute to the late Chief Ogio for his selfless service to his country and his community. I am deeply grateful to all of you.

1

The Evolution of the Oil Industry in Nigeria

Nigeria, which has been among the world's leading producers of palm oil for over two centuries, has suddenly become one of the top ten oil producing nations of the world, with an average production of 2.3 million barrels a day. Nigeria's oil industry has an interesting element in common with the country's once celebrated palm oil industry. The palm oil trade was a crucial factor in influencing the British to maintain and later annex the territory (the Oil Rivers Protectorate) in the latter part of the nineteenth century, at the peak of the European scramble for Africa. This is the same location that today harbors most of the Nigerian oil exploration (Obidake 1982).[1] As a result of its palm oil industry, this area of the country — the swampy Niger Delta with its maze of tortuous creeks and rivers — rightly earned for itself at that time the name "Oil Rivers." Since then, the word "oil" in Nigeria has become synonymous with Oil Rivers or the Niger Delta. Today the area remains an important site of Nigerian oil production, and there is a strong indication that the greatest promise for Nigeria lies in its petroleum producing region. One of the states now occupying this region proudly labels itself the "Oil Rich Rivers State." In the mid-1960s, oil enthusiasts in the region began to assert that it would emerge as the "Kuwait of West Africa," a position that has actually been maintained in a regional context. For a long time, then, Nigeria has been firmly placed on the world petroleum map. Coincidentally, it is important to note that this same region, the oil-rich Niger Delta, has once again justified its name in the second half of the present century. It is Nigeria's leading oil region just as it was during the former palm oil trade. It is, in fact, safe to claim that for Nigeria, the exploitation of oil resources seems to be the single most significant economic development for more than two decades. Although the Nigerian oil industry may be traced back to the first decade of this century, its major development has occurred only within the last three decades. The geological and geophysical report (Ayodele 1985) indicates that Nigeria has large volumes of crude oil deposits along the coastal states; moreover, by 1957, it was established through exploratory activities that the most prospective accumulation of crude oil was in areas of the Niger Delta.

Although the Nigerian oil industry itself is relatively young, it has become a very important sector in the nation's quest for socioeconomic development. The development of the Nigerian oil industry has been governed by several economic policy principles such as those related to licenses and leases signed with foreign oil companies. Prominent among the earliest oil development policies is one that was established by the British colonial government in 1914. Contained in Chapter 130 of what could be termed "the laws of Nigeria,"[2] the statement (Mineral Oil Act Laws of Nigeria, Chapter 130, 1914) specified that "the power conferred upon the Governor General to grant licenses and leases for mineral oils shall be exercised subject to the condition that no lease or license shall be granted except to a British subject or to a British company." This means that the development of the Nigerian oil industry was initially made a British monopoly; however, in light of the political developments since 1914, many oil decrees and legislative acts have emerged such that the British monopoly in Nigerian oil industry is no longer sustained. In 1969, for example, the Petroleum Decree was promulgated to repeal the entire 1914 Mineral Oil Act. This military decree vested the ownership and control of petroleum in the state government. The decree induced changes such as (1) the reduction in duration of leases from thirty years to twenty years; (2) the Nigerianization of the vital organs of the oil industry; and (3) the establishment of governmental control over oil operations. As part of its development, Nigeria's oil policy allowed foreign oil companies to engage in oil exploration in the country at their own risk. The Nigerian government would participate as a partner only if commercial production of oil was established by the contracting oil companies. Consequently, Nigeria's efforts to engage in all phases of petroleum development and control fostered the establishment of the Nigerian National Oil Corporation in 1969. By 1974 the corporation had succeeded in getting 55 percent equity participation for the government. Subsequently, in 1977 there was a merger of the Nigerian National Oil Corporation and the Nigerian Ministry of Petroleum Resources which resulted in the establishment of the Nigerian National Petroleum Corporation (NNPC) which functioned in a manner similar to the Nigerian Oil Corporation. In 1979 the Nigerian National Petroleum Corporation succeeded in raising the government's equity participation in oil company shares to 60 percent. According to the Federal Government of Nigeria Report, 1982:

The Nigerian National Petroleum Corporation is charged with the responsibility of looking after the government's interest in the oil industry as well as engaging in the exploration, drilling, production, refining and exportation of oil. The NNPC is also responsible for the installation of . . . depots at strategic points to facilitate the distribution of refined petroleum and [to] minimize oil shortages in the country.[3]

Nigeria was established as a prospective oil country in the 1950s.

Nigeria has been associated with oil product since 1956 when an Anglo Dutch Consortium, Shell D'Arcy, made the first commercial oil discovery at Oloibiri in the Niger Delta. Two years later, Shell (now Shell Petroleum Development Company) started production from the Oloibiri field in Rivers State at the rate of 5,100 barrels per day. Output rose steadily to 415,000 barrels per day by 1966 and dropped to 142,000 barrels per day during the civil war. Following the end of the war in 1970, production reached 560,000 barrels per day and in 1972 Nigeria hit 2 million barrels per day and became a major producer.[4]

The production of oil for export started in Nigeria in 1958 with the production of 1.8 million barrels, valued at about 176 million naira. Currently, the race for oil exploration and exploitation involves sixteen multinational oil corporations representing U.S., Dutch, Japanese, British, Italian, German and French interests, with the Nigerian government's continued participation.

THE EVOLUTION OF STATE PARTICIPATION IN THE OIL INDUSTRY

Prior to 1979, the Nigerian oil industry was controlled mostly by foreign oil companies.[5] These multinational oil corporations are vertically integrated: they control the oil industry from production through marketing, which enables them to maximize their profit objective and resist the transfer of technology. Hence, despite the "worthy" participation of the host government, its role has not been remarkably different from that of a passive tax collector. A semblance of progress has been made through the activities of the state-owned oil corporation in gaining some access to technology and the marketing of petroleum products, but this would seem to reflect more of a compromise than actual state control of the country's oil industry. According to Michael Tanzer (1980), the role of the state as tax collector is a product of colonialism, its production-sharing role a product of neocolonialism, and 100 percent state control a product of the drive for economic independence in underdeveloped countries.[6] This could be a reflection of the progressive phases of state participation in the oil industry, with the ultimate aim being to control its own economic destiny. The state's effort to participate in the oil industry is designed to reduce the economic power of the multinational oil companies, to share derived profits, and to allow the government to partake in all phases of petroleum development. It is an attempt to obtain the best deal on the country's oil resource.

The producer state's desire to participate and the increased nationalism in the oil industry can be traced to the behavior of oil companies with respect to resource production and pricing.

In the early 1900s through the 1950s, oil multinationals had effective control of all phases of petroleum development. The producer states did not exercise real power in either the management or operations of the oil industry except for receipts on royalties. The weakened or passive position of the producer governments at that time could be linked to their lack of knowledge about the value and uses of the oil resource; thus, the multinational companies virtually controlled the oil industry. The situation, however, began to change in the early 1960s, a period marked by political tensions between host countries and the oil multinationals. It became obvious that the oil multinationals' domination in all phases of petroleum development did not allow for equitable sharing of profits. The producer states had for a long time collected royalty payments based on "posted prices" which the oil companies deliberately kept lower than real market prices. The royalty payments to the producer states were, then, below the realized market value. This culminated in the rise of nationalism and the formation of an international oil cartel called the Organization of Petroleum Exporting Countries (OPEC).

The formation of international oil cartels (such as OPEC and the Organization of Arab Petroleum Exporting Countries, OAPEC) and the subsequent nationalization of oil companies within each producer state has led to increased state participation in the oil industry and gives those states the collective potential to raise the price of oil. Although a number of African states belong to OPEC (notably Libya, Algeria, Nigeria, and Gabon), it is regrettable that African oil producers as a group lack collective regional cooperation and coordination. This leaves African states in a precarious bargaining position. It cannot be otherwise, for oil companies are large, worldwide, interlocking conglomerates with powerful political and economic machinery which individual African nations can rarely match.[7] This added disadvantage makes African producer states particularly vulnerable to the secretive and manipulative behavior of the oil companies. However, African nations have begun to recognize the advantages of collective bargaining power. The emerging African Petroleum Producers Association (APPA), founded in 1987 and currently comprised of Algeria, Angola, Benin, Cameroon, Congo, Egypt, the Ivory Coast, Gabon, Libya, Nigeria, and Zaire may become an influential cartel akin to OPEC or OAPEC, but based in Africa.[8] As a group, it holds 7.1 percent of the world's oil reserves and 5.1 percent of its natural gas reserves. Africa holds 58,836,620 billion barrels of proven oil reserves and 226,730 billion cubic feet of natural gas reserves.[9]

Developing mineral producing countries have begun to take an active role in the development of their resource. This is evidenced not only by the collective interest demonstrated by the cartel power of OPEC and OAPEC, but also by the emergence of continental organizations such as APPA and OLADE (Organization for Latin American Development of Energy). OLADE is aimed at harnessing the cooperation and integration of Latin American and Caribbean countries to foster optimal utilization of their regional energy resources.[10]

These oil producers have joined to enhance their role in oil production and commercialization of petroleum products. In Nigeria, operating oil companies are alleged to have repeatedly engaged in price manipulation to increase company profits. Such corporate behavior inevitably leads to conflict. With traditional secrecy, the oil companies do not disclose what profits they make on Nigerian operations.[11] However, the Nigerian government has strengthened its bargaining power through increased equity participation in most oil companies operating in the country. Moreover, the state-owned Nigerian National Oil Corporation is the vehicle through which the government participates in all phases of petroleum development with specific agreements regarding profit sharing and conditions for royalty collection. The Nigerian National Petroleum Corporation (NNPC) was established by Decree 33 of 1977 to replace its predecessor, the Nigerian National Oil Corporation. As Alexander Kemp (1987) has written, "The NNPC has a major share in all new concessions. The fiscal system has been based on a package incorporating posted prices with royalty profits, tax, state participation and until 1982, a domestic market obligation at 'low' prices. The system of posted prices has been important primarily because it determines the base for royalty and income tax."

The posted price is determined according to the following formula:

Posted Price = Official Sales Price – (Profit Margin plus 15 percent of Technical Costs)/0.88

where the official sales price is the price that NNPC receives on contract sales. The petroleum profits tax is levied on values determined by the posted price minus the sum of the royalty and the national production cost allowance. The rate has been 85 percent since 1979.[12]

However, the preceding terms are no longer in force. New arrangements and agreements have been made. According to Alexander Kemp (1987), by late 1985 Nigeria had difficulty in attracting investment and proposed revised fiscal terms. First, the government took royalty plus petroleum profit tax; this was calculated using official sale prices rather than posted prices in accordance with the following formula:

Revised Government Take = OP - 0.85(TC) - ITC

where

OP = Offset Price = B x RP

RP   =   Realizable price for oil based on market values

B   = $K[(1 - r)0.85 + r]$

K   =   1.0227 or whatever is prescribed by the Minister of Petroleum Resources

r   =   royalty rate

TC   =   Annual operating costs and depreciation under the Petroleum Profits Act of 1959, as amended.

ITC   =   Investment Tax Credit Under the Petroleum Profits Act.

As a part of the government, fiscal systems respond to changes in economic conditions. The 1985 and 1986 stipulations included a new fiscal system designed to deal with the new levels of oil prices. According to the new terms, when the official price equals the realized price, the tax take is not significantly different from that in the earlier system. Again, under the 1986 agreement, oil producing companies can be required to increase the NNPC's share of production. The companies are allowed a 50 percent national profit margin on sales.[13] With these fiscal arrangements, the Nigerian government has strengthened its bargaining position by increasing its share of oil company profits.

In Nigeria, the major producer is Shell-BP, followed by Gulf, Mobil, Phillips, Agip, SAFRAP, Occidental-Tenneco, Diminex, Texaco-Chevron, and Texaco (Table 1.1). By 1979 (with the establishment of the Nigerian National Petroleum Corporation in 1977) the government of Nigeria had succeeded in purchasing 60 percent of the equity shares of all major oil companies.[14] However, with the nationalization (Ayodele 1985) of the British oil company Shell-BP (which had significant implications for the apartheid government of South Africa) the Nigerian government gained ownership of nearly 80 percent of Shell-BP (now named African Petroleum), the leader and pioneer of the Nigerian oil

Table 1.1

Nigeria: Oil Companies Operating in 1985
(list of rightholders)

			Sq. km. held as of 31 Dec. 1984	Changes in area
AGIP 1	Nigerian AGIP Oil Co. (optr)	20.0%	5,259.00	0
	Nigerian National Petroleum Corp.	60.0%		
	Phillips Oil Co. (Nigeria) Ltd.	20.0%		
AGIP EN	AGIP Energy & Natural Resource	100.0%	19,664.70	0
ASHLAND	Ashland Oil Nigeria	100.0%	1,119.00	0
ELF 1	ELF Nigeria (optr)	40.0%	8,255.60	0
	Nigerian National Petroleum Corp.	60.0%		
GULF 1	Gulf Oil Co. (Nigeria) Ltd. (optr)	40.0%	14,138.00	0
	Nigerian National Petroleum Corp.	60.0%		
MOBIL 2	Mobil Producing Nigeria (optr)	50.0%	974.00	0
	Sun DX Nigeria	12.5%		
	Tenneco Oil of Nigeria	37.5%		
NIGUS	Nigus Petroleum Nigeria	100.0%	1,025.00	0
NNPC	Nigerian National Petroleum Corp.	100.0%	21,135.00	0
PAN 1	Nigerian National Petroleum Corp.	60.0%	1,005.00	0
	Pan Ocean Oil Co. (Nigeria) Ltd. (optr)	40.0%		
PHILLIPS	Phillips Oll Co. (Nigeria) Ltd.	100.0%	232.00	0
SHELL 1	Nigerian National Petroleum Corp.	80.0%	31,909.00	0
	Shell Pet. Dev. Co. of Nigeria (optr)	20.0%		
TEXACO 1	Chevron Oil Co. (Nigeria)	20.0%	2,570.00	0
	Nigerian National Petroleum Corp.	60.0%		
	Texaco Overseas (Nigeria) Pet. (optr)	20.0%		
Former Rightholder:				
ELF NIS	ELF Aquitame Nigeria Services	100.0%	0	-23.320
	Country Total		109,938.00	-23.320

Source: Terisa Turner, "Oil Workers and Oil Burst in Nigeria," *Africa Today,* Vol. 33, No. 4, 1986, p. 36.

industry. In addition to holding equity shares, the Nigerian government owns all of the refineries, which together have a daily capacity of 260,000 barrels of oil. By 1988 Nigeria had improved its oil production to 1,238.6 million barrels per day (mbd) and its refining capacity to 270,000 billion cubic feet (bcf). Nigeria is expected to export liquified natural gas by 1995.[15]

The Nigerian federal government, then, has become a mediator between local affiliates of international oil corporations and the world market by joining OPEC in 1971 and by purchasing controlling shares in local affiliates. The government's equity interest in the oil companies appears to be in compliance with OPEC's Resolution XVI Article 90 of June 1968, which states that all member countries must acquire participation interest in the operations of the oil companies in their territories. OPEC's time table was that each member country shall acquire 51 percent participation interest by 1982.[16] On Nigeria's control of its oil and natural gas resources, Momodu Kassim-Momodu has pointed out:

In Nigeria, the entire property and control of all mineral oils and natural gas in, under, or upon any lands vest in the State. Mineral oils and natural gas under the territorial waters of Nigeria or found in, under, or upon any land which forms part of the continental shelf are also owned by the State. Consequently, any person who wishes to undertake any activity for the exploration for or production of mineral oils or natural gas requires a formal written authorization of the Minister of Petroleum Resources. Such a formal authorization is in the form of

1. an oil exploration license (OEL) which confers on the licensee the right to carry out aerial and surface geological and geophysical surveys excluding drilling below 300 feet;

2. an oil prospecting license (OPL) which grants to the licensee the exclusive right to explore, carry away and dispose of the petroleum discovered and won in the area covered by the lessee; or

3. an oil mining lease (OML) which confers on the lessee the exclusive right to search for, win, work, carry away, and dispose of all petroleum discovered and won in the lessee's operation subject to the terms of the lease. An OML also contains regulatory terms and standardization provisions which relate to the lessee's operations.

The duration of an OEL is [a] one-year term which may be renewed for one further year. The license terminates on the December 31 following the date on which it was granted. The Minister may grant it for less than one year.

The duration of an OPL is determined by the Minister but [may] not [extend] for more than five years including any periods of renewal. Before the enactment of the Petroleum Act in 1969, there were some OPLs given for seven years for continental shelf areas. Grants for territorial waters and land areas were given for five years.

For the OMLs, the current ones were granted under two legal regimes. Most were granted under the Mineral Oils Act [of] 1914, and the others under the Petroleum Act [of] 1969. Two types of OMLs were granted under the Mineral Oils Act [of 1914]. One was for the primary-term duration of 30 years for certain land and territorial water areas, while the other type was for 40 years for continental shelf areas.

Under the Petroleum Act [of] 1969, the term of an OML must not exceed 20 years.[17]

On the legal relationships in the Nigerian oil industry, Yinka Omorogbe (1987) asserts that:

Under Joint Venture arrangements, there are three separate agreements that define the relationship between Nigeria and the oil producing countries. These are:

(a) The Participation Agreement: . . . The interest acquired by the Government through [the] NNPC is referred to as "participating interest" in:
   (i)   the oil mining leases;
   (ii) the fixed and moveable assets of the Company in Nigeria . . .
   (iii) the working capital applicable to the operations of the oil mining leases . . .

Table 1.2

Concessions: Oil Prospecting Licenses (OPLs) and Oil Mining Licenses (OMLs)

Name of Company	Country of Original Incorporation	Ownership	AREA (square miles)			Location
			Onshore	Offshore	Total	
Gulf Oil Co. (Nigeria) Ltd.	USA	Gulf Oil Corp. (U.S. private) 100%	3,965	2,890	6,855	Anambra, Imo (onshore), Lagos(offshore), Rivers (onshore), Bendel (on & offshore), CRS (onshore), Oyo, Ondo, Ogun
Mobil Producing Nigeria Ltd.	USA	Mobil Oil Co. (U.S. private) 100%	–	2,025	2,025	Cross River State
Nigeria Agip Oil Co. Ltd.	Nigeria	ENI (Ente Nazionale Idrocarbum, Indian govt.) 50%	2,031	–	2,031	Anambra, Imo, Bendel, and Rivers States
Phillips Oil Co. Nigeria Ltd.	USA	Phillips Petroleum Co. (U.S. private) 100%	1,401	–	1,401	Bendel, Western States
Safrap Nigeria Ltd.	Nigeria	Societe Africaine d'Exploration Petroliere (SAFRAX) (French govt.) 50%	9,336	–	9,336	Benue, Plateau, Imo, Anambra, Kwara, Bendel, Ondo, Ogun, Oyo, and Rivers
Shell Petroleum Development Co. of Nigeria Ltd.	Nigeria	Royal Dutch Shell Petroleum Co. (Dutch, British, others)	14,992	3,906	18,898	Imo, Anambra (onshore), Kwara (onshore), Bendel (offshore and onshore)
Tenneco Co. of Nigeria Ltd.	USA	Cumberland Corp. (whollly-owned subsidiary of Tennessee Gas Transmission Co.) 50% Swiclair	1,380	–	1,380	Bendel, Rivers States

Name of Company	Country of Original Incorporation	Ownership	A R E A (square miles) Onshore	A R E A (square miles) Offshore	A R E A (square miles) Total	Location
Texaco Overseas (Nigeria) Petroleum Ltd.	USA	California Asiatic Oil Co. (U.S. private) 50%; Texas Overseas Petroleum Co. (U.S. private) 50%	—	1,931	1,931	Rivers State
Union Oil Nigeria	USA	Union Oil Co. of California (U.S. private)	—	1,000	1,000	Lagos State

Sources: "Oil and Nigerian Development," *Development Outlook*, Vol. 1 no. 3 (August 1986): 29-30.

(b) <u>The Operating Agreement</u>: The operating agreement spells out the legal relationships between the owners of the leases or concessions and lays down the rules and procedure for the joint development of the area concerned, and property jointly owned by the two parties. The term "joint property," under Nigerian operating agreements includes expenditure for practically all activities and services of the oil company, e.g. salaries, staff housing schemes, pensions, gratuities, etc. . . .

(c) <u>Heads of Agreement</u>: . . . This agreement provides *interalia,* that there shall be undivided interests in the rights granted by the applicable oil mining leases with respect to petroleum under the contract area, and that each interest owner will share therein to the extent of its equity participation. . . .

The Production Sharing Contract

The term "production sharing contract" refers essentially to arrangements where the foreign firm and the government share the output of the operation in predetermined propositions.[18]

The state has become the manager of Nigeria's national income and has maintained a tight grip on the purse strings.[19] In general, the years 1973–79 marked the use of sovereign acts by major oil producing governments. As these governments became more active in the global economic and commercial domain, they continued to claim and enjoy immunity for their activities, even in a competitive environment. In recognition of their new bargaining strength and petrowealth, producer nations were able to raise the price of oil, nationalize certain companies, dictate the agenda to operating oil companies, and generally assume political control of the international oil industry.[20] Although producer nations (like Nigeria) have made gainful strides, their relative bargaining power has been eroded by their continuous dependence on the economies and technology of oil consuming nations. In addition, their bargaining strength continues to be controlled by the demand and supply of oil and the degree of essentiality of oil in the world market. Nevertheless, a close look at the phases of negotiations and agreements between oil companies and producer governments shows that they seem to have succeeded in reducing conflict and enhancing the harmony of their mutual oil interests. Still, the issue of technology transfer remains problematic. The progress of the bargaining process between the oil companies and producer nations since 1901 is well demonstrated by Isaac Igweonwu (1988). His analysis is divided into three phases. First, the hegemony phase (1901–57) was one in which the producer nations granted full concessions to major oil companies. The oil concessionaries had effective control over the entire range of oil activities. Because the host government played a less active role, the principal features of this bargaining era were unmistakably those of a power and dependency relationship which largely benefited the oil concessionaries. Second was the direct response phase, in which the bargaining position of the producer nations began to gather momentum with the emergence of some elements of independence. During this phase, the stage was set for direct negotiations. The direct response phase contributed to the founding of OPEC in 1960.

The hegemony phase soon faded away completely and increased participation of the producer states featured concession agreements based on joint ventures and profit sharing. The direct response phase was characterized by a dramatic change in the exchange relationship between the buyer and the seller, each trying to maximize gain and minimize loss. However, the producer states still did not have adequate control over their oil industry.

Third was the tacit response phase (1966–79), a period characterized by the emergence of oil producing states as full participants seeking increased control over all phases of oil resource development. During the period 1966–73, developing countries served as the arbiters of oil resources due to their increased strength in bargaining power, assertion of sovereign rights, and increased nationalization of oil companies. The era is marked by the growing independence of the producer states and the gradual erosion of power of the oil companies. Consequently, the period resulted in a growing advantage for the governments in the terms and conditions of arrangements between various players in the international oil industry.[21] Notwithstanding these advances, the issue of technology transfer remains a stumbling block to the full control of producer nations over their oil industry.

According to Thomas Walde (1989), many governments which have nationalized petroleum production have seen their revenues decrease considerably and some have to provide considerable financial support to keep state enterprises viable.

All modern contracts illustrate that ownership does not automatically imply effective control and that the function of management can be separated from ownership. While government equity is frequent, sometimes 50 percent or even . . . 100 percent, management is often entrusted to the foreign partner.[22]

In Nigeria, despite government participation in the oil companies (according to M. A. Olorunfemi), "the country has not developed the capability to manage its petroleum resources by itself; all the crude oil is produced by foreign operators. Even though some Nigerians who work in the industry occupy important management positions, the key management roles are performed largely by foreigners."[23]

THOUGHTS ON TECHNOLOGY ACQUISITION

Nigeria is one of a number of developing countries that have not been totally successful in securing the transfer of technology from the multinational corporations. This imbalance could be the source of Nigeria's reduced relative bargaining position with the oil concessionaries whenever technology is an issue on the agenda of negotiated contracts and agreements.

State participation in the oil industry is necessary and praiseworthy, but it is not sufficient without technology acquisition. The multinational corporations resist technology transfer and the views on technology transfer are controversial. However, measures of strengthening the negotiation capacity of producer governments in their relationship with the oil companies are guided by three major viewpoints (under the aegis of the United Nations).[24] The orthodox view holds that technology produced in advanced countries is appropriate for developing countries as well. The multinational corporations could transfer technology through their commercial ventures in developing countries; through their technical support systems, the backward position of these countries could be eliminated.

A counterview holds that technology produced in advanced countries is not suitable for developing countries because of the eventual external control of their social and economic circumstances. It maintains that developing countries have different social and economic conditions and should design their own technology, and suggests that the technology dominated by the multinational corporations exists simply to increase their profits. The moderate reformist view supports an appropriate technological mix that would foster the scientific and technological capability of developing countries, and holds that the multinational corporations can play a catalytic role in the development process.[25] The multinational corporations can contribute innovatively to the national needs of host governments, and a useful solution would be to increase the host government's bargaining power with the view to increasing its technological capability. The host government should strive to import technology, and foreign investment will become a vehicle for determining which technological mix would be most suitable for the country's own development.

Even if a country has the right policy objective toward technology acquisition, resistance from multinational oil companies will limit the effectiveness of any technology acquisition policy. These companies are discouraged from any meaningful transfers of technology to host governments because these are viewed as potentially disruptive to market shares and profits in the industry.[26] Instead, development policies are encouraged which are aimed at making the producer state technologically dependent.

NIGERIA'S EFFORT TOWARD TECHNOLOGY ACQUISITION

In Nigeria, the state-owned oil company (the Nigerian National Petroleum Corporation) is vested with the responsibility of providing bilateral technical assistance to Nigeria; however, the National Office of Industrial Property (NOIP) is the only statutory body authorized to approve agreements for the transfer of technology to Nigeria and to monitor that transfer on a continuing basis. The NOIP Act has defined an equitable basis for negotiation that takes into account the legitimate interests of all negotiatng parties and the sovereignty of the country. Among the functions of the NOIP are: (1) the encouragement of a more efficient process for the identification and selection of foreign technology; and (2) the development of the negotiating skills of Nigerians so that they may secure optimal contractual terms and conditions in any agreement dealing with the transfer of technology.[27]

The measures taken by producer governments such as Nigeria in their efforts to acquire technology include their insistence on a final clause in petroleum development contracts that requires foreign operators, upon termination of the contract, to transfer to the host government, free of charge, all the petroleum installations and equipment, in good working condition.[28] In Nigeria, successive governments since 1973 have progressively acquired a majority interest in local operations of the oil companies, yet Nigerians themselves do not hold a reasonable proportion of key positions in the industry, and the foreign oil companies that operate in the country are not giving the necessary financial and technical assistance to the nation's Petroleum Training Institute.[29] The position has not shown marked improvement since 1981: in most transnational oil companies, the key and sensitive positions in management, drilling, and exploration (which involve highly technical and managerial skills) are still held by expatriates. However, according to Momodu Kassim-Momodu (1988), a solid base is being prepared for the eventual takeover of all of the operations of the oil industry.[30] Previously, no oil was produced directly by the NNPC, but in 1988 the federal government of Nigeria established an oil producing company called the Nigerian Petroleum Development Company. It is a subsidiary of the NNPC and is empowered to commercially produce and market petroleum products. It will take an active part in all the phases and the activities of the oil producing company.[31]

Since oil has become a mainstay of the country's economy, the government of Nigeria has determined to develop its in-digenous capacity in order to better absorb imported technology. Irrespective of the apparent conflicts and differences that exist between the oil companies and the producer government, their exchange relationship is harmonized to promote their common interest in the oil resource, and has been termed a "complex mixture of cooperation, conflict and compromise."[32]

OIL: THE BEDROCK OF NIGERIA'S ECONOMY

Commercial production of petroleum, which began as early as 1958, has since become a dominant factor in Nigerian national life. Oil now accounts for about 93 percent of Nigerian export earnings, 75 percent of foreign exchange earnings, 87 percent of total government revenues, and 45 percent of the gross national product. This development is not surprising, since agriculture, which has been considered by many to be the basis for a stable economy and society in Nigeria, has suffered a severe decline over the last two decades.[33] During the early post-World War II era, agricultural products dominated the export trade; Nigeria was one of the world's leading exporters of cocoa, groundnuts, and palm oil, and a notable exporter of rubber, cotton, and hides. There has, however, been a rapid decline in the size of the agricultural sector, whose contribution to the gross domestic product (or GDP) fell from around 60 percent in 1960 to about

21 percent in 1977, and eventually to less than 10 percent in 1978. Unlike agriculture, however, oil production employs a relatively small number of workers, and accounts for only 1.3 percent of the total modern sector employment in Nigeria. Consequently, the oil industry has almost displaced the agricultural economy, making Nigeria a petroleum-based single commodity reliance economy.

The Nigerian economy is dualistic in character. There has been remarkable growth in the capital-intensive oil sector while stagnation, unemployment, and decline are characteristic of the agricultural and non-oil sectors. The result is a low demand for local labor, a situation that is exacerbated during periods of economic downturn. For instance, at the onset of the oil price collapse of the 1980s, Nigeria instituted austerity measures that resulted in massive unemployment and retrenchment of workers, particularly in the public sector. But according to Jon McLin (1988), the price collapse and attendant loss of revenue have had little effect on employment in the oil industry. Throughout the economic downturn, Nigeria has maintained a surprisingly high overall employment level in the oil sector.[34] This situation affirms the dualistic structure of the economy. The country lacks the appropriate technological mix to sustain balanced growth and development in its overall economy. Moreover, the country's development plans since 1970 have been totally dependent on revenue from petroleum exports. This dependency is not void of problems. Despite the Nigerian government's ownership of shares in the foreign affiliates and the Nigerian National Oil Company's production of part of the exported petroleum the control, regulation, and daily management of the oil industry still does not rest in Nigerian hands. This is particularly true with the production of crude oil. In addition, the level of production and demand for oil is heavily dependent on western economies. For example, in 1976 the production and sale of oil dropped by 20.7 percent because of a sudden recession in Western economies. This reduction in demand cut government revenues significantly; consequently, in 1983 the oil market experienced a serious glut.

In spite of these problems, Nigeria has not diversified its export goods and continues to depend on the petroleum demand of industrialized economies to finance its social and economic development. This dependency is understandable given the fact that the Nigerian oil industry cannot and does not exist in isolation. It is a part of the global oil industry. It is therefore conceivable that changing global economic and even political conditions will have a direct bearing on its success or failure. Irrespective of oil booms, gluts, and unforeseen market circumstances, the Nigerian government's major revenue base will remain oil dependent unless there is a dramatic change in export diversification. Development plans remain totally oil revenue dependent, a limitation that is of special interest to social scientists and policy planners, particularly regarding the way in which the government allocates oil revenue to meet planned developmental objectives. In sum, since Nigeria began to increase its oil output, oil revenue has come to play a dominant role in all government economic development schemes.

The rise of oil itself is a story of the 1970s, but historically, the exploration began in 1908. As noted earlier the first serious discoveries were not made until 1956 on the shore of the Niger Delta. Commercial shipments began two years later, but were on a modest scale until the mid-1960s, when offshore production began. Expansion was then delayed by the civil war, but after the ceasefire, production increased rapidly, exceeding one million barrels a day in 1970 and passing the two million mark in 1973. By 1981 the production level was fluctuating erratically around the government target of about 2 mbd.[35]

The 1970s boom in production coincided with the surge in world prices. In turn, a shift in the balance of power enabled the government to broaden the terms on which the companies lift oil. As a result, Nigerian revenue from oil rocketed from N176 million in 1970 to N1.4 billion in 1973 and N12.86 billion by 1980.[36] According to Terisa Turner, "revenues from oil exports peaked at $25 billion in 1980 but dropped to under $10 billion in 1983 and to $7 billion in 1986. Falling oil prices averaged $14.03 a barrel in 1986 compared with $28 a barrel in 1985 [and] resulted in a 44 percent drop in government revenues."[37]

In early 1981 there were about 140 producing fields, including onshore and offshore operations located in the Niger Delta region, mostly in Bendel, Rivers, Cross River, and Imo states (Figure 1.1). Their output at the time varied widely, ranging from a low of about 300 barrels per day. Most fields were small — almost half had outputs under 14,000 barrels per day. Total proven reserves were variously estimated at between 16 and 17.5 billion barrels. The government was promoting exploration in other parts of the country as well as in the Delta region in order to increase reserves.[38]

A BRIEF HISTORY OF OIL

The origin and the quest for "black gold" (oil) and its influence on industrial development is linked to "Colonel Drake's success with his Pennsylvania well in 1859" in the United States.[39] He produced 33 barrels (bbl) per day. The exploration and production of oil was expanded in the United States. Between 1862 and 1880, the U.S. oil output increased from 3 million bbl/year to 28 million bbl/year. As a result of this expanded output the United States became an oil exporter. Soon after, the Soviet Union joined the United States, also becoming an oil exporter. By 1900 additional oil discoveries had been made in fourteen other American states and U.S. oil output reached a total of 63 million barrels.

In 1901 Spindle Top in southeast Texas recorded a "production of 100,000 bbl/day from a depth of 1,020 feet and drastically changed America's and the world's future by proving the existence of abundant oil supplies."[40] The rudimentary stage of the oil industry was dominated by the Standard Oil Company, founded by John D. Rockefeller in 1882. Later, many more oil companies were founded.

Figure 1.1

Nigeria: Oil Producing Areas

Size: 117,396 square kilometers
        12.8% of the size of Nigeria

Population: 24.1694 million or 25% of the Nigerian population

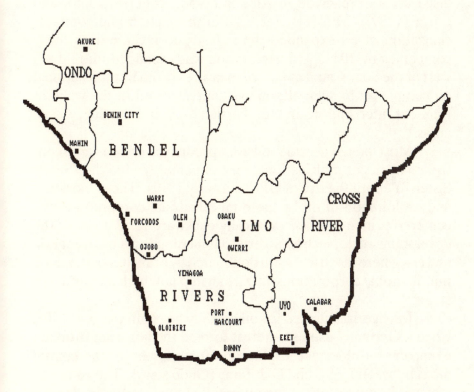

Source: Adopted from the Administration Map of Nigeria, Federal Ministry
of Information, Lagos, Nigeria, NNPC.

Through the activities of these companies, further oil exploration, discoveries and production activities took place in other parts of the world: Iran in 1908, Venezuela in 1917, Mexico and Iraq in 1927, Bahrain in 1932, Saudi Arabia in 1936 and Kuwait in 1946.[41]

Early exploration and production activities also took place also in Eastern European nations (East Germany, Austria, and Hungary). Russia had the largest share of production, second only to the United States in total world output in the early days of oil evolution.

The evolution of oil in Africa emerged when important discoveries were made in Algeria (1958), Nigeria (1958), and Libya (1959). The early increase in production and commercialization of oil expanded the industry to include over thirty companies by 1911. Oil exploration was expanded into Africa west of the Suez Canal as part of measures taken by international oil companies to seek alternative sources of oil in the wake of frequent interruptions in the   Persian Gulf and the Suez Canal areas.[42]

Most of the world's oil was produced, priced, and controlled by major multinational oil companies (called the "Seven Sisters")[43] until the rise of OPEC in early 1970s. The exploration and exploitation of oil by these multinational corporations was centered primarily in economically backward rural areas of the developing world, such as Nigeria. The scramble for oil in Nigeria and elsewhere in Africa is still dominated by branches of the same multinational corporations, in partnership now with the producer states.

In Nigeria, the race for oil actually began in the year 1908, when a German business interest formed the Nigerian Bitumen Company to undertake exploration for bitumen in the coastal areas between Lagos and Okitipupa (Ondo state). The company stopped its operations at the outbreak of the first World War.

In 1937, Shell D'Arcy (the predecessor to the present-day Shell Petroleum Company of Nigeria) reactivated oil exploration activities in Nigeria.   As Jide Osuntokun notes, Shell D'Arcy operated:

under Mineral Oil Ordinance no. 17 of 1914 and its amendments of 1925 and 1950, which allowed only companies registered in Britain or any of its protectorates the right to prospect for oil in Nigeria, and further provided that the principal officers of such companies must be British subjects. Between 1938 and 1941, Shell BP undertook preliminary geological reconnaissance. After [a five-year interruption] by World War II, it intensified and followed up this activity with geophysical surveys in the 1946-51 period. In 1951, Shell BP drilled its first Wildcat well. . . . In 1956, it made the first commercial discovery at Oloibiri in Rivers state.[44]

By the time Nigeria achieved its independence in 1960, it was already established as an oil producing country, producing and exporting over 170,000 barrels per day. This encouraging oil production potential attracted a number of international oil companies into the country, notably Texaco, Mobil, Tenneco, Gulf, Safrap (ELF), Agip Oil, and Esso West Africa. These companies were licensed to operate both offshore and onshore.[45]

PROBLEMS OF OIL AND PRODUCING AREAS

Oil, the black gold of the twentieth century and one of the most lucrative sources of wealth, is now the most important energy source of the world. Although its exploitation has created some of the largest fortunes and has helped to achieve impressive economic growth and development, little or no attention has been directed to the impact of this exploitation on the oil producing areas, particularly in developing countries.[46] This lack of attention can be attributed to the pragmatic and international orientation of oil enterprises, which are almost exclusively managed and operated by multinational corporations from a capitalistic point of view, without regard to the welfare of the producing areas. The barriers to balanced development in Africa, and Nigeria in particular, might be linked to the age-old notion that

the economic and cultural imperatives that symbolize Europe's imperialism and contemporary expansionism is the structural and cultural dependency that subjects the developing societies to being consumers of Western ideas, which in turn perpetuates their underdevelopment. The unfortunate or unholy alliance . . . emerges between the developing societies and the expansionist forces of the north.[47]

Apparently, multinational firms are no more than contemporary emissaries and purveyors of former colonial interests. They may not necessarily be concerned with genuine development for the indigenous population. They are in Africa strictly for profit, to exploit Africa's valuable raw materials for the benefit of their home economies. Nnamdi Azikiwe, the first president of Nigeria, observed in 1933 that

Amidst . . . conflicting ambitions of Europe for territorial expansion in Africa is the human factor—the fate of indigenous black Africans who dwell on this continent. They constitute an extraneous element so far as European imperialism is concerned. Their raw materials mean more to Europe than their existence to enjoy the fullest of life as do the Europeans, on their own continent, respectively. Their manpower seems only valuable for the machinery of European imperialism.[48]

The possible linkage between imperialism and underdevelopment is further noted by B. Onimode (1981), with particular reference to the British influence in Nigeria. He wrote:

British colonialism effectively blocked Nigeria's development . . . through its colossal export of national economic surplus, . . . unequal exchange in exports and imports, systematic denial of credit, neglect of education, and general distortion of the colonial economy in a perverse bilateral integration with the British system. Forced transition from a precapitalist to capitalist mode of production was about the only real development under colonialism. . . . [T]he collective consequences of colonialism constituted an effective foundation for persistent underdevelopment of the country from the colonial period to the present.[49]

In an effort to overcome the unchanging nature of colonialism, Bingu W. T. Mutharika (1988) asserts that the formulation and execution of foreign policy, especially in oil producing nations, has been deliberately tied to fighting foreign oppression, exploitation, and the trappings of imperial ambitions by multinational corporations, which are nurtured and supported by their respective imperial centers. The reaction to the experience in Africa is such that multinational corporations are regarded as being neo-colonialistic.[50] Kwame Nkrumah, past president of Ghana, stated in 1965:

Africa is a paradox which illustrates and highlights neo-colonialism. Her earth is rich, yet the products that come from above and below her soil continue to enrich not Africans predominantly, but groups and individuals who operate to Africa's impoverishment. . . . If Africa's multiple resources were used in her own development, they could place her among the modernized continents of the world. But her resources have been, and still are, being used for the greater development of overseas interests.[51]

Do Kwame Nkrumah's words of twenty-five years ago still apply today? If so, only the government of the producer state can exercise its sovereign power to reverse the imperialist trend and protect the welfare of its people. State government must make the multinationals socially accountable for their activities in the host communities if truly balanced development is to be achieved. These corporations may well intend to see genuine development for the people, but good intentions are not enough without practical evidence. It requires sound effort to implement their corporate social responsibility to the host communities, an implementation that would ensure the development of indigenous people such that all parties to the economic progress (the multinationals, government and the people) can benefit equitably. This process could reverse the trend in imperialist behavior, but a machinery for full enforcement is yet to be attained. In Nigeria, the host government and the oil corporations are partners in the exploration and exploitation of the oil resource, but there has been no significant policy change toward the welfare of the oil producing areas. The value system of the host government and that of the multinationals often differ in their objectives, but the strength of their common economic interest overrides all local rights to the mineral resource. The host government owns all subsurface mineral wealth by law. The state perceives the presence of multinationals with technology and capital as a vehicle for fostering economic growth and a relevant core process upon which all other aspects of social and economic development will depend. Hence, the host government views the intense mining of oil as a buttress for upgrading the quality of life of its citizenry. In many third world economies, however, growth does not necessarily mean actual development. The multinationals strive primarily to increase their shareholders' wealth and to maintain the interest of their parent company, usually headquartered in a foreign metropolis. The activities, then, of multinational corporations are primarily designed to benefit the absentee parent body and are divorced from the host community's welfare. Regarding these absentee owned corporations, Bock et al. (1984) wrote that they "have created a calculus of corporate welfare separate from community welfare though the corporations still require the cooperation of the government and local labor forces. . . . Even the managers who run these branch corporate bodies are [more] concerned with their careers in the larger corporate body than [with] the quality of host community life."[52] Irrespective of differences in objectives between the host government and the multinationals, there is a clear sense of their mutual economic interest converging to emphasize economic benefits with little or no regard for local welfare.

The oil producing areas of Nigeria are mostly inhabited by minority groups: the Abribas, Andonis, Edos, Effiks, Gokanas, Ibibios, Ijaws, Ika-Ibos, Ikwerres, Isekiris, Isokos, Kalabaris,

Ogonis, and Urhobos. These groups lack the power to make any political or economic decision in their favor. The balance of power in Nigeria is such that the national interest reigns supreme over local rights. In the national arena, a powerful individual or dominant group is often able to influence decisions in its favor, creating imbalance, distortion, and inequity. For example, the Nigerian revenue allocation formula ignores depreciation and other serious adverse externalities affecting the oil producing areas.

The executors of Nigeria's political policies have capital- ized on the revenue and other benefits to be derived from the oil resource. There are very few planned provisions for the welfare of the oil areas. There seems to be a direct relationship between revenue allocation and the exercise of political power; political decision-makers can apparently reverse at will the formulae for sharing national wealth. For example, prior to the oil boom in the 1950s, the formulae for revenue allocation were based on the derivation principle, whereby the resource-producing region re- ceived the greatest share. In 1982 that revenue formulae was reversed. It is now based on population, or need, with 55 percent to the federal government, 35 percent to the states, and a token 10 percent to the local government. In fact, the earlier report of the Okigbo Commission in 1980 allotted only an insignificant 1 percent toward ecological protection and 2 percent for the special problems of the mineral producing areas.[53] Comfort Briggs (1988) explains the "need" principle thusly:

Need refers to the constitutional functions and responsibilities assigned to each tier and the corresponding financial expenditures and obligations. . . .

In interregional sharing, two main indicators have been used to define the principle of need. One indicator, labeled "Minimum Responsibilities," . . . or "Equality of States," is based on the proposition that in order for a state . . . to function as a governing unit, it has to carry out a minimum number of responsibilities. Therefore, every state . . . requires an equivalent amount of revenue to do so. This type of sharing has an equalizing effect among states.

The other indicator for the principle of Need is population. It is based on the premise that government is about people, that development is about people, and that the end of government is the welfare of its people. Therefore, all citizens should have equal claim to the national revenue, regardless of [the] region [in which] they reside.[54]

Prior to the 1970s, when Nigeria relied on agrarian produce for its foreign exchange, revenue sharing in Nigeria was based on the derivation principle.

On the structure of the Nigerian revenue allocation system, J. M. Ostheimer (1973) wrote:

Financing the federation proved a thorny issue and clearly demonstrated the desire for power of each of the regions. There were two theoretical alternatives: to budget for the regions in response to their needs or according to the percentage of total revenues which they provided (derivation). Nigerians from the richer Western and Northern regions advocated the greater use of derivation. The Eastern region politicians by and large resisted this trend, at least until after the constitutional shape of Nigeria had been confirmed. Only with large discoveries of oil in the Eastern region beginning in the late 1950s did the easterners begin to prefer derivation.[55]

According to C. Briggs (1988) the fact that the central government not only collected most of the revenue but also retained the bulk of it has been criticized. Describing the system as "rampant centralism" and as even more centralized than any of the centrally planned socialist countries in the world, critics have questioned its validity and suitability in a federal Nigeria.[56]

The basis for the central government's allocation of the major portion of revenue to itself is the notion that the federal government is the repository of the national interest and therefore all efforts should be made to strengthen its finances. As one of the fiscal review boards put it, "The financial stability of the federal center must be the main guarantee of the financial stability of Nigeria as a whole. . . . By its strength and solvency, the credit-worthiness of the country will be appraised."[57]

There has been apparent misuse and misapplication of this form of fiscal federalism in Nigeria, for people tend to identify more strongly with their own localities than with the federal government, particularly when the revenue allocation principles for interstate sharing are applied.   Since 1946 a number of revenue allocation principles and the criteria for using them have been recommended by each respective Revenue Allocation Commission, but no level of satisfaction has been attained due to perceived or actual inequalities inherent in the system. A summary of revenue allocation principles for interstate sharing in Nigeria is shown in Table 1.2.

When oil became a major source of revenue in the country, the producing areas were entitled to 50 percent of the mining rents and royalties. The nonproducing areas resented it. It was argued that all sources of revenue were to be viewed as common funds; hence the Dina Revenue Allocation Commission in 1968 laid greater emphasis on the redistribution of oil revenue. To this end, oil revenue was to be distributed as follows:

1. Onshore mining rents – to be retained by states of origin.

2. Onshore mining royalties:
    (a)   15 percent -   Federal government
    (b)   10 percent -   States of origin
    (c)   5 percent -   Special Grants Account, established to finance special development projects and special emergency and contingency needs.
    (d)   70 percent -   States Joint Account

3. Offshore mining rents and royalties:
    (a)   60 percent -   Federal government
    (b)   30 percent -   States Joint Account
    (c)   10 percent -   Special Grants Account[58]

The manner in which specific allocation principles should be used, in what combination, and how much weight each should be assigned has been a most serious and intractable political issue in Nigeria.

Oil production gives rise to large state revenue. The very existence of these large sums gives impetus to class and factional

Table 1.3

Revenue Allocation Principles for Interstate Sharing

Commission (named after the Chairman)	Principle	
1. Phillipson, 1946	i.	Derivation
	ii.	Even Progress
		(a) population-proxy
2. Hicks-Phillipson, 1951	i.	Derivation
	ii.	Need
	iii.	National Interest
3. Chick, 1953	i.	Derivation
4. Raisman, 1958	i.	Derivation
	ii.	Need
		(a) population
		(b) continuity in government services
		(c) minimum responsibilities
		(d) balanced development
5. Binns, 1964	i.	Financial Comparability
		(a) need
		(b) even development
6. Dina, 1968	i.	Need
	ii.	Minimum National Standards
	iii.	Balanced Development
	iv.	Derivation
7. Various Revenue Allocation Decrees, 1967–77	i.	Equality of States
	ii.	Population
	iii.	Derivation (only 20 percent of onshore mining royalties)
8. Aboyade, 1977	i.	Equality of Access to Development Opportunity
	ii.	National Minimum Standards
	iii.	Absorptive Capacity
	iv.	Independent Revenue and Tax Effort
	v.	Fiscal Efficiency
9. Okigbo, 1980	i.	Minimum Responsibility
	ii.	Population
	iii.	Internal Revenue Effort
	iv.	Social Development Factor
		(a) primary school enrollment

(Derivation was later added to the Okigbo recommendations.)

Source: *Report of the Presidential Commission on Revenue Allocation,* Vol. 1 (Lagos, Nigeria: Federal Government Press, 1980), chapters 2 and 9. Briggs, C. (1988), 191-2.

struggle to control the state and preside over the spending of this oil revenue.[59] In Nigeria, the search for a fair and rational system of revenue allocation remains unresolved. Nigeria has attempted to resolve the problem at least eight times, but the issue has often been met with conflict rather than resolution in the political arena because policymakers are steered more by regional or political interests than by objectivity. In 1980 revenue allocation was a dominant factor in the national political debate and the conflict was mainly centered on how revenue was to be allocated among the states. The heavily populated, resource-poor states favored allocation based on population while the oil producing states favored the principle of derivation, with special provisions to compensate the areas for the ecological risks of oil production.[60] The controversy and conflict intensified as each political faction sought to control the new national oil wealth in the interest of its party or state.

Irrespective of these conflicts, the basic inequity in Nigeria's present system of revenue allocation cannot be overlooked. On the theory of justice, John Rawls (1971) wrote:

Each person [or community] possesses an inviolability founded on justice that even the welfare of society as a whole cannot override. For this reason, justice denies that the loss of freedom for some is made right by a greater good shared by others. It does not allow that the sacrifices imposed on a few [mineral producing areas] are outweighed by the larger sum of advantages enjoyed by many [nationally and internationally]. Therefore in a just society the liberties of equal citizenship are taken as settled; the rights secured by justice are not subject to political bargaining or to the calculus of social interest. . . . [T]ruth and justice are uncompromising.[61]

In light of the above, Nigeria's efforts towards social justice have not succeeded where the revenue generation and distribution system is concerned.

An apparent irony here is that the drive for parochial interest in the domestic politics of the Nigerian ruling class is not reflected in Nigeria's negotiations in the international arena with regard to oil politics. For instance, if revenue sharing based on population holds to be true and fair, why has Nigeria not convinced OPEC to increase its quota of oil production on population? Nigeria has a population nearly nine times as large as Saudi Arabia's and should not have accepted a meager 1.40 barrels per day (bpd) production quota. Considering its large population and the fact that its sagging economy is highly dependent on oil,[62] Nigeria has not negotiated effectively enough in the OPEC arena to show that human reserves should take precedence over oil reserves.

Table 1.4

Nigeria: Official Population Estimates, 1986 (in millions)

Kano	11.9
Oyo	10.8
Sokoto	9.4
Kaduna	8.5
Anambra	7.4
Cross River	7.2
Borno	6.2
Ondo	5.8
Gongola	5.4
Bendel	5.1
Bauchi	5.0
Benue	5.0
Lagos	4.2
Plateau	4.1
Rivers	3.6
Kwara	3.5
Ogun	3.2
Niger	2.1
Abuja	0.5
Total	116.2

Sources: Federal Survey Department; National Population Bureau.

Although the Nigerian Revenue Sharing plan contains the basic elements of funds allocation (any revenue sharing plan specifies four basic policy variables),[63] the struggle for power to control the national wealth within the federal structure weakens the plan's operational efficiency. It worked to the disadvantage of the minority groups in the mineral producing areas; their wealth does not necessarily enhance the fiscal capacity of their respective states because the state budgets depend on the population-based federal allocation system.

Population is an asset in heavily populated areas (Table 1.4). The heavily populated areas are not only endowed with human capital but also have a proven basis for political power and control over national wealth. Unfortunately, because effort and attention is concentrated on the oil industry and the producing areas, the nonproducing areas have been underutilized, and their full capacity for contribution to the national coffers has not been developed. Therefore, the sole reliance on oil exports to foster national and regional development may be creating an excessive burden for the mineral producing areas, who must support that development. Furthermore, if there were a diversification of the economy with improved agricultural output, sustainable growth and development could be induced that would allow the heavily populated areas to increase growth and absorption capacity without heavy reliance on the highly vulnerable and unstable single commodity export market. A diversified national economy could reduce the excessive burden borne by mineral areas as a result of the intensive extraction of oil to increase revenue and generate alternative sources of revenue within each state. Perhaps someday, a more fair and equitable means of revenue allocation will be reached with less conflict of interest and less state dependency on the federal pool. At present, however, the lack of sustainable overall economic development in Nigeria is due primarily to the failure of the government to use oil funds to transform other sectors of the economy. This is a potential source of increasing economic weakness for Nigeria and leaves the country in a greater state of foreign dependence (Table 1.5).[64]

It is clear that the quest to generate funds through reliance on oil exports has created an excess burden for the oil producing areas. While the benefits derived from the oil resource can improve human conditions nationally and internationally, we should not be so shortsighted that we overlook the many serious negative externalities borne by the oil producing areas. We must seek economic progress with environmental balance. A meager 2 percent allotment for the special problems of the mineral producing areas is inconsequential to the increased social cost suffered by the indigenous population in those areas. While the controversy in revenue allocation remains an issue, one cannot overlook the seriously disruptive effects of oil activities. It would not be unreasonable to increase the allotment for ecological

Table 1.5

OPEC: Population[*] and Oil Production Quotas[**]

	1989 quota	Population mid-year 1987	Population share (%)	Quota based on population	Oil depend-ence (%)	Depend-ence share (%)
Algeria	695	23.190	5.4	990.9	67.43	6.62
Ecuador	230	9.920	2.3	423.9	40.58	3.98
Gabon	166	1.190	0.3	50.9	71.57	7.03
Indonesia	1,240	170.530	39.4	7,286.5	35.93	3.53
Iran	2,640	51.700	11.9	2,209.1	89.53	8.79
Iraq	2,640	17.000	3.9	726.4	99.06	9.73
Kuwait	1,037	1.870	0.4	79.9	90.07	8.84
Libya	1,037	3.880	0.9	165.8	95.76	9.40
Nigeria	1,355	120.029	27.7	5,128.6	97.30	9.55
Qatar	312	.350	0.1	15.0	90.28	8.86
Saudi Arabia	4,524	13.610	3.1	581.5	85.31	8.38
UAE	988	1.430	0.3	61.1	72.81	7.15
Venezuela	1,636	18.270	4.2	780.6	82.83	8.13
OPEC	18,500	432.969	100.0	18,500.0	77.75	100.0

Source: Fadhil J. Al-Chalabi, *OPEC at the Crossroads* (Exeter, Great Britain: Pergamon Press, 1989), 38.

Notes: * Population figures in millions.
            ** Quota figures in thousand barrels per day.

disturbances and special problems of the mineral producing areas to at least 20 percent. Moreover, an additional special allotment should be provided to state and local governments of the mineral producing areas for solving problems of human settlement and fostering alternative means of promoting social and economic development.

A special funding to states and local governments is necessary and desirable since these governments in the mineral producing areas lack the fiscal capacity to respond to existing social and economic problems, and now must also tackle the extraneous problems created by the oil industry in their environment.

The author has a strong premonition that there will be a wave of change in the succeeding political order. It has already taken shape with regard to revenue allocation as reflected by the Political Bureau Report (1987). Among other things, the report stated that: (1) the government will rectify the discrepancy in revenue allocation by setting up a technical revenue mobilization commission which will in the future emphasize revenue sharing and not revenue allocation; (2) the Technical Revenue Mobilization Commission will review from time to time revenue allocation formulae and principles in operation to ensure that they conform to changing realities, thereby avoiding unnecessary political pressures; and (3) the fiscal responsibilities shared between the federal and other levels of government should be reviewed to give local governments greater latitude to collect revenue from more sources, enabling them to meet their expanded roles in the new political order proposed for the country.[65] Furthermore, the innovative revenue-sharing plan has proposed that the federal government should get 40 percent, the state 40 percent and local government 20 percent. And, specific to oil producing areas, the following recommendations are made:

1. that the dichotomy between onshore and offshore production in the allocation of revenue to the oil producing states should be abolished, as it fails to reflect the tremendous hazards faced by the inhabitants of the areas where oil is produced offshore

2. that there is a need to revise upward to at least 2 percent the present 1.5 percent allocation from the federal account for the development of mineral producing areas. The political bureau further recommends that the 2 percent from the distributive pool that is given to oil producing states be sent directly to the local governments of the areas concerned.

The local governments would thus be encouraged to play their proper role as the third tier of government whose activities have direct impact on the welfare of the rural masses. The Political Bureau opines that the local government is the basic unit for administration and development of the country, and as such, a more constitutional responsibility should be assigned in the new dispensation.

The implementation of this new initiative could possibly correct some of the structural inequities inherent in the revenue allocation system in Nigeria, and will perhaps provide some form of relief with enhanced fiscal capacity for mineral producing areas. The method of revenue allocation that has been in force over the years has very little regard for the adverse consequences of the impact of the oil industry on the oil producing areas. Nigerian public policy toward the oil producing areas seems to support the questionable view that national interest supersedes local rights. The reality is that neither the oil industry nor the government has sought an effective means of ensuring community well-being and development in the oil areas. This is understandable since the agreements between the host governments and the international oil companies emphasize a larger administrative role and an increased share of gross profits for the host government. The Nigerian state's unfair policy toward the oil areas may be consistent with this observation by critics of federalism: "The state tends to protect favored groups or special interest groups rather than general welfare of the people. . . . [T]hat federalism has worked chiefly to the advantage of elites, capitalists, absentee corporate owners and their surrogate elitist representatives."[66]

The Nigerian state benefits from oil royalties by permitting an exploitation of mineral resources that clearly results in pollution and the disruption and deprivation of farmlands and fishing ports, without providing adequate compensation or a planned mitigation policy for the affected areas. There is certainly a need to evaluate the national benefits of oil production against community concern and welfare. The production process of an exhaustible mineral resource that is accompanied by highly hazardous negative externalities should not go ignored forever; like a pendulum that swings away, it will return. The oil producing areas are already paying for the adverse effects of the oil industry, and will probably pay even more dearly for it in the future unless adequate mitigation measures are taken to minimize serious adverse impacts.

The efforts to minimize the adverse effects of the oil industry cannot be a problem for the inhabitants in the oil areas alone, but must be a major concern for the federal government and the oil industry itself, which should take a very serious look at its consequences. The oil areas have suffered enough from the seemingly benevolent aggression of the oil industry and it is time to find practical answers to the host of problems created by it.

The oil explorers and the Nigerian government cannot continue to profit from oil resources while leaving the environment and its rural inhabitants to fend for themselves, surrounded with the stink of poverty, as their wealth is ripped away to benefit other areas. Dom Helder Camara, the "brother of the poor," said, "Rural poverty is not a local problem. It is a national problem, even a continental problem. You know that the prices of our raw materials have always been set in the great decision making centers of the world."[67]

Here it is not just a demand; it is the right of the oil producing areas to benefit from their own natural resource. Despite the huge revenues derived by Nigeria from oil resources, there has been no effective plan to develop the oil producing areas. These areas deserve special attention, since they suffer doubly from the problems and deficiencies made worse by the oil industry. It is generally observed that the wealth created in the oil producing areas does not necessarily bring about improvements in the area's social and economic development.

Oil exploration areas have limited land and before oil exploration takes place, oil companies usually evacuate the inhabitants from the area and occupy such areas with their equipment. This action limits the area available to the inhabitants for their economic pursuits.

[When] it is realized that most of the companies prospecting for oil in Nigeria are partly owned by the federal government, it becomes imperative that the aid to the victim of oil exploration should fall squarely on the shoulders of the federal government and also the multinational oil companies as part of their corporate social responsibility.

Since the wealth which is derived from oil is nationally controlled, it follows that the problems of oil exploration should be nationally solved. The area where oil exploration is taking place usually becomes unsafe for human habitation because of oil pollution of water and gas pollution of air. Even where the gas is flared, the soot in the atmosphere contaminates rain water, which is one of the sources of drinking water. This disadvantage becomes strangulating if it is remembered that most drinking wells have been polluted.[68]

Yet one wonders over Nigeria's seemingly indifferent treatment of its citizens while it maintains its portrayal of care and its paternal face abroad.

Consider this account from Bendel State's Ministry of Information:

Before Bussa sprang up as the town for the people displaced as a result of the Kainji dam, and before Suleja was chosen as the new town for people displaced in Abuja, a lot of scientific research was undertaken to assess the suitability of these towns. It is surprising that even though the oil exploration hazard had been well known before oil exploration started, nobody, especially the federal government, thought it fit to undertake a study of the effect of oil exploration on the affected Nigerians. The effect of this neglect has made the solution to the problem of oil exploration look like a no man's business. The action which the federal government took to stop the contract for the disposal of waste in the sea shelf of a West African country by an American firm is commendable in terms of the international standard regarding pollution, but [it] is indefensible that the same federal government has felt unperturbed by the pollution taking place every day in her own territory.[69]

While this apparent neglect can be attributed to the purely capitalist inclinations of the multinational oil corporations, it is also true that even with the Nigerian government's participation, the situation has not significantly improved. This is understandable in view of the fact that the Nigerian government has no sustainable standing plan designed to help the inhabitants of the oil areas by providing permanent socioeconomic infrastructures and other protective facilities that would ameliorate their condition. There has been a constant cry for such a plan from the people of the oil areas and other concerned observers, but the Nigerian government has not given it serious consideration. In his article, "Oil Spillage Areas Deserve More Aid," Simon Ebare contends that

there is a crying need to provide some permanent infrastructure in the oil producing areas in order that the authorities might be able to forestall unnecessary agitation for relief materials or compensation in the future. It is clear that spillage is characteristic of oil exploration in oil exporting countries. As a result of this understanding, the natives might feel cheated if their land and economic crops are destroyed without the corresponding infrastructure in the area to sustain them.[70]

In spite of this grave concern, the almighty power of the multinational oil corporations in partnership with the government of Nigeria continues to pursue profit at the expense of the inhabitants' lives and property, environmental decay, and dislocation of indigenous economy. In February 1980, one of the years marked by frequent pollution, the National Emergency Relief Team visited Ojobotown in the oil areas of Bendel State. The people's welcoming placard read: "Our lives are threatened by oil spillage, oil has killed our fish. Our creeks are polluted. No improvement, no water and lack of electricity."[71] Furthermore, the continuous lack of infrastructure and absence of social services compounds problems for the area's inhabitants in times of oil-related mishaps, for it is a commonly known and observed fact that during oil spillage there is often an ad hoc response coupled with ill-planned relief efforts to aid victims. The result, as Simon Ebare aptly puts it, is that "the emergency relief materials are as a drop in the ocean."[72]

INADEQUATE PUBLIC POLICY FOR ENVIRONMENTAL REGULATION AND ENFORCEMENT

Further conditions of apparent neglect exist in the inadequacy of statutory regulations regarding oil exploration and the lack of their enforcement. Oil companies rarely adhere to the Industry Standard of Practice which would require them to employ up-to-date technology, and thereby minimize the likelihood of serious mishaps. Statutory Control is merely a token law, and oil mishaps are known to occur frequently. This is well reflected in Sesan Ayodele's remark on the "legal framework for environmental quality" in which he said, "It is evident that a legal framework for preventative and remedial action against oil spills was established in the Petroleum Act No. 51 of 1969. This framework made it mandatory for oil companies to adopt standard oil industry practices." To prevent oil spillage, Section 25 of this Act provided that "the licensee or lessee shall adopt all practicable precautions including the provision of up-to-date equipment approved by the Head Petroleum Inspectorate to prevent the pollution of inland water . . . of Nigeria . . . [and] where such pollution occurs or has occurred shall take prompt steps to control and if possible to end it."[73] The implementation of this requirement would mean the use of blow-out preventers, borrow and saver pits, cathodic protection of pipelines and tanks, and so on. Given that the greatest number of oil spills are caused by equipment failures, "it is more than evident that this provision has not been strictly followed."

There is no doubt that Nigeria has guidelines for oil exploration but fails to maintain effective enforcement and compliance. In certain instances there are still inadequacies observed in the statutory rules expected to protect Nigeria's inhabitants and their environment. Despite the fact that the Nigerian oil law states that the lessee (the oil firm) may not enter, occupy, or exercise any right and powers conferred by his license or lease over any private land until the permission in writing has been given and until "fair" and adequate compensation has been paid to the persons in lawful occupation of the land, this provision is seldom adhered to by oil concessionaries. According to Yinka Omorogbe (1987), further weaknesses exist in the provisions on pollution and conservation policy. He states that both are vague and imprecisely drafted, and that Nigeria has not practiced any conservation policy in the management of its oil resources.[74]

These problems are also noted by E. I. Nwogugu. He wrote that "the statutory rules for the protection of environment in the oil industry are inadequate. The rules should be made more comprehensive and the machinery for their enforcement improved."[75]

In this regard C. O. Ikporukpo (1985) also observed:

The problem is further compounded by the government's apparent unwillingness to enforce the existing laws partly due to the fact that the authority that ought to enforce the legislation is sometimes not clearly indicated. . . . [G]iven the importance of petroleum to the Nigerian economy, the laxity in enforcing the existing legislation may be due to a deliberate policy of not discouraging the operation of the oil producing companies. . . . These factors, taken together. . . [leave] no doubt that some of the incidences of oil spills have been the direct result of a lack of proper care in the various stages of production. . . . Spills have occurred through the use of old and outdated equipment.[76]

Though this book is not a forum for legal analysis, it is helpful to understand and establish the fact that there are weaknesses and laxities in the current system for which the government and the oil industry must share responsibility, and which create serious ecological and human problems in the mostly poor rural oil areas of Nigeria through their lack of adequate protection and measures for compensating the inhabitants.

Moreover, since there is currently no adequate provision of social and economic infrastructures, the inhabitants of the oil areas suffer even more greatly the negative impact of the oil industry without enjoying its direct benefits. Therefore, the current policy in Nigeria symbolically and operationally robs the natural oil resources of these regions to support and swell the economic potentials of others (nationally and internationally), with little or no regard for the regions' welfare.

There is no question that Nigeria was able to carry out successfully its developments, particularly capital projects, such as the Warri and Kaduna refineries, and expansion of the Port Harcourt refinery, due to the buoyancy that came from oil. Other projects included the Petrochemical Project (worth N300 million in 1978), the Direct Reduction Plant (N250 million), the Liquefied Natural Gas Plant (N126 million), the Murtala Muhammed International Airport, Lagos, the Delta Steel Complex, and a new federal capital territory (Abuja). In addition to these projects, Nigeria embarked on a huge network of pipeline for refined products which was constructed across the country and connected Warri refinery with Benin, Lagos, Ibadan, and Kaduna refineries, with extensions to Zaria, Kano, Jos, and Maiduguri.

According to Jide Osuntokun (1986):

The availability of money also had political consequences. The foreign policy of Nigeria during the Gowon, Muhammed, and Obasanjo years was dynamic and purposeful. Nigeria asserted herself not only in the Black Diaspora but on the African continent, and through the actions of our government, countries like Angola and Zimbabwe became independent.

Nigeria saw its wealth grow between 1970 and 1981, the time of a remarkable surge in oil revenue, which enabled it to initiate and to an extent sustain the Economic Community of West African States (ECOWAS).[77]

It becomes obvious, then, that the mining of oil in Nigeria strips the inhabitants of their natural wealth and uses it to better the socioeconomic conditions of distant lands, while the mostly rural inhabitants of the oil areas remain, despite their endowment with such a precious resource, in a state of abject poverty, neglect, and degradation. According to Chief M. O. Feyide, a former secretary of OPEC, Nigeria's oil reserve is estimated at 80 billion barrels. But according to B. Fubara (1986), the estimate is about

115 billion barrels to last at least twenty-five years from a daily production of 2 mbd.[78]   In terms of currency, this represents N7,500 for every man, woman, and child in the country. (Imagine, a country close to 100 million people.) The petroleum sector alone contributes over 80 percent of the foreign exchange earnings. Imagine how wealthy the oil areas would be if one translates the monetary value of the 80 billion barrels into per capita terms among the fewer than 25 million people of the oil areas. Imagine still how long the oil areas have suffered from neglect and underdevelopment. It becomes obvious that Nigeria and its oil industry cannot continue to ignore the special needs of the oil producing areas whose resource feeds the coffers of the nation at their own expense. The oil producing areas deserve a fair share of national development and require special attention.

There is an urgent need to establish a directed, planned policy change aimed at improving the oil areas' social and economic development. The Bendel State government, in speaking of its own area, noted that

the lack of roads has been responsible for most of the misery of the people. It is also responsible for the lack of knowledge of the people by other Nigerians. In addition to roads which will link the area to the rest of the country, intra-community socioeconomic intercourse would be given a tremendous boost by canal links. A carefully planned and well executed canal network would arouse tourist activities in those beautiful but neglected areas.[79]

Further to this, the Bendel State government emphasized the need for special developmental attention for the oil areas, stating that "the oil producing parts of the state should be declared as a special area whose development should be outside the normal allocations to the states by the federal government." The need to better the condition of oil areas is a very pressing one. Its urgency has been proclaimed by members of the National Emergency Relief Team, concerned citizens of the area, writers, and oil industry research experts. For example, on the conflict between the growth of the Nigerian petroleum industry and the quality of the environment, Sesan Ayodele contends that

it is apparent that whereas it may be time that the Nigerian oil industry is by far the most dynamic sector of the economy, the engine of growth and the most significant economic event in recent years, to which an unprecedented economic boom may be attributed, yet, its operating activities have also created an environmental disaster equally unprecedented in the country. In view of this, it is obvious that the appreciable expansion of the Nigerian oil industry which was reflected in the economic boom in the 1970s has, in reality, conflicted with environmental quality objectives of the country. As much as the crude oil is desirable, the Nigerian environmental quality cannot be traded off for whatever benefits are desirable from this material. . . . [I]t's apparent from the foregoing that the recent oil policy geared towards increased oil revenue has increased oil activities in Nigeria particularly since 1973. Such increases in operating activities have created distortions in the environment in forms of spillage, pollution and agricultural contamination. In spite of these adverse effects, experience has shown that inhabitants of these oil areas who were/are frequently exposed to those hazards have not been adequately compensated. Given the oil policy, it may be plausibly speculated that the anxiety to increase oil production in order to take advantage of the increases in oil prices has led to the governments having given little or no attention to the environment as well as to the production technologies which could safeguard exposed inhabitants.[80]

Why is it necessary for the inhabitants of the oil areas to live under such deplorable conditions and neglect, remaining unsettled, while the revenue derived from their own natural resource settles others? A. J. Koyonde noted that:

one can hardly appreciate the immeasurable injustice being done to the people who live in the oil producing areas until one remembers that [it was revenue] from oil that was used to build the Kainji Dam [and to settle] permanently the people [who were] removed from their usual homes; that [it] is the oil money that is being used to develop the Baklori farm project and [to pay] compensation that is running into millions of Naira to the people affected by the execution of that gigantic project . . . that [it] is the same oil money that is being used to build a new federal capital at Abuja and [for] the settlement of the people removed from the project.[81]

In view of the serious problems created by the Nigerian oil industry with respect to the oil producing areas, it is imperative that Nigerian oil policy and its developmental priorities be thoroughly questioned, appraised, and reexamined in the light of balancing national goals with regional interest. And it is clear that Nigeria's past and present development strategies offer very little as a potential guide for the future of the oil producing areas.

Since the inception of the oil industry, the oil producing areas have borne the brunt of a series of negative externalities without receiving adequate compensation. This distributive injustice does not make sense because "inequalities of wealth go hand in hand with inequalities of power, the essence of [a] growing distance that separates the progress of some . . . [from] the stagnation of some, not to say the regression of others."[82] This inequality should not be allowed to prevail. As noted earlier, the oil areas are predominantly inhabited by minority groups who are particularly vulnerable to the political and economic power of the oil multinationals and the government of the producer nation.

According to United Nations University (UNU) research (1988), an examination of the relationships between minority cultures and the larger societies in which they are immersed revealed the effects that different development policies might have on the survival prospects of the world's minority cultures.[83]

UNU project director on ethnic minorities and human and social development, Rudolfo Stavenhagen, commented that:

the process of nation-building might have negative consequences on the ethnic groups throughout the world, who number in the thousands. Most of the world's countries, in fact, are multiethnic nations, composed of peoples of differing origins, cultural traditions, religions, and even languages. These differences, which have so often hindered centrally planned development in the past, have become more openly exposed in a resurgence of ethnic and cultural demands by minority peoples. . . . The existing standards for the protection of human rights are oriented towards the individual, and do not take account of the rights of collectivities.[84]

He proposed an alternative ethno-development based on the demands of minority groups.

On the social consequences of economic development, the World Bank Report (1982) states that:

Tribal minorities in all parts of the world have suffered for centuries from [the] adverse effect of expansion from outside into territories that were formerly entirely tribal and once supported larger tribal populations. This process has often led to the decimation and even to the extinction of these populations. This was generally accepted as [an] inevitable though by no means always intentional byproduct of development.

The tribes of human beings must not be sacrificed to the goals of economic development . . . nor should the technically more powerful abuse the rights or way of life of the technically less powerful.[85]

To this end, it has become necessary that all concerned parties in the oil production process integrate their efforts to avert any possible calamities or misfortunes that could affect the communities of the oil producing areas. By taking a serious look in this way at the oil impact, a basis will be formed for determining a meaningful socioeconomic and environmental mitigation policy. It will be a step toward the respect for and preservation of environmental integrity, and will also accelerate any action taken by the oil industry to ameliorate the adverse socioeconomic and environmental effects of their action.

STATEMENT OF THE PROBLEM

In this introduction, a considerable amount of background information has been delineated. However, the basic problem in this study is to examine the impact of the oil industry on the indigenous population of the oil producing areas of Nigeria with particular reference to selected ecological factors.

The introduction of a new technology in a third world society to stimulate the engine of growth calls for changes either for better or for worse. The oil industry in Nigeria is no exception; it has created positive externalities, or derived benefits, along with negative externalities, or social costs, to the society.

The term "oil impact" refers to changes in patterns of interaction and social structures: depersonalization, invasion, unwanted mobility, and loss of property.[86] There are also economic changes revealed in the levels of industrial output, employment, unemployment, and gross receipts. In addition, there are the biological and environmental consequences of the resultant pollution, posing hazards to health and to the ecology of the area.[87] For the purpose of this study, however, the term "impact" will refer to selected social and economic factors that are directly measurable and attributable to the oil industry. The measurable variables specific to this study are:

1. The impact X represents the production of oil measured in barrels per day for each year from 1964 to 1984. It is assumed here that the intensity of oil production is an indicator of impact activity. Hence, oil production represents the independent variable.

2. The dependent variables selected are social and economic indicators of societal well-being such as housing, water, power, roads, health, and education. There are also social costs to the society characterized by pollution. Therefore Y represents the set of socioeconomic dependent variables as indicators of development or underdevelopment attributable to the presence of the oil industry in producing areas.

Apparently there is excessive emphasis on the economic significance of oil production in Nigeria, to the extent that human consequences coupled with local costs to oil producing areas are ignored or forgotten. As O. Ogbonna puts it:

We need to know not only how profits are shared between industry and government, but also how the benefits are disposed of in the domestic economy, and especially how the rural majority fit into the scheme of things. Primary activities should have assessment of their net impacts [and] must necessarily consider what they do to local communities of the region of production as an important segment of [the] national economic and political system.[88]

The above statement is a valuable inspiration to the concern of this study. No one has seriously and explicitly addressed the question of the oil industry's impact on the oil producing areas. We cannot afford to concern ourselves solely with strategic economic interests without regard for local implementations and community welfare. Thus the purpose of the present study has this principal aim: to investigate the impact of the oil industry on the indigenous population in the oil producing areas. From this study, we will gain perspective on the specific problems. Moreover, the study will sensitize the reader to the necessity of planning carefully for the affected communities. Finally, this study is an attempt to determine if the oil industry has impacted measurably upon the indigenous population of oil producing areas, and if it will it be necessary for that population to continue to be the primary bearers of the economic and social costs of Nigerian development and corporate profit.

Many previous studies on the Nigerian oil industry have been primarily concerned with trends in production, markets, revenue, and economic growth. These studies have no doubt proven helpful to the oil companies and the government, but insufficient attention has been given to determining the industry's impact on the indigenous people.

Is it not desirable that relief materials reach the victims of oil spillage and other oil mishaps through planned community-based service systems instead of the hasty and inefficient ad hoc relief programs? Is it not possible that substitute industries could be established in oil areas so that the social and economic livelihood of the indigenous people may be improved? Finally, what will be the future of oil producing areas in the post-oil era?

Is it not possible that Nigeria could reduce the imbalance in its development by creating an improved socioeconomic infrastructure for the special needs of the oil areas? Or could it be said that, just as Britain colonized Nigeria and exploited its resources for the benefit of British metropoles, Nigeria is exploiting in like manner the resources of its mostly rural oil areas for the benefit of its own and other metropoles, at the costly expense of rural degradation? These are some of the basic issues that this study seeks to address.

Significance of the study

The significance of this study will lie in the difference it is capable of making in the quality of lives of the people; its premise is that human value should supercede the profit motive. As R. A. Carpenter puts it, "the conservation of species and habitats [should] be [a] major responsibility in development planning."[89] One assumes that when a country realizes profit from its natural resources that its indigenous population will also benefit; as a country improves its wealth, the quality of life of its inhabitants should also improve. Whether this relationship holds true in Nigeria is yet to be seen from the findings of this study of the impact of the oil industry on its producing areas.

Limitations of the study

Although this oil impact assessment study is intended to be complete and comprehensive, there were a number of constraints in reaching the ideal goal in terms of cost, data, resources and time, and nonquantifiable factors and methodological limitations with regard to the time series/ordinary least square model; the complex nature of the study organization and its relationships with human subjects; and measurement difficulties in integrating all the conceivable levels of the dependent variables (socioeconomic indicators and environmental changes) into the assessment process. In spite of these constraints, the study seems feasible and promising.

NOTES

1. Yeri Obidake, "The Impact of the Nigerian Petroleum Industry on the Transportation Pattern," unpublished manuscript (Syracuse University, New York, 1982), 1.

2. J. K. Offomey, "The Oil Industry in Nigeria," address delivered to the Nigeria–British Association at Nigerian Institute of International Affairs, Lagos, July 13, 1983.

3. Federal Ministry of Information, Federal Government of Nigeria Report (Lagos, Nigeria, 1982).

4. J. Nwokedi, "Nigeria's Oil Business" in *Nigerian Handbook* (Lagos, Nigeria: Patike Communications, 1985).

5. Paul Lubeck, "Nigeria: A Political Economy,"*Africa Today*, Volume 24, no. 4 (October 1977), 6-10.

6. Michael Tanzer, *Oil Exploration Strategies: Alternative for the Third World in Oil and Class Struggle*, Peter Nore and Terisa Turner, eds. (London: Zed Press, 1980), 90.

7. Nicholas Sarkis, director of the Arab Petroleum Research Center and adviser on oil matters to several African states, in *OPEC Review* (Summer 1988), 182.

8. *OPEC Bulletin* (Vienna, Austria), March 1989.

9. *OPEC Bulletin* (September 1989): 26.

10. Sanchez G. Sierra, "Latin American Energy Organization," *OPEC Bulletin* (September 1989): 28.

11. I. C. Igweonwu, "A Theoretical Perspective on Negotiations with Reference to the International Oil Industry," *OPEC Review* Vol. 11, no. 2 (Summer, 1988): 177.

12. Alexander Kemp, *Petroleum Rent Collection Around the World,* (Halifax, Canada: Institute for Research on Public Policy, 1987), 49.

13. Ibid., pp. 51, 52, and 196.

14. *Petroleum Intelligence Weekly,* July 7, 1980.

15. International Petroleum Encyclopedia (Tulsa, Oklahoma: Pennwell Publishers, 1988), 68-70.

16. B. Fubara, "The Ethics of Nigeria's Proposed Withdrawl from OPEC," *Journal of Business Ethics* 5, no. 4 (August 1986): 353.

17. Momodu Kassim-Momodu, "The Duration of Oil Mining Leases in Nigeria," *Journal of Energy and Natural Resources Law* 6, no. 2 (1988): 103-4.

18. Yinka Omorogbe, "The Legal Framework for Production of Petroleum in Nigeria," *Journal of Energy and Natural Resources Law* 5, no. 4 (1987): 277-9.

19. Paul Lubeck, "Nigeria: A Political Economy," 6-10.

20. I. C. Igweonwu, "A Theoretical Perspective," 189.

21. I. C. Igweonwu, "A Theoretical Perspective," 177-93.

22. Thomas Walde, "Third World Mineral Development in Crisis," *Journal of World Trade Law* 19, no. 1 (January-February 1985), pp. 12-13.

23. M. A. Olorunfemi, "Managing Nigeria's Petroleum Resources," *OPEC Bulletin* (December/January 1986), 25.

24. Miguel S. Wionczek, "Measures of Strengthening the Negotiation Capacity of Governments in Their Relations With Transnational Corporations," UN Technical Paper ST/CTC/11, New York.

25. Ibid.

26. Momodu Kassim-Momodu, "Nigeria's Transfer of Technology," *Journal of World Trade* 22, no. 4 (August 1988):52.

27. Ibid., 58-59.

28. Hassan Zakariya, "Transfer of Technology Under Petroleum Development Contracts," *Journal of World Trade Law* 16, no. 8 (1982): 215.

29. Statement by Lawrence Amu, managing director of NNPC Platts *Oilgram News*, New York (September 1, 1982), 2.

30. Momodu Kassim-Momodu, "Nigeria's Transfer," 54-55.

31. Momodu Kassim-Momodu, "The Duration of Oil Mining Leases," 114.

32. Howard Lax, *States and Companies: Political Risks in the International Oil Industry* (New York: Praeger, 1988), 173.

33. Olufemi Fajani, "Trade and Growth: Nigerian Experience," *World Development* (January 1979).

34. Jon McLin, "Petroleum Price Roller Coaster: Some Social and Economic Effects on Producing States," *International Labor Review* 127, no. 4 (1988): 409-29.

35. Christopher Stevens, "The Political Economy of Nigeria," *The Economist* (London: Cambridge University Press, 1984).

36. Ibid., 13.

37. Terisa Turner, "Oil Workers and Oil Burst in Nigeria,"*Africa Today,* Vol. 33, no. 4 (October 1986): 36-37.

38. Ibid., 36.

39. H. R. Linden, "World Oil — An Essay on its Spectacular 120-Year Rise, Recent Decline, and Uncertain Future," *Journal of Energy Systems and Policy* 11, no. 2 (1987-88): 251.

40. Ibid., 253.

41. Ibid., 254.

42. Ibid., 257.

43. According to H. R. Linden (1987: 255), the Seven Sisters' corporate names were: Exxon, Standard Oil, Mobil, Gulf, Texaco, Shell, and British Petroleum.

44. Jide Osuntokun, "Oil and Nigerian Development," *Development Outlook* 1, no. 3 (August 1986): 40.

45. Ibid.

46. S. Roberto, "The Impact of Oil Operations on the Producing Regions of Southern Mexico," *Third World Planning Review* 5, no. 1 (February 1983): 57.

47. John W. Forje, "Modernization, Development, and Alien Penetration," *Journal of African Studies* 2, no. 3 (Fall 1984): 125.

48. Nnamdi Azikiwe, *Renascent Africa* (New York, Negro Universities Press, 1969), 7.

49. B. Onimode, "Imperialism and Nigerian Development," in *Path to Nigerian Development,* O. Nnoli, ed. (Dakar, Senegal: Codesria Book Series, 1981), 91.

50. Bingu W. T. Mutharika, Chief of the Africa Trade Centre of the United Nations Economic Commission for Africa in "A Theoretical Perspective on Negotiations, with Reference to the International Oil Industry," by Isaac Igweonwu, *OPEC Review* 11, no. 2 (Summer 1988): 181.

51. Kwame Nkrumah, past president of Ghana, *Neocolonialism: The Last Stage of Imperialism* (London: Thomas Nelson and Sons, Ltd., 1965): 1-2.

52. B. Bock et al., *The Impact of the Modern Corporations* (New York: Columbia University Press, 1984), 164.

53. *The Report of the Presidential Commission on Revenue Allocation: Main Report ,Vol. 1* (Lagos, Nigeria: Federal Government Press, 1980), 86.

54. Comfort A. Briggs, "Fiscal Federalism in Nigeria Through the Second Constitutional Government: A Study of Political Influence on Revenue Allocation" (doctoral dissertation, George Washington University, 1988), p. 195.

55. Ibid, 188.

56. Ibid.

57. Ibid.

58. J. M. Ostheimer, *Nigerian Politics* (New York: Harper and Row Publishers, 1973), 39.

59. Petter Nore, *Oil and Class Struggle* (London: Zed Press, 1981), 2.

60. W. Zartman, *Political Economy of Nigeria* (New York: Praeger, 1983), 49.

61. John Rawls, *A Theory of Justice* (Cambridge, MA: Harvard University Press, 1971), 3

62. D. Muruako, "OPEC: Population vs. Oil Reserves," *African World News* (July/August 1988): 22. Muruako showed that Iran, Saudi Arabia, and Nigeria quotas would have been different if population had been used for production allocation. Iran has a population approximately four times that of Saudi

Arabia, but has a reserve of 0.33 times in oil quota for production and produces 0.50 times more than Saudi Arabia. Nigeria has nine times the population of Saudi Arabia, 0.105 times the oil reserves of Saudi Arabia, but with quotas of barely 0.30 times that of Saudi Arabia. Then, using Saudi Arabia as the base for calculation, he showed that if Saudis produce 4.353 bpd, Iran should be allowed a quota of 5.979 bpd and Nigeria 4.189 bpd. The derived calculation is as follows:

Factors	Population	x	Reserves	x	Base	=	Quotas
Saudi Arabia	1.000	x	1.000	x	4.353	=	4.353
Iran	4.162	x	0.330	x	4.353	=	5.999
Nigeria	9.165	x	0.105	x	4.353	=	4.189

63. According to David Hyman, *Public Finance (Intergovernmental Fiscal Relations)* (New York: Dryden Press, 1987), 582. The revenue sharing plan should include:

1. a formula determining the total amount of federal revenue to be distributed among the states per year

2. a formula specifying the allocation of total revenue to be shared among the alternative states

3. a formula stating the percentage of funds that should go to local governments in each state and the levels of local government that should be included in the sharing arrangement

4. a specification of any restrictions to be placed on expenditure of the federally shared funds

64. O. Nnoli, *Path to Nigerian Development* (Dakar, Senegal: Codesria Book Series, 1981), 148.

65.   Federal views on the Political Bureau Report in *National Concord Newspaper,* August 11, 1987.

66. A. E. K. Nash, *Oil Pollution and Public Interest* (Berkeley, CA: Institute of Governmental Studies, University of California, 1977), 10-24.

67. The South Publication: *Third World Magazine,* December 1980; and *Industrialization and Economic Development,* P. T. Buer, ed. (London: Warden and Nicolson, 1984), 74-76.

68. Ministry of Information, *Hazards of Oil Exploration in Bendel State* (Benin City, Nigeria, 1981), 34.

69. Ibid.

70. Simon Ebare, "Oil Spillage Areas Deserve More Aid," *Sunday Times* (Port Harcourt, Nigeria), July 27, 1980.

71. Ministry of Information, *Hazards of Oil Exploration in Bendel State* (Benin City, Nigeria, 1981), 14.

72. Ibid., 23-35.

73. Sesan Ayodele, "The Conflict of the Growth of the Nigerian Petroleum Industry and Environmental Quality," *Socioeconomic Planning Science* 19, no. 5 (1985): 295-301.

74. Yinka Omorogbe, "The Legal Framework for the Production of Petroleum in Nigeria," *Journal of Energy and Natural Resources Law* 5, no. 4 (1987): 273.

75. E. I. Nwogu, "Law and Environment in the Nigerian Oil Industry," *Earth Law Journal* (Netherlands) 1; 2 (May 1985): 91-105.

76. C. Ikporukpo, "Management of Oil Pollution of Natural Resources in Nigeria," *Journal of Environmental Management* 20, no. 1 (1985): 204.

77. Jide Osuntokun, "Oil and Nigerian Development," 34.

78. B. Fubara, "The Ethics of Nigeria's Proposed Withdrawal from OPEC," *Journal of Business Ethics* 5, no. 4 (August 1986): 327.

79. Ministry of Information, *Hazards of Oil Exploration in Bendel State* (Benin City, Nigeria, 1981): 22-30.

80. Sesan Ayodele, "The Conflict of the Growth of the Nigerian Petroleum Industry and Environmental Quality," 300.

81. Simon Ebare, "Oil Spillage Areas Deserve More Aid," *Sunday Times* (Port Harcourt, Nigeria), July 27, 1980.

82. P. T. Buer, *Industrialization and Economic Development* (London: Warden and Nicolson, 1984), 75.

83. United Nations University Research, *Human Rights and Conflict Resolution Network Update,* United Nations University, Tokyo, Japan (June 1988), 2.

84. Ibid.

85. *World Bank Report* (Washington, D.C.: World Bank, May 1982), 2.

86. Wiber Moore, *The Impact of Industry* (Englewood Cliffs, NJ: Prentice Hall, 1965), 4-10.

87. William H. Mathews, *Man's Impact on the Global Environment: Assessment and Recommendations for Action* (Cambridge, MA: MIT Press, 1970), 141.

88. O. Ogbonna, "The Geographic Consequences of Petroleum in Nigeria With Special Reference to Rivers State" (doctoral dissertation, University of California, 1979), 12.

89. R. A. Carpenter, *Natural Systems for Development* (New York: Macmillan Press, 1983).

2

Overview: Nigeria in Modern Times

GEOGRAPHY

Nigeria is a developing country and Africa's most populous nation. The country is physically set on the easternmost part of the Gulf of Guinea in West Africa. It lies within the tropics, between latitude 4 degrees and 14 degrees north of the equator and 3 degrees east of the Greenwich meridian. It is bounded on the west by the Republic of Benin, on the north by the Niger Republic, on the east by the Republic of Cameroon, and on the south by the Atlantic Ocean.[1]

Nigeria has an area of about 913,072.64 square kilometers (some 357,000 square miles). The country is well watered by the Rivers Niger and Benue and their tributaries. There are only two well-defined seasons, the dry season (from November to March) and the rainy season (from April to October). The average temperature is about 32 degrees centigrade. Nigeria takes its name from the Niger River. There is a popular, though mistaken, belief that Nigeria is connected with the word "niger," from which the word "negro" is derived. It has been established, however, that the word Niger traces its origin to local African and pre-Roman expressions for a "Great River" so that literally Nigeria means "land of the great river."[2]

Modern Nigeria was born in 1914 when the two British protectorates of north and south were amalgamated by Sir Frederick Luggard. Though Nigeria is a racially homogenous society, it is socially, religiously, and linguistically heterogenous (Figure 2.1). There are well over 300 languages and dialects in Nigeria, and it is divided into nearly as many ethnic groups. Nigeria's current population is estimated to be nearly 100 million with a projected population of 341 million by the year 2020. The tenth-most populous country in the world in 1986, the United Nations has forecast that Nigeria will rank fourth (exceeded only by China, India, and the Soviet Union, but ahead of the United States) by the 2025.[3] The major ethnic groups are the Hausas, Ibos, Fulanis, Yorubas, Edos, Effiks, Ijaws, Tivs, and Kanuris.

Mineral producing areas

Nigeria is blessed with a number of important mineral resources. In different parts of the country, you will find limestone, columbite, lignite, iron ore, lead, zinc, tin, bauxite, diatomite, gypsum and oil. There are also traces of uranium, gold, and liquified natural gas in certain areas, particularly Bauchi State, Sokoto State, and the Chad Basin in Bornu State.

Mining has played an important role in the country's economy. Before the rise of the oil industry, extraction of solid minerals was centered around two major producing areas:

1. The Udi Hills (near Enugu and Abakaliki) in the east central part of the country in present-day Anambra State. The specific elements mined were coal, zinc, and lead.

2. The Plateau areas (near Jos) in the present-day Plateau State. The specific elements mined were tin and columbite.

In the last two decades, the mining of solid minerals has declined, partly due to decreased demand in the world's market and partly, of course, to the rise of oil displacing their importance.

Figure 2.1

Nigeria: Major Ethnic Distribution in Mineral Regions

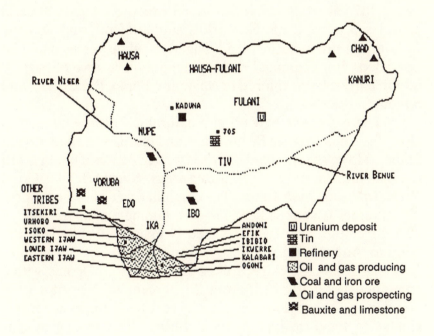

Sources: J. R. Prescot, *Nigerian Geographical Journal,* June 1958; Ogbonna Okoro (1979); John M. Ostheimer (1973).

Oil producing areas

Nigeria began oil production in 1956 when the first discovery was made at Oloibiri in the Niger Delta. Since then, oil exploration and exploitation has expanded into many areas (both onshore and offshore) within the Niger Delta Basin. The Niger Delta is the main producing area with seventy-eight oil fields, the largest of which is at Forcados Yorki. There are a total of 158 oil fields in operation in Nigeria, of which 18 percent are offshore, and 2,187 oil wells, of which 1,563 are producing. Nigeria provides 3 percent of the world's supply of oil, and was the fifth-largest producer in 1985.[4] Nigeria's oil resources could be upgraded. It is estimated that a potential oil reserve of over 30 billion barrels is unexplored in Anambra, Benin, Bida, Chad, and Sokoto.[5]

There are also new oil and natural gas prospecting areas along the Chad Basin in Bornu State, and in Anambra and Sokoto States. However, this study, for reasons of data availability, will focus on the following oil producing areas: Rivers, Bendel, Cross River, Imo and Ondo States. The combined size of these oil-producing areas is about 117,396 square kilometers, or roughly 12 percent of the country. The area is mainly inhabited by the Abribas, Andonis, Edos, Effiks, Gokanas, Ibibios, Ijaws, Ika-Ibos, Ikwerres, Irhobos, Isekiris, Isokos, Kalabaris, and Ogonis, with a combined population of about 25 percent of Nigeria's total population. The region is marked by very thick equatorial forest similar to the Brazilian Amazon Basin. The coastal area is mangrove forest interspersed by a network of creeks and rivers. Beyond the mangrove belt lies a stretch of tropical rainforests. This area has been the hotbed of Nigeria's oil industry since the early 1950s.

Political development

Nigeria is a British invention formed by the amalgamation of the two former British northern and southern protectorates in 1914. The unification of the two separate administrations was effected by the British for their administrative convenience. The country was then divided into four provinces: the northern, western, and eastern provinces, and the colony of Lagos (Figure 2.2).[6] Nigeria was ruled under a unitary system of government until 1922, when the first constitutional legislative council was formed, but representation was limited to the colony of Lagos and Calabar in the eastern province. A new constitution, formed in 1946, gave the provinces the responsibility of advising the colonial central government, but only as to matters affecting the provinces. However, the adoption of the later 1951 constitution empowered the regional administration in each province to become regional government for the province. This new provision gave rise to the birth of three political parties in the country: the National Council of Nigeria and the Cameroon, the Northern Peoples Congress, and the Action Group.

These three emergency political parties set the pace for Nigeria's active drive toward independence. Their leaders participated in a number of conferences that led to the establishment of both regional and national assemblies, and finally to the attainment of independence on October 1, 1960. On October 1, 1963, Nigeria became a republic, thus severing all ties with the British crown but retaining its membership in the Commonwealth.

POLITICS AND GOVERNMENT OF NIGERIA SINCE 1963

In Nigeria, socially conditioned values have had a major influence on political behavior. Under the 1963 constitution, the Federation of Nigeria consisted of the capital territory Lagos, as

Figure 2.2

Nigeria: Before 1967

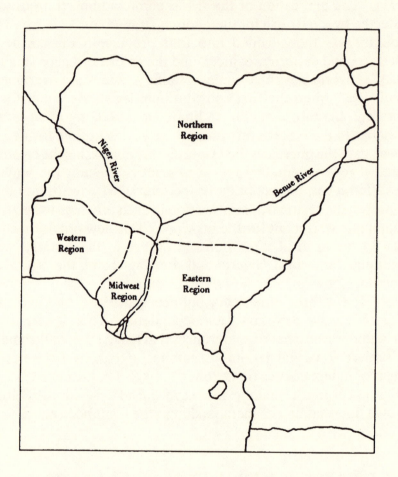

Source: J. M. Ostheimer, *Nigerian Politics* (New York: Harper and Row, 1973).

well as the northern, western and eastern regions. Later, a mid-western region was carved out of the western region to become the fourth region (Figure 2.3). Nigeria's first government after independence from Britain in 1960 was patterned after the Westminster model, or a cabinet form of government (Dundley 1982)[7.] The chief executive branch was part of the legislature and wielded its power as a participant there. The first republic lasted about five years.

In January 1966 (Dundley 1982), the military seized power from the civilian administration in a coup d'etat. The country's first prime minister, Sir Abubaker Tafawa Balewa, and a number of other high-ranking government officials lost their lives. General Aguiyi Ironsi became Nigeria's first military ruler in 1966. He ruled only six months before being killed along with several top military offers in a counter-coup. He was succeeded by Lt. Col. Yakubu Gowon (later General Gowon). Gowon's military administration divided the country into a twelve-state structure. That particular structure was the basis for governing the country for the next nine years. General Gowon's military government led the nation through thirty months of civil war (1967-70).

OIL AND POLITICS – THE CIVIL WAR

The existenae of oil was an influential factor in the politics of the Nigerian civil war. Both the federal government and the secessionist government had interest in oil royalty payments. The multinational oil corporations were trapped in a dilemma about the distribution of royalties and taxes.[8] The secessionists demanded that royalty payments be made to their coffers. But the federal government threatened to revoke licenses and concessions to oil companies if such payments were made. It was reported that the multinational oil companies resolved the dilem-

Figure 2.3

Nigeria: Political Transition, 1963–89

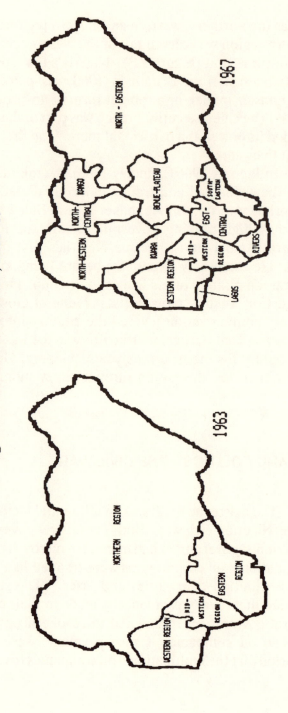

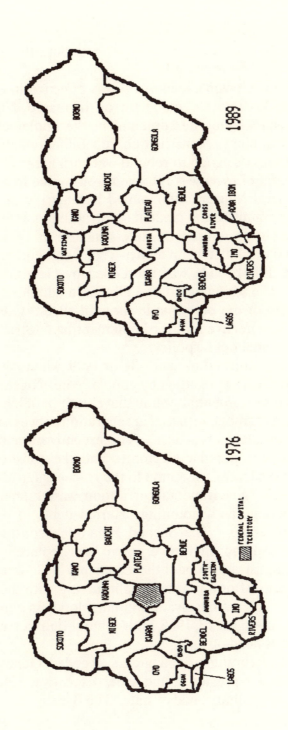

ma by making royalty and tax payments to both the federal and the secessionist governments.

General Gowon's leadership was effective in ending the civil war in 1970. As demand for oil increased, Nigeria's oil resources were highly instrumental in the implementation of federal government reconstruction, rehabilitation, and resettlement programs designed to rebuild war-torn areas. On July 29, 1975, General Gowon was removed from office in a bloodless coup. General Murtala Muhammed became the new head of state. His administration created seven additional states, bringing the country to a nineteen-state structure in 1976. General Muhammed was killed in an abortive coup on February 13, 1976 (Olayiwola 1984).[9] He was succeeded by General Olusegun Obasanjo. The Muhammed and Obasanjo administrations enjoyed the era of the oil boom in the mid-1970s. Oil became a lucrative and effective tool for implementing Nigeria's national and international public policy.

Nigeria returned to civil rule in 1979, when Alhaji Shehu Shagari was elected president by popular vote. Nigeria's second republic was a presidential system that closely paralleled the U.S. system of government, with a clear separation between the executive and legislative branches.[10] The executive branch derived power from the popular electorate and the constitution. In December 1983, the army came to the rescue again after allegations of massive governmental corruption, wasteful management of the economy, and mounting external debts in the face of declining revenues. The Second Republic's constitution was suspended and the civil government was replaced by a new military administration under the leadership of General Mohammadu Buhari. After a year and eight months with the country's economic problems unsolved, another bloodless counter-coup took place on August 27, 1985, and General Buhari was removed from office as head of state.

General Ibrahim Babangida succeeded General Buhari and was named president and chief executive. He became Nigeria's sixth military head of state. The Babangida administration dealt with the problematic scenario of the oil burst and the oil glut with declining revenues and mounting deficits.

The custodian theory is put forward by the military itself, which claims that it is the custodian of the nation's constitution, and as such is being flouted. This theory was employed, for example, by Major General A. A. Afrifa, to explain the overthrow of President Nkrumah in 1966, and later by General Murtala Muhammed to explain the overthrow of General Gowon. Military involvement in a developing democratic state is apparently the most stable of several practical alternatives utilized when parliamentary democracy falters.[11] In Nigeria, the search for political development coupled with economic stability continues. A new political blueprint was drawn by the Babangida military administration to return the country to civil rule by the year 1992.

In African states, during any civilian rule, each political party strives to ensure personal control of the national treasury and revenue-producing resources. When the elections are won by a political party, the government becomes no more than a holding company of the bourgeoisie, which is solely intent on sharing the national booty. From historical observations of political transformation processes in the country, we see that the origin of leadership and adherents of a given political party identify with past political parties, although there may be a symbolic change of party name or slight modifications of political ingredients in an effort to comply with the new guidelines for political behavior formulated by the custodian military government.

Mineral resources are key to national wealth and the politics of distribution has always been controversial. The extraction of oil itself takes place in minority areas and the minorities by nature lack a strong influence on the national political machinery. They are simply aggregated into a political buffer state and, by their political behavior, seek to benefit from a greater portion of the revenue derived from their mineral resources on the basis of the derivative principle (Onoh 1983), which presupposes that mineral producing areas should have a greater share of the revenue derived from the resource.[12] In order to achieve their fair share of the revenue, minority groups throw their political weight behind any one of the major groups. The minorities try to ally with a major group to gain attention in the bid to meet their demand, although not necessarily with one collective voice. But on the whole, minorities strive to maintain a sense of balance in the Nigerian political system. However, the question of what political system will thrive well for Nigeria is still open to debate. As Uzor M. Uzoatu puts it, "Nigerians talk politics better than they play it." Since October 1960 the country has had only nine years of civil rule and seventeen long years of military government. Against two democratically elected heads of state, Nigeria has had a roll of six military rulers. All of this spells instability, and it is little wonder that the present military head of state, President Babangida, on January 13, 1986, set up a nineteen-member bureau to develop a political system for the country to break the cycle of instability.[13] President Babangida's innovative political order is the establishment of a two-party system under government supervision. He has named two parties: the Social Democrat Party, which would promote the ideals of a welfarist principle; and the National Republican Convention, which would promote the principles of regional compromise and free enterprise.[14] An advantage to be derived from the new two-party system is that ideological divisions will not be allowed to become social divisions, and the regional configurations that were evident in past political behavior will, it is hoped, be eliminated from the national political forum. Therefore the hope for a viable political system for the country, one that will ensure stability for 1992 and beyond, is widely held by the Nigerian people.

As President Ibrahim Babangida puts it, "For us it is a challenge we shall face with resolve and fortitude, characteristic of our military profession. We are committed to laying such foundations for political stability as will render unnecessary military intervention as a vehicle for alternating or changing governments."[15]

THE ECONOMY

"Progress is made in capitalist society according to the law of personal profit which leads to competition, which in turn contributes to productivity; it is also the law of the jungle."[16] Nigeria's economy during its colonial era was mainly export oriented. The production of cash crops was encouraged by the colonial government for the purpose of encouraging European industrial development.

When Nigeria emerged as an independent state in October 1960, its economy was largely agrarian. Its exported cash crops were: palm oil, groundnut, cotton, and cocoa. Mining also played a role in the country's economy. Among the minerals mined were iron, tin, columbite, limestone, and coal. The oil industry also began to develop at that time.

However, more than 70 percent of the people were employed in agriculture or related fields. This was the structure of the Nigerian economy before the oil boom of the 1970s. Nigeria has begun to enjoy the sudden upsurge of oil wealth. The oil production quickly climbed from a low of 0.14 mbd in 1968 to 1.08 mbd at the start of the decade.[17] Thus the world market demand for oil greatly influenced the internationalization of Nigeria's domestic economy, and its social and economic development became largely dependent on oil earnings.

The abundance of oil resources attracted a number of foreign multinational oil companies and related firms from Europe, the United States, and Japan. As Gottfried Haberler noted long ago, it is the ancient rule again: "Those who have [oil deposits] shall receive foreign capital."[18] The influx of foreign capital and technology catalyzed the rapid growth of the Nigerian oil industry, whose activities are highly centered in the oil producing areas of Nigeria. The lucrative nature of oil resources influenced the need for expanded production in the 1970s through the 1980s which was blessed with a dramatic rise in oil prices; all worked together for the benefit of Nigeria. For example, "like other oil producers, Nigeria increased its prices substantially in

1979/80 and by July 1980 there was a tag of $37 a barrel on its market crude (Bonnylight). This price was too high, and production fell. The mini-slump was quickly ended by the Iran–Iraq war and Nigerian oil prices were pushed up yet again to $40 a barrel in January 1980."[19] This resulted in a buoyant revenue for Nigeria until the sudden slump of world oil prices in 1983 (Figure 2.4). But oil still remained the big earner for Nigeria, because production itself had not declined dramatically in face of the slump. Despite the past boom and gluts, oil has remained the principal source of funding for the country's development plans. Oil wealth helped Nigeria by increasing the value of exports at an annual average rate of 30 percent between 1970 and 1980, and oil has also financed huge public investment programs such as the Kainji Dam, superhighways, steel plants, development of the nation's seaports, airports, and a new federal capital at Abuja.[20]

Nigeria practices a form of mixed economy wherein virtually all the firms in the private sector have connections with foreign capital under the glorified name of "technical partners." The foreign investment may have some positive value if it is limited to small areas in which foreign capital can be of help, but instead the influx of foreign capital has generated an economic dependency that has stifled local initiative for autonomous self-development. Moreover, the foreign sector is highly capital intensive, which operates to the country's disadvantage by creating massive unemployment. Foreign control and consequent economic dependency has displaced the capacities of the indigenous population in the development of autonomous innovative techniques for production and self-sustained growth. For instance, oil production and its pollutant effects are blamed for the agricultural decline. The agricultural sector offered major employment opportunities for the masses in the pre-oil growth era, but oil pollution on farm lands has generated unemployment in affected rural areas. The oil sector employs less than 5 percent of the labor force and the rest of the private sector lacks the absorption capacity to reduce unemployment. Nigeria has recorded an impressive average annual GNP growth rate of 3.7 percent, or GDP

Figure 2.4

Trend in Nigerian Crude Oil Prices, 1972-89
(U.S. dollars per barrel)

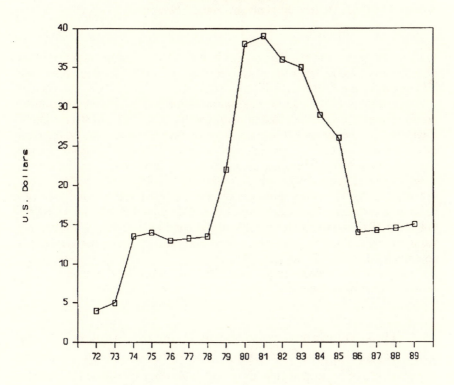

Sources: Sesan Ayodele, 1983, 300; British Petroleum, *Statistical Review of World Energy* (London, 1986), 5; *OPEC Bulletin*, February/March 1989.

$72,632 million dollars,[21] and a per capita income of $884 (Fubara 1986).[22]

The economic scenario is well summarized by *African Heritage* magazine:

Since the early 1970s the petroleum industry has been the mainstay of the Nigerian economy and the major determinants of the country's economic growth. It contributed to more than 95 percent of the total export earnings and provided just over 90 percent of all government revenue.

With the collapse of the world oil market in 1981, the revenue of the government of Nigeria declined. The Federal Revenue which in 1980 stood at an all time high of 15.2 billion, fell to 12.1 billion in 1981 to 11.7 million in 1982. The current exchange rate is U.S. $1.00 = 4.04 naira (October 1987). The government policy response, rather than rationing expenditures, looked for external loans. That was how the nation got into the external debt bondage. Today, the total external public debt is Trend in Nigerian Crude Oil Prices 1972-1989$22 billion out of which some $12.9 billion is medium and long term debt. Simultaneously, domestic public debts also grew from a modest 7.9 billion in 1980 to 27.9 billion in 1985. Side by side with mounting debts was the deterioration in the country's balance of payment. External reserves of 5648.2 million in 1980 fell to 1065.3 million in 1982 and to an all time low of 885.2 million in 1983. With reserves barely enough to finance a month's import and with the international financial community skeptical of the country's viability, creditors became worried. Soon, credits needed to sustain imports were cut off, throwing the economy into serious economic dislocation.[23]

Thus Nigeria has faced a drastic decline in revenue since 1981, compelling the government to impose austerity measures to restructure its economy. Nigeria has low foreign asset investment and diversification; hence it has no adequate protection against shocks in oil revenue or uncertainty over oil market stability (Table 2.1).

Nigeria has a high degree of external dependence but low internal dependence which, coupled with high debt service, makes it more vulnerable to economic instability. A study on economic policy with fluctuating oil revenues (A. Markandya and

Table 2.1

Nigeria: Real Exchange Indices and Consumer Price Indices

Year	Exchange Rate[*] 1970-89	Consumer Price Index 1970-84
1970	1.26	83.8
1971	1.40	97.3
1972	1.52	100.0
1973	1.51	106.0
1974	1.60	119.2
1975	2.00	159.3
1976	2.33	198.1
1977	2.52	236.3
1978	2.81	280.4
1979	3.97	311.7
1980	3.20	344.0
1981	3.10	415.6
1982	3.90	447.6
1983	3.22	551.5
1984	4.03	769.9
1985	4.05	n/a
1986	4.04	n/a
1987	4.30	n/a
1988	4.695	n/a
1989	7.05	n/a

Sources: OPEC Bulletin (Sprint 1989): 28-29, Tables 2 and 3; West Africa, February and July 1987, and March 1989.

Note: [*] U.S. dollar/naira exchange rates.

M. Pemberton 1988) showed that Nigeria has an external dependence of 97 percent, an internal dependence of 18 percent, foreign assets holding of 16 percent and a debt service ratio of 25 percent.[24] Nigeria's real exchange rate has declined and the country is battling with inflation in a time of dwindling oil revenues (Figure 2.5). Markandya and Pemberton (1988) defined external dependence to mean the export of minerals as a percentage of total exports, and internal dependence to mean the export of oil as a percentage of GDP in current market prices; net foreign assets are defined as the percentage of GDP and interest on public debt as the percentage of the export value of goods and services.

According to Yinka Omorogbe (1987), oil accounts for 98.2 percent of total revenue in a given fiscal year.[25] The value of petroleum exports was estimated to have risen to $6,700 million in 1987 and $7,100 million in 1988. 1989 earnings were expected to be $1,400 million more than forecast. Oil production costs for Nigeria are up to seven times as high as those of the Middle East, but the low sulphur content of Nigerian oil places it at the upper end of the OPEC price scale.[26]

Oil had been instrumental to Nigeria's economic achievement since the 1970s, but mere economic aggregates by themselves are of little use for the masses since they are hardly relevant to their needs. In essence, the wealth did not get to the people. Distributive justice did not emerge to favor them. Apparently, economic growth as measured by GNP is not synonymous with social welfare. Scholars are beginning to wonder if conventional economic theories and practice are indeed suited for Africa. Nigeria was credited with an impressive growth rate in the 1970s, but was reduced to poverty status in the late 1980s. By 1989, it earned the status of one of the world's poorest nations by the World Bank, with a foreign debt of $30.5 million.[27]

Western economic practice is governed by individualism, and its application seems to interfere with the African traditional mode of brotherhood, collective progress, and well-being. African societies need to modify the alien economic tradition

Figure 2.5

Nigeria: Oil Production 1964-87 (millions of barrels per day)

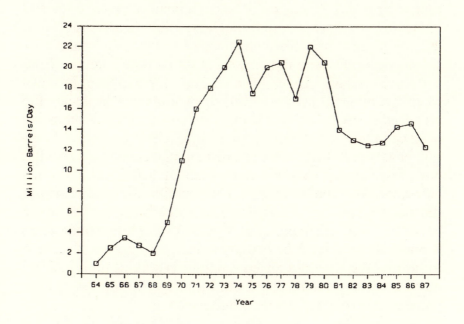

*Sources:*Ministry of Petroleum Resources, Lagos, Nigeria; British Petroleum, *Statistical Review of World Energy* (London, 1986), 5; *Petroleum Encyclopedia* (1988), 248.

which is geared toward individualism and should perhaps stop mimicking Western economies, which are strictly market oriented. It is possible to incorporate certain positive aspects of capitalism into the African system without losing sight of traditional African values. (The Japanese have been able to incorporate capitalism into their system without losing sight of their tradition.) Nigeria was credited with economic progress but its people for the most part did not benefit. African capitalist mixed economic systems such as Nigeria's should be adaptive to traditional communalism, in which each community has the collective right to prioritize ecological balance (human needs) and societal interest. Economic growth through exploitation and progress of the privileged class without elements of stewardship for the masses is unethical within the African tradition of brotherhood and collective welfare. Indeed, we all hope for the glorious dawn when the ethical imperative will reign supreme, displacing the greed inherent in the profit motive and seeking a sustainable balance between economic growth and human ecological interest. Nigeria still finds itself in a neocolonial economy which has not effectively tapped the country's human and material resources for the benefit of its people. The benefits of economic growth did not trickle down sufficiently to make the average citizen better off. The vast majority of Nigerians were losers rather than winners as a result of the country's economic growth. Suffice it to say that the Nigerian mixed economy is nothing more than an alloy of socialism and capitalism, with negative aspects of each enmeshed in a sort of jungle economics.

THE STATUS OF WELFARE

Chief Obafemi Awolowo, premier of western Nigeria in the 1950s, once stated, "The provision of education and health in a developing country such as Nigeria is as much an instrument of economic development as the provision of roads, water supply, electricity, and the like."[28] There is an age-old disparity in the delivery of social services in Nigeria. The provision of social amenities has remained unequal to the disadvantage of the needy rural majority since colonial times. Colonial administration of the social service system mostly favored the urban rich and powerful over the rural poor. R. Stock (1985) notes that the British colonial administration did not ensure a comprehensive social service delivery system.[29] That legacy has held to this day. After twenty-eight years of self-rule, there still exist disparities in the provision of social services. The spatial distribution or network of social facilities remains relatively sparse and unbalanced. The capitalist mode of economic development in the third world generated more underdevelopment than development through policies that alienated the indigenous peoples from their environment either by force or imposition. The result is that people have been displaced from their subsistence agricultural economy in favor of a cash-based economy, which has led to foreign dependence. Subsequently, the people became vulnerable to a variety of new socioeconomic problems such as food shortages, new health hazards, loss of land, environmental pollution, forced migration, unemployment, and other negative byproducts of industrial expansion. These conditions call for the provision of an adequate social service infrastructure.

Nigerian social service indicators

These indicators seem to affirm the continued existence of disparities in the social service delivery system (Table 2.2). Nigerian social statistics indicate that the average monthly cash income of a rural household is N96.79 as compared with N228 for urban areas.[30] In the housing sector, it is noted that 80 percent of Nigerians live in mud and thatch dwellings, with or without toilet facilities. Only 17 percent live in block buildings and the rest (3 percent) live in other forms of buildings.[31]

Table 2.2

Nigeria: Actual and Projected Social Indicators

Indicators	1965	1970	1975	1980	1985	1990	1995	2000
Population Total[1]	58.5	66.2	74.9	84.7	90	103	115.2	158
Rural pop./ 1000	47,129	53,715	61,356	20,985	89,891	89,891	99,903	–
Urban pop./ 1000	9,218	11,947	11,726	70,193	37,657	50,062	–	–
Life Expectancy	41.2	43.7	46.2	48.6	53	52.5	55	57
Dependency Ratio/100	887	890	902	917.7	945	946.7	971.5	963.7
Health[2]	44,990	24,670	17,630	12,550	8,059*	–	–	–
Infant Mortality Rate/1000	170.4	158.0	146.3	135.2	120.0*	–	–	–
Crude Death Rate/1000	13	12	10.3	7	5.6	16.7	14.3	11.2
Crude Death	49.1	47	46.2	40.2	35	49.6	40.2	33

Income Distribution 1976–1977: Lowest 20%: 5.6   Highest 10%: 34.1

Sources: 1. *World Development Report* (Washington, DC: International Bank for Reconstruction, June 1987): 252-64. 2. *Selected World Demographic Indicators, 1950-2000* (New York: United Nations Department of Economic and Social Affairs, May 1975): 55. 3. *Demographic Indicators of Countries,* United Nations Dept. of International Economic and Social Affairs, ST/ESA/SER,A/82.

*1983, Federal Office of Statistics: 1985, *Economics and Social Statistics,* Table 37, p. 36.

Notes: [1]In millions.
[2]Population per physician.

Water. In the rural areas, 63 percent of the people get their water from streams, 26 percent from private wells, and only 6 percent use pipe-borne water. In urban areas, 58 percent use pipe-borne water and 31 percent use wells and streams or bore holes.

Power. Ninety-two percent of rural households are without electricity, whereas 75 percent of urban household have access to it.

Education. Nigeria's educational philosophy is to mold each child into a sound and effective citizen and to offer equal educational opportunities for all. It is also designed to ensure that adequate steps are taken to make education relevant to national needs and objectives. To this end, the Universal Primary Education scheme was launched in 1976 and primary school enrollment rose from 5 million to nearly 12 million. There was also a remarkable rise in secondary and post-secondary school enrollment.[32] The Universal Primary Education philosophy remains, but empirically it has been abandoned in recent times due to the government's dwindling financial resources. Although the country has eighteen established universities, the number of available positions in those institutions is limited, and they are unable to meet the rising demand for higher education. With a growing population of nearly 100 million; there is a need for more educational facilities.

Health. Health facilities in Nigeria remain most spatially disproportionate, a situation that poses the utmost disadvantage to rural residents. The better-funded and equipped health facilities are located in urban areas. There is also a dual health care system. Western scientific medicine exists side by side with traditional health care systems, and they are often in direct competition with each other. Moreover, there is unequal access to Western medicine. Many people, particularly those in the rural areas and the low-income group, rely on traditional herbal medicine because it is easier to get, and herbalists are more plentiful than doctors in the less populated areas. This dualism in health care facilities has a significant impact on the country's morbidity. Statistics show that the infant mortality rate is 193 per 1,000 for rural areas and 94 per 1,000 for urban areas (Federal Office of Statistics, 1985). The average ratio of physicians per capita is one in 12,550 people. Nigerian average life expectancy is 48.6 years. However, efforts are under way to integrate Western and traditional medicine and, through cooperation, to minimize the disparities in the health care system.

Roads. African countries, with the coming of independence in the 1960s, went on a veritable road-building spree. Nigeria was no exception to this rule, because good highways were seen as the umbilical cords of rapid economic growth. In 1946 colonial Nigeria had 24,000 miles of roads, only 700 miles of which were bituminized, but from 1951 to 1972 the distance and number of paved roads increased more than tenfold.[33] Table 2.3 shows the history of road infrastructure in Nigeria from 1962–80. Oil revenue made it possible for the government to embark on massive road construction, but the building of roads was highly disproportionate; rural infrastructure lagged behind intercity and intracity constructions. There was little or no attention given to road development in rural oil producing areas. The country has roughly 98,200 kilometers of roads of all categories. All interstate roads are called "Trunk A" roads and are the federal government's responsibility.[34] Trunk A roads, including bypasses and four-lane expressways, were built between and within major cities during the 1970s oil boom. Twenty-six percent of the network are state roads categorized as either Trunk B or Trunk F roads. Some of the roads are bituminized or asphalt, but many sections of the country still have gravel or earth-surfaced roads. There are some 43,000 kilometers of these rural roads under local authority control. They constitute 44 percent of available roads in the country but receive minimal attention and maintenance, and during the rainy season, the roads are hardly passable. Many rural areas are still inaccessible by road, particularly in the Riverine areas of the Niger Delta. The residents of these areas rely heavily on waterways, some of which are not navigable in the

Table 2.3

Summary of States' Road Programs, 1975–80

States	Total kilo- meters	Estimated total cost	1975–76	1976–77	1977–78	1978–79	1979–80
Benue-Plateau	2,417	93,960,	14,390	20,470	24,620	21,620	12,860
East-Central	1,755	86,698	19,218	19,385	18,615	19,725	9,755
Kano	1,043	55,340	9,640	11,180	10,960	13,520	10,040
Kwara	1,347	61,780	7,840	16,740	16,209	13,291	7,700
Lagos	573	31,265	6,130	7,410	6,850	5,845	5.030
Mid-Western	1,821	187,920	59,210	52,360	37,320	26,260	12,770
North-Central	2,063	59,723	13,300	16,700	14,900	11,200	3,623
North-Eastern	2,496	117,926	21,225	29,439	32,831	20,596	13,835
North-Western	1,791	106,150	20,450	34,700	25,150	11,400	14,450
Rivers	296	41,150	13,650	12,000	7,950	4,900	2,650
South-Eastern	990	67,064	13,045	18,330	11,683	12,951	11,055
Western		75,500	12,700	15,340	16,070	16,880	14,510
Total	19,166	984,476	210,798	254,054	223,158	178,168	118,273

Sources: 1. Nicholas Balabkins, "Indigenization and Economic Develop- ment: Nigerian Experience" in *Contemporary Studies in Economic and Financial Analysis,* vol. 33 (London: JAL Press, 1982), 73; 2. Federal Ministry of Economic Development, Lagos, Nigeria.

Note: Planned investment in roads in the 1962–68 Plan was N150.6 million shared between the federal, northern, eastern, and western govern- ments of the time. The respective allocations were N70.9 million, N49.2 million, N17.7 million, and N12.7 million for the four govern- ments in that order. The three regional governments together dis- bursed N51 million, while the federal government made substantial progress on its program. With the creation of the mid-western region in 1963 an allocation of N5.1 million was made for transport projects, out of which N3.7 million was disbursed. The 1970-74 Second National Plan allocated N332.6 million to roads. Various factors like inflation, changes in project scope, and midstream addi- tion of new projects accounted for many plan revisions, such that by 1973, the revised size of the road program was N883.7 million, made up of N643.7 million for the federal government and N240 million for the twelve states' roads programs. By 1974 total capital cost of the federal road program had risen to an all-time high of N926.8 mil- lion, thus bringing the total national road program to N1.2 billion by that date.

dry season. It is difficult for the residents to transport goods and services to desired markets.

Condition of social services in oil producing areas

Given the structural imbalances and the severe limitations of the social service delivery system, the residents in oil producing areas suffer doubly due to already poor conditions which are exacerbated by oil industry activities, and the lack of adequate measures to alleviate them. Further, the inadequacy of infra-structural facilities is a formidable barrier in transporting relief materials to victims of oil-related mishaps. The special needs of oil producing areas were well described by Johnson Koyonda:

One problem of the oil producing areas is that the people live in very small and isolated areas that render their voices [too] faint to be heard by those who should be responsible for their welfare. Because of their size and population these communities cannot attract social and welfare services like pipe-borne water, health care facilities, schools, electricity and markets. This is the case of places . . . where large quantities of crude oil are being extracted daily. If the small pockets of settlement are brought together and settled permanently in suitable places within their usual cultural environment, sufficiently removed and safe from the ravages of oil spillage, it will be easier to provide for them most of the social services they are now denied. . . . The people in the oil location areas must be made to have . . . and to enjoy the good things provided by the money from the oil whose production renders their lands unproductive, pollutes their drinking water, rivers, fish ponds and lakes. The oil money must provide schools for their children, health care centers, industries for alternative employment and pipe-borne water, light, roads and bridges for the people on whose land it is extracted.[35]

THE ROLE OF OIL AND STRATEGIES FOR DEVELOPMENT

One of the outstanding features of British colonial rule which influenced the economic development of Nigeria as a colony was the introduction of an alien administration and economic organization. This innovation laid the foundation for the development and expansion of a dual economy, with activities in the private sector identifying more closely with foreign than with local interests. Consequently, indigenous participation in the foreign sector became a question of compulsion and necessity rather than of choice and interest. Thus the modus operandi of this system was foreign, its philosophy incomprehensible, its tactics coercive, and its design exploitative.[36] To the British (Lugard 1922),[37] this new system was a complement to the prevailing traditional pattern of economic organization, and held as a high ideal the leading of the backward races to a higher place of social organization. The colonial strategy for Nigeria was not that of instituting comprehensive reforms for development purposes but rather the imposition of a system that would guarantee future British interests. Those preconceived interests are still maintained. The character of Nigerian development in its metropoles (which serve as foreign hegemony centers) reflect the dual economic system. Despite nearly three decades of independence, Nigeria has not moved away from a colonial dependent development model. Nigeria has not effectively instituted an integrative approach to development that would allow the benefits of its rapid economic growth to filter down to the rural majority. This pattern of unbalanced growth and development is characteristic of most third world nations. Development features, to date, have centered around building up the metropolis (industrial parks, highways, turnkey factories, and telecommunication systems).

Chinweizu, in an article on decolonizing the economy, states that Nigeria must cultivate "an industrial mode of organizing and distribution with the appropriate family and social structure to support and benefit from industrial organization."[38] To this end he wrote:

the practice of referring to Third World countries as developing countries is misleading. . . . In fact, developing countries are so few among them that it would be more correct to refer to the Third World as the maldeveloping world. An example of the few developing countries of the Third World is China. During the first 30 years of the People's Republic, it concentrated on total social transformation, which placed great emphasis on the development of a national industrial culture anchored to agriculture and heavy industries. . . . In stark contrast to China is Nigeria, an excellent example of the maldeveloping majority. In its 23 years of independence, Nigeria has concentrated on developing its consumer appetite for imports, and has used its vast oil revenues to feed this habit. . . . Any . . . fundamental social transformation to prepare its citizens for a national industrial culture has gone unrecognized. The paramount desire of the Third World elites is not development but the perpetuation of their rule, with minimum disruption to their enjoyment of its perquisites. However, to legitimize their rule in the minds of people hungry for material prosperity, these elites have found it necessary to proclaim development as the principal enterprise of the state. . . . Third World development strategies have tended to concentrate on . . . importing cargoes of western consumer goods and on building the infrastructures for distributing and using them. This sort of 'development' naturally suits a West which is interested in markets and raw materials, but not the emergence of competing productive capacity.[39]

True development should bring tangible benefits to the vast majority of people. The current practice of commodity production for export to generate funds to buy imported goods in most part fulfills the interest of the elites who have a craving for foreign goods. It is a cycle that fosters continual economic dependency and conditions the people to look to outsiders for support and guidance. The elites, endowed with foreign goods through consumption, have strengthened their position as society's "upper class." The acquisition of foreign gadgets has become the standard for assessing individual value and collective well-being. For this reason, many multinational firms have entered into a collaborative arrangement to enhance the dominant groups' political position, to the disadvantage of the rural majority and the urban poor. The multinational corporations

encourage the development of an external orientation among the elites that exacerbates preexisting elite–mass estrangement [and reduces any] links that may exist between urban and rural. Also, increased wage differentials result in uneven income distribution and widening [of the] elite–mass gap. The resulting impact is [a] reduction of economic capabilities that interferes with the objective of full and integrated development.[40]

The result has been the creation of enclaves of prosperity amid poverty. The presence of the multinationals and foreign investment could be a valuable source of growth and development for a third world country if it was mutually beneficial to all parties within the guiding principles of comparative advantage in international commodity exchange. However, a notable observer of multinational activities in developing countries (V. Bornschier 1978) asserts that "multinational penetration lowers investment growth in less developed countries,"[41] in sharp contrast with the popular view that multinationals with capital and technology could generate economic growth and development. But the differential mode of penetration by multinationals into third world countries may render the growth and development patterns unequal or unsustainable.

On the study of multinationals, economic penetration, and growth in developing countries, Ram D. Singh (1988) found that although "the penetration of multinationals in less developed countries increased, but not uniformly, notable exceptions include Nigeria as among the less developed countries. Between 1972 [and] 1980 . . . there was a decline in foreign investment."[42] Ironically, one can recall that during roughly the same period, Nigeria was credited with an impressive growth rate, which might have been linked to the distorted follies of mere growth in economic aggregates due to growth and boom in the oil sector. The growth was perhaps selectively sectoral and did not attract the diversified foreign investment in other sectors that would induce sustainable growth and balanced development. Apparently, the mere existence of multinational enterprises do not bring about needed development. A critique on multinational corporations in Nigeria (T. J. Biersteker 1982) noted that the multinational corporations require and support local comprador groups in both their investment and trade activities. The self-interest of these local groups occasionally conflicts with Nigeria's declared policies.[43] There appears to be a causal relationship between multinational activities and inequalities of development in the third world. For instance, Nigeria used its vast oil wealth in the 1970s to embark on extravagant expenditures, only to find itself making huge profits for special interest groups within the country and abroad. There was no authentic development. There was virtually no integrated approach to incorporatng the needs of the rural areas into the developmental dimension. Instead, there was a concentration of development in the metropoles. Nigeria's urban centers could mimic the impressive skyline of industrialized cities of the West, but the country was still unable to provide basic amenities such as water, housing, roads, and power to its rural areas. Dr. Halfdan Mahler has said that water is life and safe water means better

Table 2.4

Nigeria: Direct Foreign Investment 1970–88 (in million U.S. dollars)

Year	Amount
1970	205.0
1971	285.0
1972	305.1
1973	373.1
1974	257.4
1975	417.7
1976	339.4
1977	438.4
1978	213.3
1979	310.0
1980	739.8
1981	546.1
1982	429.8
1983	353.5
1984	188.8
1985	469.6
1986	195.1
1987	600.1
1988	836.4

Sources: *World Debt Tables 1989* and *World Debt Tables 1990*, World Bank, Washington, DC.

Table 2.5

Nigeria: Investment (percent of GDP), 1981–88

Year	GDFI/GDP	Private I/GDP	Public I/GDP
1981	21.4%	6.0%	15.4%
1982	15.3%	4.7%	10.6%
1983	11.4%	3.3%	8.1%
1984	6.0%	1.7%	4.3%
1985	7.7%	1.8%	5.9%
1986	9.9%	2.5%	7.4%
1987	12.3%	4.3%	8.0%
1988	13.3%	4.5%	8.8%

Source: *World Debt Tables, 1989,* World Bank, Washington, DC.

life.[44] The number of water taps per 1,000 persons is a better indication of health than the number of hospital beds.

Authentic development can be obtained if there is provision of social and economic services that bring tangible benefits to all segments of the nation, urban and rural alike. The entire nation should be viewed as a system, and the government as the agency of balancing the system by keeping the interests of all constituents in mind, for a degeneration in part will ultimately affect the rest. It is possible for the government, in cooperation with the multinationals (as part of their corporate social responsibility), to attain balanced development. As J. J. Haas (1973) wrote, "it is the responsibility of corporations to render assistance beyond the natural parameters of its structure. It has the obligation to maintain community stability and integrity."[45]

There is a need for a policy change away from the unbalanced development pattern of urban growth and rural stagnation. The imbalance in development has created two faces of oil wealth: growth in Western hegemonic centers in urban areas, and continued stagnation and underdevelopment in rural areas. The facade of a Western skyline in urban metropoles as a symbol of development should not be allowed to take precedence over much-needed rural development. There is a need for change, to eliminate the formidable barriers to balanced social and economic development. Hence the basic question is, what role can the oil industry play in the overall infrastructural development of the oil areas, given the fact that national and regional development plans are mostly financed by oil revenue or petrorevenue? Given the existing inequality in the regional distribution of infrastructural facilities, can the oil industry help to ensure a new strategy that would induce a balance there, in spite of the fact that the oil producing areas that give the nation the most revenue are largely industrially backward?

Since the 1960s, Nigeria's infrastructural development has been concentrated and developed largely in a few major zones (e.g., Lagos and Kano), and industrial development has been localized. It appears that the public policy of effecting better regional location of industrial and infrastructural facilities has been ineffective (Anusionwu 1978).[46] The federal government has expressed a commitment to the strategy of balanced regional industrial development, but there has been no visible evidence of change in the government strategy of indirectly encouraging industry concentration. The government's assurances in this area, it seems, have been largely lip-service. This is unfortunate, because it would be advantageous for the government to ensure that a more balanced regional distribution of public infrastructure is effected. There is no doubt that a more balanced spatial distribution of infrastructural facilities is necessary to ensure a more reasonable and better balance of income, wealth, and other economic opportunities. Previous studies and writers have acknowledged the backward nature of the oil producing areas, but no one has come up with a plan that will improve the socioeconomic development in a way that will serve the needs of the local population. In the long run, the plan must also improve the physical quality of life in the area, if provided with an effective supporting system by way of developing social and economic infrastructures. Other studies have tended to center on the development of special strategic interests (Emembolu 1975).[47] For instance, the modernization of the port facilities at Warri, Port Harcourt, and Calabar (all major cities in oil producing areas) might be well intentioned, but it would seem to serve the needs of the multinational companies for access to major national and international trade centers, rather than the needs of the indigenous population of the oil areas.

Indeed, government control and management of oil resources have made a significant difference. For instance, according to Emembolu (1975) the Nigerian government oil revenue in the 1960s was derived from such elements as rentals, profits, taxes, and royalties.[48] From 1958 to date, Nigerian participation in OPEC, coupled with the latter's pricing policy, contributed to a measure of stability and even an acceleration in the rate of government receipts from oil. Growth in government revenue has been attributed to increased production as well as improved prices. Thus oil has contributed to increased foreign exchange earnings (accounting for about 95 percent), apart from the global oil glut in the 1980s which eroded government revenues. Prior to the growth of the oil industry, Nigeria relied on agricultural exports for foreign exchange. Agriculture was the most important economic sector, accounting for more than 50 percent of the GNP and providing employment for over 70 percent of the labor force. However, there has been a steady decline of agricultural contributions to GNP due to the increased importance of the oil sector. On the other hand, the growth in government revenue has made increased government expenditures possible in various supporting sectors of the economy. The consequence has been the generation of considerable economic activity, particularly new strategies for economic development, and the development of social and economic infrastructures through planning.[49] Since 1946 Nigeria has adopted developmental planning as a strategy for accelerating economic and social development. Hence it is important to note that oil has provided Nigeria with the necessary budgeting flexibility with respect to its development programs.

The growth of oil revenue enabled Nigeria to embark on a number of development projects and provided the main source of their financing. Nigeria's reliance on external help to finance its development was highly reduced, particularly in the 1970s. As noted above, Nigeria adopted development planning in 1946. There have been three major plans since 1962. The first two plans were constrained by a lack of adequate capital. Thus, the scale of projects, particularly in the public sector, has been largely determined by the ability of the government to elicit external financial help.

The dependence on external financial assistance began to disappear with the increasing development of the oil industry, as demonstrated by the features for the three plans. For example, in the First Development Plan (1962–68), 50 percent of the planned N1,354 million expenditure was expected to be financed from external sources (Table 2.6). However, this plan experienced many setbacks due to underspending, structural distortion, and underfulfillment.[50] In contrast, N1,452 million for the second plan (1970–74) involved very little foreign aid (Table 2.7). This plan emphasized a higher level of agricultural output, rural development, and improvement of the nation's infrastructure. The plan promoted Nigerianization of the economy and also took measures to combat unemployment. The total investment was N5,300 million. The 1970–74 plan had a projected growth rate of 7 percent, but the growth was at 8.2 percent per annum in real terms.[51] The Third National Plan (1975–80) envisaged a total investment of N30,000 million, out of which N70,000 was to be raised from the public sector. The plan emphasized rural development, increased food production, and improvement of the overall social infrastructure. The target growth rate was about 9.5 percent. From the foregoing, it was evident that the success of the Fourth Development Plan (1981–85) depended on the continual growth of oil revenue.[52] However, this expectation was hindered by the oil glut and erosion of oil prices. Still, the developmental plan for 1981–85 was not abandoned, in spite of the oil-dependent financing strategy.

Table 2.6

First National Development Plan and Implementation, 1962–68

Section	Federal (N million)			Northern Region (N million)			Eastern Region (N million)			Western Region (N million)			Total for Federation (N million)		
	Est.	Act.	Ach.	Est.	Act.	Ach.	Est.	Act.	Ach.	Est.	Act.	Ach.	Est.	Act.	Ach.
Primary production	40.9	21.9	53.5	49.9	22.1	44.2	60.7	31.7	52.2	36.8	29.1	79.0	183.5	105.0	57.2
Trade and industry	88.0	24.8	28.1	19.7	21.9	111.1	25.8	20.5	79.4	46.8	27.7	59.1	180.5	95.0	52.6
Electricity	196.2	140.0	75.9	3.0	–	–	1.2	0.7	58.3	3.0	11.5	383.3	203.4	161.3	79.3
Transport	207.9	191.3	92.0	49.3	24.5	49.6	17.7	11.0	62.1	12.7	15.3	120.4	287.6	242.2	90.5
Communication	60.0	22.0	36.0	–	–	–	–	–	–	–	–	–	60.0	22.0	36.6
Water	3.7	1.3	35.1	14.8	15.6	105.4	10.2	10.0	98.0	19.7	18.4	93.4	48.5	49.4	101.8
Education	58.3	49.3	84.5	37.8	20.0	52.9	17.7	5.7	2.2	25.7	16.1	62.6	139.5	91.3	65.4
Health	20.6	5.9	28.6	6.6	6.2	93.9	3.6	1.4	38.8	3.2	1.2	37.5	34.1	14.9	43.6
Town and country planning	46.3	29.8	64.3	12.0	0.6	5.0	6.6	3.4	51.5	18.5	5.3	28.5	83.4	39.2	47.0
Cooperative and social welfare	5.3	1.1	20.7	4.8	4.1	85.4	1.0	0.7	70.0	6.0	1.4	23.3	17.3	7.4	42.7
Information	4.7	4.4	93.6	0.1	1.2	1200.0	0.9	3.0	333.3	1.5	0.9	60.0	7.3	9.3	127.3
Judicial	0.5	1.5	300.0	–	–	–	0.5	0.3	60.0	0.8	0.6	75.0	1.9	2.4	126.3
Administration	87.8	181.0	206.1	1.9	8.0	421.0	4.1	5.2	126.8	2.2	12.6	572.7	98.1	207.0	211.0
Financial obligation	4.4	9.5	215.9	–	1.2	–	0.2	2.8	1400.0	3.2	12.0	375.0	7.8	25.7	329.4
Total	824.6	692.8	–	199.9	125.4	–	150.2	96.4	–	180.1	152.1	–	1352.9	1072.1	79.2

Source: Federal Ministry of Economic Development, *Second National Development Plan 1970-74* (Lagos: Federal Government Printer, 1970), 13.

Table 2.7

Development Plans 1970–80 (in N million)
Revised Public Capital Program: 1970–74

Sector (1)	Total (2)	Federal government (3)	All states (4)	Benue-Plateau (5)	East-Central (6)	Kano (7)	Kwara (8)	Lagos (9)	Mid-Western (10)	North-Central (11)	North-Eastern (12)	North-Western (13)	Rivers (14)	South-Eastern (15)	Western (16)
Economic															
Agriculture	267.960	69.866	198.094	8.527	20.321	47.278	9.453	7.334	19.667	5.600	15.002	9.358	11.956	19.005	24.593
Livestock, forestry and fishing	63.670	9.619	54.051	2.173	5.100	2.734	1.360	6.520	6.313	1.972	4.598	5.314	6.967	2.988	8.012
Mining	36.661	36.661	–												
Industry	192.384	67.394	124.990	10.000	16.287	7.360	9.460	5.720	30.398	5.216	8.055	3.028	7.106	7.226	15.134
Commerce and finance	45.337	13.192	32.145	1.684	1.332	2.720	5.000	0.500	2.574	0.904	1.256	3.830	6.849	5.020	0.476
Fuel and power	108.570	90.650	17.920	0.540	–	1.630	2.100	–	0.400	1.600	0.400	0.250	2.000	2.000	–
Transport/ inland waterways	901.829	645.492	256.337	32.155	10.202	11.000	12.20	60.104	29.045	18.892	29.028	10.050	11.370	12.660	19.711
Communication	129.209	129.209	–												
Resettlement and rehabilitation	33.408	18.800	14.608										11.454	3.154	
Subtotal	1,779.028	1,080.883	698.145	55.079	53.242	72.722	39.493	80.178	94.997	32.984	59.539	31.980	44.498	60.353	73.080
Social															
Education	399.965	152.064	247.901	14.500	33.111	16.200	7.385	11.690	35.745	19.081	21.046	21.237	10.478	8.428	49.000
Health	152.625	37.690	114.935	3.003	18.176	9.820	7.408	10.680	16.857	5.045	12.934	8.978	6.424	4.186	11.424
Labor and social welfare	41.361	16.058	25.303	1.449	2.956	2.056	3.114	1.000	0.558	2.511	2.849	1.496	2.586	0.800	3.928
Information	86.773	65.000	21.773	2.999	2.000	–	1.210	0.200	6.811	0.581	0.530	0.164	2.827	1.080	3.371
Town and country planning	63.970	22.569	41.401	1.100	7.957	3.200	0.350	1.000	1.491	6.807	7.606	0.790	2.100	4.000	5.000
Water and sewerage	144.777	–	144.777	12.266	10.321	9.000	9.692	11.376	20.724	23.988	5.395	6.755	8.070	4.100	23.090
Subtotal	889.471	293.381	596.090	35.317	74.521	40.276	29.159	35.946	82.186	58.013	50.360	39.420	32.485	22.594	95.813

Revised Public Capital Program: 1970–74 (cont.)

Sector (1)	Total (2)	Federal government (3)	All states (4)	Benue-Plateau (5)	East-Central (6)	Kano (7)	Kwara (8)	Lagos (9)	Mid-Western (10)	North-Central (11)	North-Eastern (12)	North-Western (13)	Rivers (14)	South-Eastern (15)	Western (16)
Administration															
General administration	261.650	137.630	124.020	16.497	8.502	6.552	9.244	42.360	5.738	2.309	–	15.536	7.612	3.670	6.000
Defense and security	346.183	346.183	–	–	–	–	–	–	–	–	–	–	–	–	–
Subtotal	607.833	483.813	124.020	16.497	8.502	6.552	9.244	42.360	5.738	2.309	–	15.536	7.612	3.670	6.000
Financial															
Financial Obligations	73.601	73.601	–	–	–	–	–	–	–	–	–	–	–	–	–
Subtotal	73.601	73.601	–	–	–	–	–	–	–	–	–	–	–	–	–
Total	3,349.933	1,931.678	1,418.255	106.893	136.265	119.550	77.896	158.484	182.921	93.306	109.899	86.936	84.595	86.617	174.893

Table 2.7 (cont.)

Summary of Public Sector Capital Programs: 1975–80

Sector (1)	Total (2)	Federal government (3)	All states (4)	Benue-Plateau (5)	East-Central (6)	Kano (7)	Kwara (8)	Lagos (9)	Mid-Western (10)	North-Central (11)	North-Eastern (12)	North-Western (13)	Rivers (14)	South-Eastern (15)	Western (16)
Economic															
Agriculture	1,645.852	750.845	895.007	64.768	95.408	142.556	66.303	14.824	63.521	68.139	73.754	65.441	48.150	63.526	128.617
Livestock	344.046	173.176	170.869	10.314	15.227	24.682	7.299	17.090	8.383	12.280	20.801	20.080	5.700	10.648	18.365
Forestry	109.730	30.014	79.716	9.055	5.355	4.610	9.300	0.500	4.975	5.826	8.438	4.530	2.000	12.701	12.426
Fishery	101.554	58.561	42.993	3.367	1.398	1.600	1.700	15.451	2.289	0.100	1.397	0.751	5.538	5.639	3.763
Minings and quarrying	2,680.428	2,680.425	–	–	–	–	–	–	–	–	–	–	–	–	–
Manufacturing and craft	5,315.871	4,907.227	408.644	28.938	69.271	23.966	37.804	32.246	43.500	21.289	22.463	8.200	36.228	39.419	45.320
Power	1,075.238	932.038	143.200	12.000	10.000	8.000	15.000	0.200	10.000	10.000	20.000	20.000	8.000	10.000	20.000
Commerce and finance	559.355	323.433	235.922	16.900	25.700	16.086	28.650	15.500	12.180	14.175	19.600	10.305	43.100	23.573	10.153
Transport	7,303.068	6,274.342	1,028.726	98.990	88.728	55.340	63.990	36.265	200.000	59.723	119.956	108.180	51.650	69.184	76.720
Communications	1,338.944	1,338.944	–	–	–	–	–	–	–	–	–	–	–	–	–
Subtotal	20,474.082	17,469.005	3,005.077	244.332	311.087	276.840	230.046	132.076	344.848	191.532	286.409	237.487	200.366	234.690	315.384
Social															
Education	2,463.822	1,656.193	807.629	71.702	78.239	68.647	46.129	30.642	60.807	75.600	90.511	63.264	74.300	65.931	81.857
Health	759.928	314.160	455.768	30.670	62.621	32.430	28.500	53.901	39.690	23.810	42.900	30.550	34.805	22.850	43.041
Information	380.225	234.341	145.884	9.415	19.837	6.500	15.900	5.300	5.900	6.193	16.137	16.170	12.310	15.110	17.112
Labor	43.187	43.187	–	–	–	–	–	–	–	–	–	–	–	–	–
Social development and sports	139.603	24.950	114.653	8.148	22.592	6.203	5.760	19.266	3.920	3.770	11.501	6.751	9.350	8.778	8.614
Subtotal	3,786.765	2,272.831	1,513.934	119.935	183.289	113.780	96.289	109.109	110.317	109.373	161.049	116.735	130.765	112.669	150.624

Summary of Public Sector Capital Programs: 1975–80 (cont.)

Sector (1)	Total (2)	Federal government (3)	All states (4)	Benue-Plateau (5)	East-Central (6)	Kano (7)	Kwara (8)	Lagos (9)	Mid-Western (10)	North-Central (11)	North-Eastern (12)	North-Western (13)	Rivers (14)	South-Eastern (15)	Western (16)
Regional Development															
Water supply	930.038	317.413	612.625	58.120	57.540	40.000	45.500	44.400	73.975	41.100	42.201	43.489	7.600	31.200	127.500
Sewerage, drainage, and refuse disposal	428.495	154.499	273.996	9.706	28.000	13.240	6.000	70.000	58.000	9.200	7.500	4.500	26.000	4.600	37.250
Housing	1,837.430	1,650.000	187.430	5.000	20.500	30.930	8.000	11.000	30.000	10.000	18.000	10.000	10.000	10.000	24.000
Town and country planning	754.867	250.453	504.414	24.299	70.706	21.243	9.200	117.525	31.007	23.102	31.087	38.730	55.500	35.009	47.006
Cooperative and community development	193.294	16.187	177.107	12.782	17.000	17.773	6.500	35.344	11.851	10.548	23.516	16.644	1.200	13.655	10.294
Subtotal	4,144.124	2,388.552	1,755.572	109.907	193.746	123.186	75.200	278.269	204.833	93.950	122.304	113.363	100.300	94.464	246.050
Administration															
Defense and security	3,325.517	3,325.517	–	–	–	–	–	–	–	–	–	–	–	–	–
General administration	1,124.128	709.210	414.918	24.809	35.955	46.421	25.250	34.960	27.092	36.617	39.866	50.472	40.877	34.160	18.439
Subtotal	4,449.645	4,034.727	414.918	24.809	35.955	46.421	25.250	34.960	27.092	36.617	39.866	50.472	40.877	34.160	18.439
Nominal total	32,854.616	26,165.115	6,689.501	498.983	724.077	560.227	426.785	554.414	687.090	431.472	609.628	518.057	472.308	475.983	73.477

Source: Federal Ministry of Economic Development, *Second National Development Plan 1970-74* (Lagos: Federal Government Printer, 1970)

97

The Fourth National Development Plan, like its predecessors, was an apparent instrument for harnessing the country's national resources for the benefit of its people (Table 2.8). To this end, its specific objectives were: an increase in the real income of the average citizen; a more even distribution of income among individuals and socioeconomic groups; reduced levels of unemployment and underemployment; an increase in the supply of skilled labor; reduced dependence on a narrow range of activities; and a balanced development of the different sectors of the economy and the various geographical areas of the country. Increased participation by citizens in the ownership and management of productive enterprises and greater national self-reliance would also result, as would a real shift toward optimum utilization of human and national resources, development of technology, increased productivity, and the promotion of a national orientation conducive to greater discipline, better attitudes toward work, and a cleaner environment. The government expected to finance this developmental plan from oil revenue since more than 80 percent of the anticipated national revenue would come from the oil resource.

There is still an urgent need to develop the socioeconomic infrastructures for the oil producing areas so that the people of those areas can benefit from the national development plans. In 1990, Nigeria moved into a new national planning program called the First National Rolling Plan (1990-1992). Its fundamental objective is to strengthen the foundation for true national development. The first phase of the plan seeks to address the issues of exchange rate instability, inflation, unemployment, intergovernmental fiscal imbalances, and social problems. True development efforts seek to improve agriculture and the quality of life in rural areas as well as to achieve diversification of the country's export base.[53] The second phase of the three-year plan will be geared toward the maintenance of infrastructural facilities in both urban and rural areas. The third phase will focus on ways to ease structural adjustment for vulnerable groups. To this end, the government seeks to maintain and expand primary health

Table 2.8

Fourth National Development Plan:
January 1981–December 1985 Investment Program (in million naira)

Sector	Allocation
Agriculture	5,588.9
Power	3,278.7
Electricity distribution	271.0
Rural electrification	1,345.4
Transport	10,504.1
Roads	8,863.0
Railways	1,630.0
Air transport	653.1
Water transport	988.0
Communications	2,000.0
Telecommunications	1,700.0
Postal services	300.0
Education	7,533.5
Teacher training institutions	782.7
Secondary education	1,908.6
Technical education	1,077.3
Scholarships	752.8
Health	3,066.6
Labor and social welfare	178.5
Information	624.1
Regional development	4,869.9
Housing	2,661.7
Water supply	2,940.4
Defense and security	3,940.0
General administration	2,247.0
Public sector investment	70,500.0
State governments	28,000.0
Private sector investment	11,500.0

Source: Central Planning Office, Lagos, Nigeria.

Note: Under the Plan, GNP at constant 1973/74 factor cost is projected to rise from about N18,740 million in 1979/80 to N27,941 million in 1984/85, implying an average annual growth rate of 8.3 percent.

care delivery and mass transportation systems, improve educational facilities, develop means to increase employment, and encourage family planning.

The overall cost of the plan for the three-year period is estimated at N142 billion, out of which 65 percent or N92 billion is meant for the public sector and 35 percent or N50 billion for the private sector. Furthermore, the federal government will invest about N32 billion under joint venture arrangements in oil exploration while the state and local governments will have N20 billion and N7 billion respectively. Finally, a Special Projects Fund worth N3.5 billion will be executed under the Ecological Fund and the Fund for Mineral Producing Areas.[54]

Nigeria, like most developing countries, practices a mixed economy, and developmental planning is the usual route to the attainment of its socioeconomic objectives. A mixed economy (Tudaro 1981) is an "economy characterized by the existence of an institutional setting in which some of the productive resources are privately owned and operated and some are controlled by the public sector."[55] The private sector is typically comprised of four distinct forms of individual ownership: the traditional subsistence sector, consisting of small-scale private farms and handicraft shops, selling a part of their products to local markets; small-scale individual or family-owned commercial businesses and services; medium-sized commercial enterprises in agriculture, industry, trade, and transport, owned and operated by local entrepreneurs; and large jointly owned or completely foreign owned manufacturing enterprises, mining companies, and plantations, primarily catering to foreign markets, but sometimes with substantial local sales (the capital for such enterprises usually comes from abroad and a good proportion of the profit tends to be transferred overseas).

In the context of such an institutional setting, we can identify two principal components of development planning in mixed economies. The first is the government's deliberate utilization of domestic savings and foreign finance to carry out public investment projects and to mobilize and channel scarce resources into areas that can be expected to make the greatest contribution toward the realization of long-term objectives (e.g., the construction of railways, schools, hydroelectric projects, and other components of economic infrastructure, as well as the creation of import-substituting industries). Second, governmental manipulation of economic policy (e.g., taxation, industrial licensing, the setting of tariffs and quotas, wages, interest rates, and prices) can be used to stimulate, direct, and in some cases, even control private economic activity in order to ensure a harmonious relationship between the desires of private business and the social objectives at hand. Thus planning is an integral part of modernization. Gunnar Myrdal (1979) wrote that "modernization ideals should include rationality: The substitution of modern methods of thinking, acting, producing, distributing and consuming for age old traditional practices."[56] According to the first Indian prime minister, Jawaharal Nehru (1961),

what underdeveloped nations need is a scientific and technological society. It employs new techniques whether it is in the farm, in the factory, or in transport. Modern technique follows modern thinking. You cannot get hold of a modern tool and an ancient mind; it would not work. The quest for rationality implies that opinions about economic strategies and policies should be logically valid inferences rooted as deeply as possible in knowledge of relevant facts. Hence, planning the search for rationality is a coordinated system of policy measures that can bring about and accelerate economic growth and development; a mechanism for social and economic equalization that promotes more of equality in status, opportunities, wealth, income, and level of living.[57]

According to Arthur Livingstone, a national plan is both an act of government and a response of the people, requiring the authority of the first to give it shape and the participation of the second to make it work.[58] Nigeria has also employed development planning to achieve a more efficient social and economic infrastructure, committing capital to work on roads, railways, airways, and other forms of transportation and communication, water supplies, financial institutions, electricity, and public services such as health and education. However, in formulating a plan, development strategists should consider the fact that the introduction of a new technology and industry into a community can cause the breakdown of the traditional socioeconomic fabric and potentially incapacitate the ability of the local people to cope and compete with the new form of sophisticated economy, and the technological power and wealth of outsiders. Industrial impact on the host community is problematic in this regard. This effect is even greater in an enterprise economy, in which a producer adjusts production in order to maximize profit. Unfortunately, these problems are neither provisionally planned for, nor adequately dealt with after the fact; community welfare remains secondary to the drive for profit. Nigeria is a prime example of this.

The overall importance of infrastructural development (Anusionwu 1978) to the success of Nigeria's national or regional economic development cannot be overemphasized.[59] A successful economic development plan largely depends on whether or not the country's roads, communication facilities, railways, ports, and waterways can support the growth and development of agriculture, commerce, and industry with the efficient movement of people, goods, and information throughout the country. No one region should be left behind in the quest for development. Nigeria has invested heavily in its infrastructural system in an attempt to stimulate economic development and achieve greater social justice and political expediency.

Investment decisions regarding the infrastructural system will determine its use for many years to come, and may influence subsequent decisions of private and corporate industry. In essence, economic considerations persuade investors to locate their industries in areas with at least a basic infrastructure. The need for infrastructural facilities is, to a great extent, a spatial problem. For instance, the use of transportation involves a framework of spatial flows, and transportation systems are one of the critical influences on location and specialization of the country's socioeconomic activities. According to Y. Obidake (1982), it is important to be aware that policymakers, or special groups in power, will sometimes distribute resources to their own advantage.[60] Therefore the spatial pattern of the infrastructure can also be a reflection of the distribution of power and wealth in the society. Research has shown (Oyebanji, 1984) that, although results are contraindicative, Nigeria has expressed unequivocal commitment to the balanced development strategy. National development plans since about 1970 have consistently emphasized that an unbalanced situation (in which some parts of the country experience rapid economic growth while others lag behind) would no longer be tolerated, and that interregional disparities would be resolved, for the sake of social justice and egalitarian principles, in favor of disadvantaged regions. The Nigerian federal government has also promised that as it pursues the balanced development strategy, adequate attention would be given to providing basic needs (i.e., water, housing, medical and educational facilities, good roads, higher life expectancy, adequate calorie intake, etc.) to the poorer areas. Ironically, the major mineral producing or prospecting areas in Rivers, Cross River, Plateau, Bauchi and Bornu States, areas which have the greatest potential for increasing the wealth of the nation, were among the areas identified as the most distressed and slowest in development in Oyebanji's study (1984).[61] Such an uneven distribution of resources in a country "unequivocally committed" to a balance there calls for the need to investigate the neglected relationship between socioeconomic development and the spatial patterns of infrastructure in the country. In all phases of national development, the proportionate attention accorded infrastructural development in oil areas has been minimal. The Nigerian petroleum industry, in partnership with the government of Nigeria (which has controlling interest in the oil industry), should work on developing the infrastructural network in areas where it remains weak and poorly developed. Understanding the interaction of these factors — socioeconomic development, spatial patterns of infrastructure, and the politics behind them — is important to the study of the impact of the oil industry on the indigenous population of oil producing areas.

NOTES

1. Government of Nigeria, *Facts and Figures About Nigeria* (Lagos, Nigeria: Federal Office of Statistics, 1986),1-4.

2. Government of Nigeria, *Handbook of Nigeria and Our Heritage* (Lagos, Nigeria: Department of Information, 1953).

3. Paul Hackett, "Nigeria: Economy," in *Africa South of the Sahara, 1990,* 19th ed. (London: Europa Publications, 1989): 775.

4. Ibid.

5. Richard Adelu, "Nigeria's Oil Resources Could Be Upgraded," *OPEC Bulletin* (June 1989): 63.

6. Department of Information, Government of Nigeria, Office of the President (Lagos, 1982).

7. B. Dundley, *An Introduction to Nigerian Government and Politics* (Bloomington, IN: Indiana University Press, 1982), 129.

8. L. Turner, *Oil Companies in the International System* (London: Royal Institute of International Affairs, 1985), 75.

9. P. Olayiwola, *Petroleum and Structural Change in a Developing Country: The Case of Nigeria* (New York: Praeger, 1984).

10. B. Dundley, *An Introduction to Nigerian Government and Politics,* 129-30.

11. A. A. Afrifa, *Ghana Gold* (London: Peak Cass Press, 1966).

12. J.K. Onoh, *The Nigerian Oil Economy: From Prosperity to Glut* (New York: St. Martin's Press, 1983), 107.

13. Uzor M. Uzoatu, *This Week Newsmagazine* 1, no. 11 (September 29, 1986): 33.

14. *West Africa* (October 23-29, 1989): 1756.

15. *West Africa* (July 13, 1987): 1336.

16. Rene Dumont with Marcel Mazoyer, *Socialism and Development* (London: Andre Deutsch, 1983), 28.

17. Christopher Stevens, "The Political Economy of Nigeria," in *The Economist* (London, Cambridge University Press, 1984).

18. G. Haberler, "International Trade and Economic Growth," in *Economics of Trade and Development,* James Thebberge, ed. (New York: John Wiley and Sons, 1958).

19. Christopher Stevens, "The Political Economy of Nigeria," 2.

20. Ibid.

21. *Development Outlook* (an international socioeconomic magazine published in Lagos, Nigeria)(August 1986).

22. B. Fubara, "The Ethics of Nigeria's Proposed Withdrawl from OPEC," *Journal of Business Ethics* 5, no. 4 (August 1986) 351-63.

23. *African Heritage Magazine* (September/October 1987): 7.

24. A. Markandya and M. Pemberton, "Economic Policy with Fluctuating Oil Revenues," *OPEC Review* (Spring 1988): 17.

25. Yinka Omorogbe, "The Legal Framework for Production of Petroleum in Nigeria," *Journal of Energy and Natural Resource Law* 5, no. 4 (1987): 273.

26. Paul Hackett, "Nigeria: Economy," 775.

27. *West Africa* (January 9-15, 1989): 32.

28. Obafemi Awolowo, *Autobiography of Chief Obafemi Awolowo,* (Cambridge, England: Cambridge University Press, 1960): 268.

29. R. Stock, *Social Impact Analysis and the Development of the Third World* (Boulder, CO: Westview Press, 1985), 216.

30. Federal Office of Statistics, Lagos, Nigeria, 1984.

31. Federal Office Statistics (Household Survey), Lagos, Nigeria, 1985.

32. Department of Information, Government of Nigeria, Office of the President, Lagos, Nigeria, 1983.

33. Nicholas Balabkins, "Indigenization and Economic Development: Nigerian Experience in Contemporary Studies in Economic and Financial Analysis," Vol. 33 (London: JAL Press, 1982), 73.

34. *Country Profile: Nigeria* (Washington, DC: U.S. Government Press, 1982).

35. Johnson Koyonda, "Oil Spillage Problem! Answer Lies in Building Permanent Settlements," *Sunday Tide,* July 27, 1980.

36. E. J. Usoro, "Economic Transition From Colonial Dependency to National Development: The Nigerian Experience," *Nigerian Journal of Economic and Social Science* (July 1982): 210.

37. L. Lugard, *The Dual Mandate in British Tropical Africa* (London: 1922) in E. J. Usoro, "Economic Transition From Colonial Dependency to National Development: The Nigerian Experience," *Nigerian Journal of Economic and Social Science* (July 1982).

38. Chinweizu, "Western Economic Order: The Plunder of Africa," *Third World Magazine* (South Publication, February 1984): 46.

39. Ibid.

40. Thomas J. Biersteker, *Distortion or Development? Contending Perspectives on the Multinational Corporation* (Cambridge, MA: MIT Press, 1981), 24.

41. V. Bornschier, *Multinationals in the World Economy and National Development* Butten no. 32 (Zurich: Soziologisches Institut der Universtat, 1978).

42. Ram D. Singh, "The Multinational's Economic Penetration, Growth, Industrial Output and Domestic Savings in Developing Countries: Another Look," *Journal of Development Studies* 25, no. 1 (October 1988).

43. Thomas J. Biersteker, *Distortion or Development?,* 156.

44. Halfdan Mahler, director, World Health Organization, International Drinking Water Supply and Sanitation Decade (1971-81) Geneva 27, Switzerland.

45. J. J. Haas, *Corporate Social Responsibility in a Changing Society* (New York: Theo Gaus & Sons, 1973).

46. E. C. Anusionwu, "Management of Industrial Location Through Infrastructural Development: Nigerian Experience," *Nigerian Journal of Economic and Social Science* 20, no. 5 (November 1978): 351.

47. G. Emembolu, "Future Prospects and the Role of Oil in Nigerian Development," *Journal of Energy and Development* (August 1975): 135.

48. G. Emembolu, "Petroleum and the Development of a Dual Economy: The Nigerian Example" (doctoral dissertation, University of Colorado, 1975).

49. Government of Nigeria, Federal Ministry of Economic Planning, *National Development Plan, 1962–1968,* 6.

50. *Africa South of the Sahara 1981–1982* (London: Europa Publications, 1981), 773.

51. U.S. Department of Agriculture, *Sub-Saharan Africa, 1982–1983,* (London: Europa Publications, 1983), 785.

52. Federal Republic of Nigeria, *Nigeria 1983* (Lagos, Nigeria: Department of Information, Executive Office of the President, 1983).

53. Ibrahim Babangida, president of Nigeria, "Government Unfolds Budget of Development Sustenance," *The Guardian,* January 1, 1990: 10.

54. Ibid.

55. M. Tudaro, *The Meaning of Development: Economic Development of the Third World* (New York: Longman Publications, 1981), 115-16.

56. Gunnar Myrdal, *The Challenge of Wealth and Poverty, Part I* (New York: Pantheon, 1979).

57. Michael Tudaro, *The Meaning of Development,* 116.

58. Arthur Livingstone, *Social Policy in Developing Countries* (London: Humanities Press, 1969), 97.

59. E. C. Anusionwu, "Management of Industrial Location."

60. Y. Obidake, "The Impact of Nigerian Petroleum Industry on the Transportation Pattern" (unpublished manuscript, Syracuse University, 1982), 6.

61. J. O. Oyebanji, "Identifying the Distressed Areas: An Integrated Multivariate Approach," *Socioeconomic Planning Science* 18, no. 1 (1984): 53-57.

## 3

The Impact of Extractive Economies Around the World

Although this study is concerned with oil areas in Nigeria, still it is useful to examine past studies done in other areas of the world to enable us to learn from their experiences and examples. These studies, in combination with previous research on the Nigerian oil industry, could provide a valuable resource in shaping the direction of this study. We may be able to note certain similarities and differences among the impacts of various extractive industries on given communities. For this reason, examples are provided from industrialized countries as well as developing countries.

Social assessment of technological impact is a systematic interaction and feedback tool used to measure the impact of energy development on a given community. However, the socio-economic and environmental impacts of extractive activities on host communities may differ, particularly between communities in industrialized nations and those in developing countries.

STUDIES ON OIL IMPACT ASSESSMENT IN THE UNITED STATES

A study was made on the impact of energy development and industrial expansion on the Unalaskan Indian community on the

Bering side of the Fox Islands in Alaska (Palinkas et al. 1985).[1]
The Unalaskan people had a unique historical relationship with
their traditional socioeconomic environment. The influx of outsiders changed their value system and created social
heterogeneity, leading ultimately to modernization. This was the
experience of Aleutian Indians of Alaska. Their traditional
values were rooted in their subsistence economy until it was
displaced in favor of increased commercial fishing and the development of the oil industry. They viewed the new cash-based
economy as unstable and insecure, and oil development in particular was considered merely a temporary support. Hence, their
hopes in oil remained secondary. Meanwhile, the industrial
growth brought population growth, and this put a strain on available community resources. The need for more social infrastructure in terms of roads, housing, transportation, water
resources, power, and sanitation became evident, while at the
same time conditions requiring professional assistance were on
the rise because of increased morbidity rate and other problems.
It is predicted that the cost of health care, education, and other
social services in Alaska will escalate in the 1990s through the
year 2000. Industrial expansion and outside influence have contributed to a steady decline in traditional Aleutian values, which
may be completely absent by the year 2000 due to increased social
heterogeneity. The study findings also show that the dual value
systems (traditional versus modern) is likely to create genera-
tional conflict among the Aleutian people. Moreover, increasing
socioeconomic and cultural variation from tradition setting may
result in competition for access to scarce resources and social
facilities, and possible political conflict in the community. The
intervention of industry in Alaska has alienated the Aleutian
people from their territory and tradition, the ultimate cost of
which will continue to accrue for many years.

In America's second largest state, the findings were different. On the impact of the oil industry in west Texas, Moore (1965)
contends that

before the depression three areas of west Texas were invigorated by oil discovery. . . . [T]he benefits of oil discovery were not limited to the land owner
with oil on his property or the company which drilled the oil wells. But also, the
land leased in every county provided a yearly added income to ranchers and
farmers alike.[2]

Moore's findings revealed that despite the impact of the oil
industry on the economic and, consequently, social history of west
Texas, the basic tradition and character of the region remains
agricultural; that is, the oil industry did not replace or displace
agriculture in west Texas communities.

J. H. Copp (1984) studied the social impact of oil and gas
developments on the small rural community of Caldwell in central Texas and found that the

local community businesses were more prosperous and larger, the number of
workers in the community and county had at least doubled, community institutions were stronger, more services were available, community leadership was
stable and the level of community satisfaction was high. . . . That the new oil
and gas money has broadened and deepened the distribution of wealth and
power in the community.[3]

STUDIES IN THE UNITED KINGDOM

In examining oil's contribution to Britain's self-sufficiency,
Colin Robinson and Eileen Marshall traced British consumption
of oil in the 1950s and 1960s. During this period, consumption
rose while output declined, but with the discovery of North Sea
oil in 1975, the trend was reversed. The United Kingdom became
an oil exporter, because production now exceeded consumption.
In the face of change and the uncertainty of the oil market, Britain
seeks various means of achieving oil self-sufficiency in any given
oil production demand scenario.[4] It has compiled guidelines for

depletion control, deferred production, and repletion policy, and has therefore increased the likelihood that the British oil industry will sustain its self-reliance. Another interesting study on British oil industry is based on the success story of the Shetland community of Scotland. On the social impact of oil on the Scottish community, Dan Shapiro et al. (1980) assert that the continuous involvement of the local authority as the agency maintaining control over the direction of oil-related development has enabled the local residents to profit from the presence of oil industry through specific agreements favoring community interest.[5] Residents of the community took steps to safeguard their interests through their communal power to refuse, permit, or delay any company activity within their area. On the whole, the Shetland community maintained its interests and oil firms complied.

STUDIES IN CANADA

Further reflection on oil impact assessment can be seen in the Canadian case study of East Coast offshore petroleum exploration. The purpose of the study (Voyer and Gibbons 1974) was to demonstrate the potential consequences of applying technological capability for exploration and exploitation of petroleum, and to assess the physical, economic, political, and social consequences of technological development on the Canadian subregion.[6] The governments of the Canadian Atlantic provinces saw the potential exploration of petroleum as a way of boosting the economy of the subregion, but would not undertake the project without a specific environmental protection policy. The Oil and Gas Production and Conservation Act and the Oil and Gas Land Regulation gave the federal government the responsibility for ensuring that all offshore operations meet certain standards designed to protect those working in offshore activities and to protect the marine environment from the risk of pollution resulting from offshore petroleum exploration and exploitation activities. In addition, the effective participation of area residents forced the Mobil oil operation on Sable Island to conform to a rigorous set of environmental guidelines.

THE MEXICAN EXPERIENCE

The mining of oil in a developing country reflects a deep contrast, as shown by this Mexican example. Roberto (1983) found that the impact of oil operations on the producing regions of southern Mexico has been essentially disruptive in terms of price increases, income distribution, bottlenecks in social and economic infrastructure, and deterioration of the environment.[7] The strong negative effect has been due primarily to the rapid expansion of oil industry, disproportionate regional investment, and the steep increase in population of those urban centers most affected by oil activities. Consequently, there has been a persistent scarcity of housing, basic infrastructure, and food. Moreover, the expansion of the oil industry was insufficient to absorb the rapid increase in the labor force. Manifestations of further oil related problems for the producing regions are documented in a report by the United Nations Research Institute for Social Development (UNRISD) which states that the "oil boom precipitated a crisis in the producing regions in agriculture and food systems."[8]

THE BRAZILIAN EXPERIENCE

The extractive activities in host communities in a developing country continue to generate a dualistic character of unequal exchange and uneven development in the producing regions. This inequality and underdevelopment is also demonstrated by

S. Bunker's 1985 study of extractive activities in Brazil's Amazon region. He observed that

> when natural resources are extracted from one regional ecosystem to be transformed and consumed in another, the resource exporting region loses value that is in its physical environment. These losses eventually decelerate the extractive region's economy, while the resource consuming communities gain value and their economies accelerate. Extractive appropriation impoverishes the environment on which local populations depend both for their own reproduction and for the extraction of commodities for export.[9]

Extractive activities, particularly with respect to "red gold" and the exploitation of rubber, sugar, and other cash crops, established a locally dominant class which created a mode of extraction that so fully exploited labor and nature that neither could fully recover. The dominant class organized various modes of extraction in response to international market opportunities, but the rates of exchange for their exports were so diverse that the cycles of extraction and trade ultimately impoverished not only the physical environment and the labor force but also the dominant classes that depended on them.

THE ZAIRIAN EXPERIENCE

Samuel Ochola (1975) has argued that the exploitation of the mineral resources in Zaire has failed to establish forward and backward linkages that often accompany the opening of mines. His data were analyzed by estimating the percentage share of mining contribution to gross domestic product (GDP), employment, and foreign exchange earnings. His results showed that employment in the mining sector has been declining in percentage terms relative to other sectors, although in numeric terms it has been increasing.[10] In 1966 mining accounted for 10.9 percent of wage earners employed by enterprise, in 1967 10.3 percent, and in 1968 9.4 percent. However, mining's contribution to total government revenue and foreign exchange earnings saw a dramatic increase in the same period. From 1966 to 1968 mining contributed over 50 percent of total government revenue and about 85 percent of its foreign exchange earnings. However, its contribution to GDP showed a decline of 2 percent during this period. The finding that mining's contributions to GDP and employment were lower than its contributions to government revenue and foreign exchange earnings led Ochola to conclude that the mining sector has promoted economic growth rather than economic development.[11] He attributed the cause to the influence of foreign interests in Zaire's mining industry and the consequent export of all mining outputs to the advanced capitalist countries. He supported his argument by listing the names of multinational and international agencies that dominate the mining operations in Zaire.

OIL IN THE VENEZUELAN ECONOMY

Venezuela, a founding member of OPEC, has been an oil producer since 1917. It has one of the world's largest reserves in the Orinoco Tar Belt.[12] The exploration and exploitation of oil has significantly influenced Venezuela's economy for several decades. The most profitable operation was carried out by a subsidiary of Standard Oil of New Jersey which was then known as Creole Oil. Creole Oil and other multinational oil companies have played a major role in Venezuelan social and economic development.

The Venezuelan Oil Corporation, the first state-owned oil company, was formed in 1960. It accounted for about 3 percent of Venezuela's hydrocarbon output in 1974. The Venezuelan oil industry itself was nationalized in 1976, bringing the oil industry and its activities under state control. The role of the nationalized oil industry in Venezuela was expected not only to maximize revenue for the government, but also to boost the country's overall economic development by assisting in:

      - providing oil and maximizing the return on investment in oil;

      - producing oil and providing a preferential market for Venezuelan goods and services;

      - the development of the production of goods and services used by the oil industry;

      - the economic development of the areas in which the industry operates; and

      - the development of a wide range of energy related activities.[13]

It is interesting to note that the multinational oil companies, before and after nationalization, assumed an active role in providing the basic social infrastructures (water, education, housing, power, and so on) for the oil producing areas. From the onset, special consideration was given to the social and economic development of the producing areas; the interests of the host communities were integrated into the development of the resource.

THE IMPACT OF MINING IN IRAQ

The impact of the mining sector (oil) on Iraq's economic development has been presented by Al-Eyd Kadhim (1979). The data on sectoral contribution to GDP (in percentages at current prices) and the structure of employment were presented and analyzed. The results showed that the oil sector accounted for more than one-third of the country's GDP between 1953 and 1973. Following the rise in oil prices, the share of the oil sector in Iraq's GDP rose sharply, amounting to 53 percent in 1974, 57 percent in 1975 and 60 percent in 1976. The author also found that while the share of oil in total output rose, that of agriculture declined.

Furthermore, the diminishing role of agriculture and the growing dominance of oil were not accompanied by similar changes in the pattern of employment. For example, agricultural employment as a percentage of Iraq's total employment increased from about 49 percent in 1963 to 56 percent in 1973. During the same period, the oil industry's share of total employment declined moderately. Kadhim therefore argued that "the oil industry, in other words, failed to play the role of leading sector."[14] The reasons for this failure, he argued, are: (1) the oil industry is capital intensive and therefore cannot absorb a substantial percentage of the labor force; (2) the foreign oil companies confined their operations to extraction and export and as such refrained from investing in downstream operations such as refining; and (3) the inability of the government to establish petrochemical and other oil-based industries.

Kadhim's conclusion was that "the link between the oil industry and the rest of Iraq's economy is very weak."[15] The fact that oil sector employs less than two-thirds of 1 percent of the labor force means that its direct contribution to income and aggregate demand is minor.

STUDIES ON CANADIAN NATIVE PEOPLE

A Poison Stronger Than Love is a true story about the causes of suffering among the Ojibwa Indians in Northwestern Ontario, Canada.[16]

The Ojibwa tribe had a very deep attachment to their land and their natural environment, and traditional respect for human dignity. They were self-sufficient, independent, and highly stable people who lived in a traditional family setting. Then, the Ojibwa came in contact with the Europeans. The European search for colonies ended with the Ojibwas' signing of the Northwest Angle

Treaty of 1873. The European intrusion on the native Ojibwa way of life resulted in a forced acculturation which displaced of their traditional economy and caused dependency, relocation, and contamination. The Indians became exposed to a new type of livelihood in a wage-earning economy. The European expansion into their land brought about industrialization. Both personal and communal losses were suffered by the Ojibwa tribe, from weakened social relationships to their eventual social collapse. The government of Canada did not embark on a comprehensive plan designed to better the welfare of the Indians. Instead, they reinforced dependency. Moreover, the Indians were not effectively compensated for their suffering. The culprit, the Reed Paper Company, and the Canadian government both disclaimed all legal, social, and moral responsibility for the pollution. Neither the federal government, the state government, nor Canadian politicians could or would help the Indian people, and adequate justice was not rendered.

It is important to note that poor indigenous people, whether in a third world nation or existing as an enclave in a developed nation, share the experience of exploitation and distributive injustice. The following examples are substantive studies on extractive activities specific to developing countries.

A STUDY ON NEW GUINEA

Another example of problems posed by extractive activities is reflected in the study of the social impact of the OK Tedi Mine in Papua, New Guinea.[17] OK Tedi, begun in 1980, was a $1.5 billion project in one of the world's most remote and inhospitable regions. It was hoped that when OK Tedi was in full production, it would bring about changes in the area ranging from expanded employment and business opportunities for the people to developmental changes in the overall economy. Notwithstanding these potential benefits, environmental conservation and other responsibilities were spelled out as part of the public policy objective. In this regard, New Guinea's Constitution of 1975 declared:

We declare our fourth goal to be for Papua New Guinea's natural resources and environment to be conserved and used for the collective benefit of us all, and be replenished for the benefit of future generations.

We accordingly call for:

1. wise use to be made of our natural resources and the environments in and on the land or seabed, in the sea, under the land, and in the air, in the interests of our development and in trust for future generations;

2. the conservation and replenishment, for the benefit of ourselves and posterity of the environment and its scenic and historical qualities; and

3. all necessary steps to be taken to give adequate protection to our valued birds, animals, fish, insects, plants, and trees.[18]

The findings of the study on OK Tedi show, among other things, that the most damaging social impact of the mine has been the generation of various inequalities in the region. Nevertheless, the study acknowledged that the rural residents possess a clear sense of natural justice based on their traditional values. If prevented from seeking redress in a Western-style legal system, the likelihood of costly social disruption may increase.

THE INDONESIAN EXPERIENCE

Further lessons are learned from increased timber extraction in the Indonesian tropical forest between 1968 and 1980, which resulted in serious ecological consequences including large forest fires. The extractive impact assessment indicates that there has been: (1) "extinction of several species of flora and fauna through direct destruction and loss of habitat; (2) hydrological damage including loss of natural drainage . . . and increased sedimentation of rivers; (3) widespread soil degradation through increased erosion and mineralization; and (4) climatic change caused by destruction of thick rain forest canopies."[19]

Indonesian officials perceived that the large foreign investments in the timber sector did not create the expected number of jobs for Indonesians. Apparently, the mere existence of extractive activities in a host community in a developing country does not bring about growth and development for the indigenous population. Instead, it generates a malignant growth of social inequalities, environmental decay, deprivation, and under-development.

PETROLEUM INDUSTRY IN THE PEOPLE'S REPUBLIC OF CHINA

China is blessed with an abundance of such mineral resources as coal, crude oil, and gas, with verified reserves of about 137 mineral deposits distributed in over 15,000 deposit areas throughout the country. The production of crude oil alone reached 130.69 million tons in 1984, the fourth largest in the world. Although mineral deposits are unevenly distributed in China, records show that 78 percent of proven coal reserves are located in the north and northwest region, while 85 percent of proven crude oil reserves are located around the eastern part of the country and north of the Changjiang river.[20] These mineral producing areas tend to supply most of China's energy needs. According to Xia Xiamin (1988), the estimated worth of the minerals "in situ" alone is comparable to the value of all the minerals in the United States. China has a population of 1.06 billion people and ranks eighty-fourth in the world in per capita reserves.

China has a planned mineral development program. The main features of the plan are aimed at a comprehensive development of its energy and mineral resources, and a rational utilization policy that seeks to emphasize minimal consumption and the protection of resources and imports on the basis of domestic needs.

China desires to maintain political stability so as to ensure economic growth for the benefit of its people. Foreign capital investment in the energy industry is expected to play a significant role in its development effort, but will be subject to laws and regulations with regard to foreign economic relations. For instance, Chinese laws permit Chinese and foreign joint ventures but provide strict regulations regarding foreign exchange control and management of the labor force. The Chinese government requires that joint venture pacts include a technology trade combination as a basis for the transfer of advanced technology, because the exploration and exploitation of China's mineral resources had been low for many decades due to a lack of state-of-the-art technology.

The major energy source of China has always been coal, but there is a strong prospect for the development of the oil and gas industry; however, an increase in proven reserves would remain key to that development. Since 1984 the country's proven reserves have increased to over 700 million tons per year, and it is expected to rise because the influx of foreign venture capital could catalyze the development process.

China expects domestic energy utilization to increase and has taken steps to ensure an adequate supply for the support of its reformed economic outlook. Although in the past the performance of the petroleum sector was quite small, China has improved its output since the 1960s. In 1973 China became an oil exporter; by 1985 the volume of exported oil had risen to over 30.6 million tons. The nation's per capita consumption of oil is still low due to a preference for coal as its major energy source. In fact, the supply of oil to most oil consuming units is controlled by quotas, so the oil exported is conserved from domestic consumption. Why does China export oil? China exports to balance its bilateral trade with friendly countries and, of course, to generate foreign currency needed for the importation of technology.

China's mineral development strategies are carried out in accordance with the nation's five-year plans and annual economic plan. A state planning commission is vested with the responsibility for maintaining an overall balance in the national economy and for meeting social development needs. Above all, it is interesting to note that China has an enforceable regulatory policy. It has enacted thirty-seven Articles of Control on the exploration and exploitation of petroleum resources. As a matter of interest, the most recent Article is headed: "Regulation of people in exploration of petroleum resources with specific rights and obligations of the parties to petroleum contract for the purposes of maintaining sovereign rights and environmental protection."[21]

The government of China has taken specific measures to protect the rights and interests of its indigenous population, including the minority population of the mineral producing areas in the eastern region of the country. The Chinese government was not only concerned with environmental pollution but also with the possible moral and spiritual pollution that could result from the interaction of its indigenous population with an expatriate work force and foreign ideas.

THE MALAYSIAN EXPERIENCE

Another interesting example is drawn from the Malaysian oil industry. Malaysia, with a population of 15 million people is a modest producer of oil. The country is classified as the twenty-first world class producer. Its crude oil production has reached 500,000 barrels per day. Malaysia's oil production dates back to 1910 in the Sarawak region; however, most of its current oil production is centered offshore, accounting for about 44 oil fields and 47 gas fields. The government of Malaysia derives 30 percent of its revenue from oil exports and 95 percent of the country's energy needs are met by oil. The country also has a gas reserve estimated at 70 trillion cubic feet, enough to last at least 100 years.

The main oil producing areas in Malaysia are the Sarawak Peninsula and Sabah. These areas were formerly backward in development but oil has boosted their respective local economies. Malaysia's oil reserves are moderate in comparison with the reserves in a major oil producing country; hence, depletion control and energy diversification are encouraged by the government.

The Malaysian national oil corporation is called Petronas. Petronas is vested with the responsibility of planning for the orderly exploitation and use of Malaysia's petroleum resources so as to satisfy both present and future needs.[22] In order to encourage local participation and maintain a balanced economic development, the petroleum industry is involved in the development of the agrobased sector of the economy. This is an encouraging policy, designed to induce the spread of spillover benefits to the vast majority of its people through the promotion of agriculture. A policy like this would prove helpful in a country like Nigeria, where agrobased industry has declined to the point of food crises as a result of the rapid development of the oil industry. Malaysian policy sets a further example with the establishment of economic research units and agriculture and industrialization research units aimed at seeking to maintain a healthy balance between agriculture and industrial development. These units carry out socioeconomic impact and perception studies in an effort to minimize problems of traumatic social change.

The country's depletion policy restricts annual oil production and allows production deferments of up to five years. It is the desire of the Malaysian government to see that the fast-growing petroleum sector is in line with national objectives, including conservation policy and environmental protection.

Petronas has helped to encourage the participation of the local labor force and businesses in petroleum activities and their derived benefits. Its management of socioeconomic impacts has helped to generate employment and business opportunities for its people and the material standard of living has improved. Hence petroleum disruption and dislocation of traditional mode of life is kept at barest minimum. Direct benefits to the people are made possible through provision of infrastructures such as power, communication, health services, water supply, transportation, and other essential social services. Although the oil producing states ceded all oil rights to the national government, the states receive half of the oil revenue or royalties,[23] and are free to spend the money as they see fit to boost development. In addition, they still receive federal allocation for development projects. Thus, increased general development along with oil development is part of Malaysia's aim to improve the overall quality life of its citizenry, rural and urban alike.

The foregoing analyses reveal differences in the impacts of extractive industry on host communities in developed economies and those in developing economies. The problem of inequalities and distributive imbalances continues to plague most third world areas, as well as traditional communities existing as an enclave in developed economies. China and Malaysia are exceptions, and seem to have better programs and policies for the improvement of overall quality of life for all their citizenry, particularly the indigenous populations of the producing areas.

NOTES

1. L. Palinkas et al., *System Approach to Social Impact Assessment: Two Alaskan Case Studies* (Boulder, CO: Westview Press, 1985).

2. R. R. Moore, "The Impact of Oil Industry in West Texas" (doctoral dissertation, Texas Technological College, 1965).

3. J. Copp, *Social Impacts of Oil and Gas Developments,* (College Station, Texas: Texas A&M University, Center for Energy and Mineral Resources , 1984).

4. Colin Robinson and Eileen Marshall, "Oil's Contribution to U.K. Self-Sufficiency" (London: Policy Studies Institute and the Royal Institute of International Affairs, 1984).

5. Dan Shapiro, *Social Impact of Oil Industry in Scotland* (Hart, England: Gower Publication, 1980), 161.

6. R. Voyer and M. Gibbons, *Technology Assessment: A Case Study of East Coast Offshore Petroleum Exploration* (Science Council of Canada, Background Study no. 30, March 1974).

7. S. Roberto, "The Impact of Oil Operations on the Producing Regions of Southern Mexico,"*Third World Planning Review* 5, no. 1 (February 1983): 57.

8. "Oil and Related Problems for Producing Regions," UNRISD Research Note no. 7, Geneva, 1985, 23.

9. S. Bunker, *Extractive Economies: The Underdevelopment of the Amazon* (Urbana, IL: University of Illinois Press, 1985).

10. Samuel A. Ochola, *Minerals in African Underdevelopment* (London: London Viller Press, 1975), 130, as discussed in L. A. Azubuike, "The Role of the Mining Industry in the Economic Development of the Less Developed Countries: The Case of Zaire," master's thesis, Atlanta University, Atlanta, Georgia, 1985.

11. Ibid, 135.

12. Gilbert Jenkins, *Oil Economists Handbook* (London: Applied Science Publishers, 1977): 79.

13. Laura Randell, *Political Economy of Venezuelan Oil* (New York: Praeger, 1987): 22.

14. Al-Eyd A. Kadhim, *Oil Revenues and Accelerated Growth: Absorptive Capacity in Iraq* (New York: Praeger, 1979), 29. Also, L. A. Azubuike, "The Role of the Mining Industry."

15. Ibid, 35.

16. Anastasia M. Shkilayk, *A Poison Stronger than Love: The Destruction of Ojibwa Community* (New Haven: Yale University Press, 1986).

17. Jackson, "OK Tedi: Pot of Gold," in *Multinational Corporations, Environment and the Third World*, C. Pearson, ed. (Durham, NC: Duke University Press, 1987), 52.

18. William Pintz, "Environmental Negotiations in OK Tedi Mine in Papua New Guinea," in *Multinational Corporations and the Third World*, Charles S. Pearson, ed. (Durham, NC: Duke University Press, 1987): 35.

19. Malcom Gillis, "Multinational Enterprises and Environmental and Resources Management Issues in the Indonesian Tropical Forest," in *Multinational Corporations, Environment and the Third World*, C. Pearson, ed. (Durham, NC: Duke University Press, 1987), 70.

20. P. Dorian and D. Fridley, *China's Energy and Mineral Industry* (Boulder, CO: Westview Press, 1988), 93-96.

21. Peter Hills and Paddy Bowie, *China and Malaysia: Social and Economic Effects of Petroleum Development* (Geneva, Switzerland: International Labor Organization, 1987), 70-80.

22. Ibid.

23. Ibid., 132.

4

Selected Studies on the Oil Industry in Nigeria

The Nigerian oil industry has undergone considerable study. The oil industry by nature encounters many socioeconomic, political, and environmental problems, which is understandable in light of the fact that it is traditionally operated by privately owned oil multinationals with headquarters in industrialized nations. These multinationals (Prast 1964) produce most of the world's crude oil, extracting it mainly from economically developing areas.[1] The oil exports provide foreign exchange and government income for these nations. Many studies on the oil industry focus on issues affecting economic growth and derived benefit for the multinationals and the producer nations. There have been a number of studies by economists and other social scientists on the Nigerian oil industry. The first study was by L. H. Schatzl (1969), and focused on the importance of oil in relation to the future energy needs of Nigeria as the country moves into self-sustained growth.[2] A second study by S. Pearson (1970) took a different approach, emphasizing the current and future impact on the Nigerian economy of the flow of oil-related investment.[3] Other economists studied different aspects of the Nigerian oil industry. E. Emembolu (1975), for instance, focused on petroleum and the development of a dual economy.[4] His study revealed that the heavy reliance on petroleum resources for growth and the high rate of oil exploitation would lead to diminished consumption. His study also pointed out that investment in a dual economy could become inefficient beyond a certain point. He recommended that the rate of oil exploitation be consistent with the optimal rate of investment or absorption of capital in the economy. Dare Odofin (1979) focused on the impact of the multinational oil corporations on Nigeria's economic growth.[5] Odofin demonstrated that multinational capital investment has catalyzed Nigeria's rapid economic growth. The increased earnings from the oil sector offered some relief for Nigeria's balance of payments and allowed for a rapid rate of growth in the domestic economy. His findings also revealed that there is a positive and significant relationship between indirect employment (public sector), domestic savings, and net foreign oil capital inflows. His study concluded that foreign investment during the period 1963–75 had a profound effect on the rapid growth of the Nigerian economy. However, the short-term economic growth could not bring about a long-term balance-of-payments equilibrium unless specific measures were taken to curtail import expenditures. He predicted that Nigeria might experience substantial debt and deficit (of course, this was true by the time of this writing—the economic boom was short-lived and Nigeria has become a debtor nation). His findings also acknowledged the economic disparity between the "haves" and the "have-nots" and the twin problems of poverty and unemployment in the country. He pointed out that during the oil boom, Nigeria was doing well, but the Nigerians were not. Nigeria epitomized a classic case of growth without development.

J. K. Onoh (1983) studied the Nigerian oil economy from prosperity to glut, and examined the role played by oil in the domestic economy and its relationship with the international political economy of the 1970s and the 1980s.[6] He analyzed the differential access to oil revenue by the local, state, and federal governments under the controversial federal revenue-sharing formula. Oil was highly instrumental in Nigeria's economic prosperity and foreign policy in the 1970s, but the shrinkage of oil revenue and the oil market gluts have seriously weakened its position.

Finally, B. E. Okogu (1986) in a study entitled "The Outlook for Nigerian Oil: 1985–2000," predicted the future of Nigerian oil output and revenue under four different market scenarios: weak, optimistic, defensive OPEC, and OPEC breakdown.[7]

These studies are by no means exhaustive, and other economists have contributed useful insights into the Nigerian oil industry, but at this juncture let us move into studies by other social scientists. For instance, O. Ogbonna (1979) has studied the geographic consequences of petroleum in Nigeria.[8] His findings acknowledged that the oil industry there has disturbed the environmental balance of the producing areas and has failed to provide adequate compensation for the resulting problems. From a public policy standpoint, P. Olayiwola (1986) portrays Nigeria as a country of growth without positive change in his thesis "Petroleum and Structural Change in a Developing Country: The Case of Nigeria."[9]

According to Paul Collier (1978) the oil industry and the inequalities it has created in Nigeria do paint a picture of economic growth without progressive change. Over 60 million people live in the rural areas of Nigeria, exceeding the combined population of Tanzania, Uganda, Zaire, Kenya, Ghana, and Mozambique. The wealth that oil brought to the country seemed to be the fulfillment of a dream, the dream of poverty eradication. In 1978, Nigeria's per capita GNP stood at $560, the highest in Africa. From 1960–78 the country recorded a growth rate of 3.6 percent per year. It was considered Africa's success story. However, the dream wealth from oil was unequally distributed.

During the oil growth and its subsequent boom, agricultural output became stagnant and has remained so for a long period of time. The socioeconomic status of the people was determined by access to land, and oil had displaced part of the arable land on which rural people depend. The rapid export of oil actually reinforced income reduction in the rural areas; naively, one would have expected their income to have risen. The rural population, then, suffered both relative and absolute decline in quality of life, even as the oil industry was creating the Nigerian "success story."

It is clear that rapid growth at the national level did not automatically benefit the rural poor in Nigeria. Where massive income derived from the oil boom could have transformed the living standards of its people, the money was diverted to other beneficiaries. The rural residents and the urban poor were the real losers.[10]

There have been a few limited studies done to address the socioeconomic and environmental impact of oil industry in Nigeria. For instance, on the economic and social impacts of environmental regulations on the petroleum industry in Nigeria, E. C. Odogwu wrote:

Since there is always going to be generation of wastes and since getting regulations entails costs [for] the regulated, it is obvious that the question confronting everybody is: how clean and at what cost? In view of this, cost benefit analysis is an important factor in environmental standard setting.[11]

To elucidate his view, Odogwu traced the impact of some major oil spillage incidents in Nigeria and raised a number of interesting issues. He emphasized that "there is an obligation on the part of the government to assure [that] the public will not be harmed by industrial operations. Likewise there is an obligation by government to provide employment opportunities and [an] improved standard of living which results from industrial activity."

Overzealous environmental controls adversely impact the growth of a nation. However, no one would need to wrestle with this dilemma if government and industry had effective ways of harmonizing economic interest with environmental integrity, particularly with respect to the human side of industrial growth. In that light, Odogwu's study concluded with a recommendation to seek a cooperative environmental program that endeavors to benefit the nation without harming the industry.[12] The real issue is to find a well-balanced environmental program that benefits the industry, the nation, and the special needs of the people in the area. None of the previous studies, including Odogwu's study, shows adequate concern for the special needs of the people.

From an environmental perspective, A. D. Ikpah (1981) examined the environmental pollution control policies and practices of the Nigerian oil industry.[13] He asserts that pollution itself is an inherent part of economic operation, but that the magnitude of spillage events can be minimized through good industry management practices. Nigeria's efforts to extract its mineral resources (oil) should therefore seek to balance production needs with environmental quality in the quest for national development. Ikpah emphasized that greater government and industry cooperation for the detection, prevention, and control of environmental pollution could minimize pollution levels now and in the future.

All of these studies have contributed highly useful insights into problems, challenges, and opportunities in the oil industry, but it seems that within the array of oil literature, the main concern has been overly centered on production, growth, price trends, and revenue. This no doubt interests the multinational oil companies and the national government, but no one has stopped to assess the impact of oil production on the oil producing areas. The Nigerian oil industry has not adequately addressed the problems created by its impact on the inhabitants of the oil areas. There is still a dearth of research with respect to addressing those problems. Therefore a wide range of issues are yet to be addressed, particularly from the perspective of social policy and the human side of energy development.

THE PROBLEMS OF OIL SPILLAGE

Oil spillage and pollution are some of the negative byproducts of the petroleum industry and its effect on environmental quality is a source of major concern. Oil spill impact assessments have provided a useful means for estimating costs to the affected community since the Torrey Canyon ran aground off Lands, England in 1967, causing a spill of 117,000 tons. However, it has always been difficult to assign a monetary value to the ecological damage sustained as the consequence of an oil spill. Often, the costs are reported to be extensive but nonquantifiable.[14]

Numbers of oil spills have been reported around the world. In 1977 the Mexican National Oil Company began drilling an exploratory well, Ixtoci, in the Bay of Campeche in the Gulf of Mexico. On June 3, 1979, the well blew out and caught fire. By July 18, 1979, the blowout became one of the world's worst oil spills, having released 1.31 million barrels of oil into the environment. By 1980 an estimated total volume of 3.3 million barrels had been spilled, spreading as far as coastal areas of Texas in the United States. The damage was extensive. Earlier, on March 16, 1978, the Amoco *Cadiz* went ashore on the rocks at Port Sall on the western part of Brittany, spilling 223,000 tons of crude oil and spreading weathered oil along 400 kilometers of the French coastline. The estimated loss amounted to some $15.6 to $59.6 million. It caused the rapid depletion of fish stocks, worsened the economic condition of fishermen, and degraded the biomass.[15] In estimating the nonmarket economic losses from oil spills with reference to the Amoco *Cadiz*, Brown (1982) contends that about 60 million noncommercial organisms and about 30,000 tons of noncommercial macro and micro fauna were destroyed. Some 19,000 to 37,000 sea birds were lost in the Amoco *Cadiz* spill incident. Nine years previously, in January 1969, a Santa Barbara well blowout caused an oil spill estimated at 112,900 tons. The cost of cleanup alone was about $10.6 million. A comprehensive damage assessment of these and other spills has not been easy. Yet a number of studies have attempted to estimate the extent of economic and social cost to the affected areas.

Let us now turn to studies done on oil spillage in Nigeria. In an analysis of oil spill incidents in Nigeria between 1976 and 1980, S. A. Awobajo wrote:

Within the period . . . this country experienced seven hundred and eighty-four (784) oil spill incidents. These spills resulted in the loss of 1,336,875 barrels of oil. . . . [I]t is also informative to note that in 1981 alone (January–May) 121 incidents of oil spills were reported; again with another loss of 9,750 barrels to the national economy.[16]

Awobajo's study also examined the magnitude and distribution of oil spill incidents by geographic area and by company. The study pointed out the possibility that pollution spillover costs could extend to Nigeria's southeastern neighbors. In another study on the problem of environmental pollution and control in the Nigerian petroleum industry, Nwankwo et al. (1981) examined the complex nature of the oil industry in Nigeria and its complex pollution problems. The researchers identified the following sources of pollution in the oil industry: onshore and offshore exploration and production; transportation and marketing operations; and petroleum refining. However, the main causes of pollution peculiar to the Nigerian situation are specifically known to have occurred from:

- flow line leaks;
- over-pressure failures;
- sabotage to well heads and flow lines;
- hose failures on loading systems; and
- failures along pump discharge manifolds.

The Nigerian oil industry is still confronted with problems in pollution control and enforcement because of the lack of adequate administrative, technical, and other necessary infrastructural facilities. Nevertheless, the Nwankwo study offered some recommendations for effective management of these problems, particularly stressing the need for development and implementation of effluent limitation guidelines and the importance of instilling an environmental consciousness into all operating personnel.

On human health hazards associated with petroleum-related pollution, O. S. Olusi (1981) identified various sources of petroleum pollution and the specific health hazards known to occur.[17] He drew his assumptions from the epidemiological studies done in the United States, which suggest that there is a correlation between exposure to oil pollution and the development of cancer. Related health problems in Nigeria have not been fully documented, but his laboratory studies on rats indicate a potential for mutagenic and carcinogenic effects. In addition, in a preliminary survey, oil workers showed abnormalities in blood counts, increased malaria outbreaks, respiratory tract infections, urethritis, conjunctivitis, dermatitis, and other symptoms. Olusi concluded that communities and oil workers who are exposed to petroleum pollution ought to be protected from its health hazards. He called on the oil industry and the government to help provide funds for future research.

On the study of environmental and socioeconomic impacts of oil spillage in the petroleum producing riverine areas of Nigeria, G. Angaye et al. (1983) contend that although the petroleum industry has created an economic boom for the entire nation, it has also led to environmental and socioeconomic problems. The study states that "the inhabitants of the ecological zones of the riverine areas of Nigeria where petroleum is produced are the most obvious victims of the environmental and socioeconomic hardships that oil mining and spillage have produced in the country."[18] Through field survey methods, the researchers were able to determine the impact of oil spillage on a number of selected communities in the oil producing areas. The study identified a number of human, environmental, and economic hardships to area residents caused by the effect of spillage on fishing, farmlands, soil, climate, and water, and magnified by the helplessness of the inhabitants. The study also revealed that oil producing countries in the third world (such as Nigeria) lag behind the industrialized world in the provision of much-needed laws to protect their citizenry and control the multinational oil companies. The paper offered a number of policy plans to effect mitigation and also affirmed the fact that "petroleum exploration and exploitation have brought not only economic boom to Nigeria but also political power, especially within Africa. Ironically, the areas where . . . resources are naturally located suffer evident deprivation and lag behind in development of socio-economic development."

Another serious threat posed by oil-related pollution is its effect on the ground water, which is a source of drinking water for area residents. On the effects of oil spills on ground water, A. U. Oteri (1981) asserts that groundwater contamination resulting from hydrocarbon spills is a widespread phenomenon.[19] His study of a major oil blowout in the Rivers State of Nigeria revealed that extensive environmental degradation existed eighteen months after the incident, and that ground water in particular was contaminated with crude oil and will remain so for a long time. He concludes that ground water pollution resulting from spills cannot be totally cleaned up; the only real solution lies in prevention.

Finally, A. M. A. Imevbore et al. (1981) also studied the problems of pollution control in the Nigerian oil industry and found that the industry has played a prominent role in improving economic development in Nigeria. Like the others, however, he contends that the environmental pollution associated with the industry is now an important and sensitive issue that demands that all those concerned take a sensible and practical view of it.[20] The paper goes on to examine the specific problems of pollution and proposes that a monitoring and control program could best prevent further environmental degradation.

These and many other studies on the effects of oil spillage and pollution in Nigeria stress the need to establish measures for pollution control, prevention, and a comprehensive mitigation policy.

NOTES

1. W. G. Prast, "The Role of Host Governments in International Petroleum Industry" (doctoral dissertation, Pennsylvania University, 1964), 7-10.

2. L. H. Schatzl, *Petroleum in the Nigerian Economy* (Ibadan, Nigeria: University of Ibadan Press, 1969).

3. S. Pearson, *Petroleum and the Nigerian Economy* (Stanford: Stanford University Press, 1970).

4. G. Emembolu, "Petroleum and the Development of a Dual Economy: The Nigerian Example" (doctoral dissertation, University of Colorado, 1975).

5. D. C. Odofin, "The Impact of Multinational Oil Corporations on Nigeria's Economic Growth: Theoretical and Empirical Explorations" (doctoral dissertation, American University, Washington, DC, 1979).

6. J.K. Onoh, *The Nigerian Oil Economy: From Prosperity to Glut* (New York: St. Martin's Press, 1983).

7. B. E. Okogu, "The Outlook for Nigerian Oil: 1985–2000" *African Review* (December 1986).

8. O. Ogbonna, "The Geographic Consequences of Petroleum in Nigeria with Special Reference to Rivers State" (doctoral dissertation, University of California, 1979.

9. P. Olayiwola, *Petroleum and Structural Change in a Developing Country: The Case of Nigeria.* New York: Praeger, 1984.

10. P. Collier, *Oil and Inequalities in Rural Nigeria* (Geneva, Switzerland: International Labor Office, 1978), 191-217.

11. E. C. Odogwu, "Focal Point Environmental Affairs Shell Petroleum Development Company of Nigeria in Petroleum Industry and Nigerian Environment," *Proceedings of the 1981 International Seminar* (Lagos, Nigeria: NNPC, 1981), 49.

12. Ibid.

13. A. D. Ikpah, "Oil and Gas Industry and Environmental Pollution: Application of Systems Reliability Analysis for the

Evaluation of the Status of Environmental Pollution Control in Nigerian Petroleum Industry" (doctoral dissertation, University of Texas at Dallas, 1981).

14. R. L. Freeman et al., "Measuring the Impact of the Ixtoc Oil Spill on the Visitation at Three Texas Public Coastal Parks," *Coastal Zone Management Journal* 12 no. 2 (1985): 77-107.

15. Richard Congar, "Estimation of Production Lost by Small Scale Independent Fishing as a result of Amoco *Cadiz* Oil Spill," in *The Cost of Oil Spills* (studies presented to the Organization for Economic Cooperation and Development, Paris, 1982), 189-91.

16. S. A. Awobajo, "Oil Spillage in Nigeria: 1976–1980," *Proceedings of the 1981 International Seminar* (Lagos, Nigeria: NNPC, 1981).

17. O. S. Olusi, "Nigerian Oil Industry and the Environment," *Proceedings of the 1981 International Seminar* (Lagos, Nigeria: NNPC, 1981).

18. *Proceedings of the 1983 International Seminar* (Lagos, Nigeria: NNPC, 1983).

19. A. U. Oteri, "A Study of the Effects of Oil Spills on Ground Water," *Proceedings of the 1981 International Seminar* (Lagos, Nigeria: NNPC, 1981).

20. A. M. A. Imevbore et al., *Proceedings of the 1981 International Seminar* (Lagos, Nigeria: NNPC, 1981).

5

Assessment Methodology

This chapter contains the purpose, formal exposition of impact assessment methodology, data collection, model applied, research design, hypotheses, and method of analysis adopted for this study.

IMPACT ASSESSMENT METHODOLOGY IN EXTRACTIVE ECONOMIES

The impact of extractive activities has always posed a major concern not only for local residents, but also for many concerned social scientists. Several conceptual and empirical approaches have been developed to measure socioeconomic and environmental changes effected by extractive activities in a given community.

Below are some of the previous approaches to assessments of extractive impacts. In a study of energy values in unequal exchange and uneven development, S. Bunker (1985) applied "an ecological model" to achieve a historical analysis of the underdevelopment of Brazil's Amazon Basin (where extractive activities included exploitation of rubber, Brazil nuts, sugar, lumber, gold, etc.):[1]

    – by organizing history into periods that correspond to the predominance of particular commodities in the Amazon export trade;

    – by describing how extraction and production of these commodities were organized either through reorganization of prior modes of production and extraction or through organization of new modes; and

    – by analyzing how the demographic, organizational, infrastructural, and ecological effects of each of these modes of production and extraction established the potential for limits on later modes of extraction.

The ecological model is useful in explaining the persistent poverty in the resource region.

    In a study of attitudes toward energy development in the northern Great Plains of the United States, James G. Thompson et al. (1983) adopted survey techniques to determine the extent to which residents in the northern Great Plains would accept rapid social change and the degradation of their physical environment in exchange for perceived economic benefits of development.[2] The study's findings suggest a considerable variance of attitude within the population surveyed. Finally, on the economics of mineral extraction Anders et al. (1980) employed two basic models—the standard hosteling mineral depletion model and Harberger's model of investment—in an attempt to estimate the extent of factor substitution and technical change in the Canadian metal mining industry.[3] The two models are considered a useful guide to mineral industry policy analysis. These studies and many other approaches have contributed a useful understanding of extractive impact assessment, but at this juncture, let us turn to impact assessment methodology in oil production and related activities.

IMPACT ASSESSMENT METHODOLOGY IN THE OIL INDUSTRY

A number of impact assessments have been performed in the oil industry. Here we will discuss some examples and problems from previous works on oil impact assessment. Previous studies show that oil impact assessment was often confronted with conceptual, methodological, and empirical problems. For instance, the difficulties associated with socioeconomic impact assessments of the oil industry are within the nature of the industry itself. According to Leistritz and Chase (1982), there are four specifically identified problems: (1) information; (2) the integration of diverse petroleum activities; (3) examination of interindustry linkages; and (4) developing realistic projections of petroleum activity. Another problematic area of oil impact assessment is the nature of uncertainty inherent in the oil industry.[4]

According to Leistritz and Chase (1982), given the inherently dynamic quality of the oil industry and the uncertain nature of the resource, realistic projections of future activity within the development region are extremely difficult. Nevertheless, the authors suggest that the implementation of several monitoring systems should provide for the periodic collection of data, identification of emerging problems, and reformulation of impact projections on the basis of monitored information. Implicit within any monitoring program is the provision of accurate and timely information as the basis for rational planning, growth management, and impact-mitigation in most host communities.

While conceptual and methodological issues involved in socioeconomic impact assessment of oil remain problematic, generally there are some well-developed tools of socioeconomic impact analysis. A number of these models and methods have proven empirically useful in researchers' understanding of oil impact assessment and analysis. First, the gravity allocation model is a widely used technique for projecting the settlement patterns of energy-related workers. The underlying premise of its use is that larger communities closer to the project sites will gain more population from the project than smaller and more distant places (Murdock and Leistritz 1981).[5]

This model goes further as a useful tool in estimating the magnitudes of secondary economic activity (that is, employment, income, and business volume) resulting from petroleum activity. This is an important aspect of any comprehensive social and economic impact assessment. A second mechanism often utilized in estimating the secondary effects of an initial economic stimulus on an area's employment, income, and output is the input/output model. This model, with quantitative estimates of the interdependencies of an area's economic sectors as suppliers of inputs and purchasers of products, provides the basis for tracing the multiplier effects of a dramatic increase of petroleum activity in the economy (Chase et al. 1982). In addition, some studies have adopted survey techniques useful to understanding the social and economic impact of energy related development on a community (Copp 1984; Leistritz and Chase 1982; Murdock and Leistritz 1981; Voyer and Gibbons 1974). These studies provide examples of the methodology of oil impact assessment.

PURPOSE

The purpose of this study was to measure the impact of the oil industry on the inhabitants of the oil producing areas as measured by certain ecological factors. The purposes are to:

1. identify socioeconomic factors that are thought to influence the people and their environment in selected areas in Nigeria

2. explain how the identified factors are influenced by the oil producing activities in the area

3. perform an impact assessment study of the area in an attempt to quantify the effect of the identified factors on the inhabitants

4. draw a realistic policy conclusion based on the observed interaction between the identified factors and the results of the impact assessment study of the area

The results of this impact study could shed some light on the ways and means of implementing community impact agreements. It will further provide a mechanism for monitoring policy in Nigerian oil industry. Finally, it serves as an example for other areas in which similar problems are found.

PROCEDURE

Formal exposition of impact assessment methodology

The general steps followed by most impact analyses (OECD Report 1978) are to:

– define the issues and current status;
– identify possible features and their likelihood of occurrence;
– identify possible actions and their suspected impact; and finally
– evaluate alternatives and select desirable courses of action.[6]

It is necessary to have precise information about sources of impacts, likelihood, timing and duration, magnitude, diffusion, and the probability breaking-point of reactive behavior and policy. Hence, a formal procedure becomes very important to the effort to improve understanding. In essence, the analysis could disclose new facts that could change the attitudes of decision-makers.

Data collection

The data collected for this study were basically secondary data sources from archival records of federal and state governments, oil industry records, published and unpublished writings of previous researchers in the oil industry and related fields. However, when actual figures were not available, estimates were derived from available raw data.

Impact assessment model applied in this study

In view of the secondary data sources and the trend of oil production, the application of time series seems appropriate for this study. Time series involves periodic measurements on some variable or variables obtained at equally spaced points in time. The time series analysis determines if a given event had any significant impact on the existing trends (given the point in which the event occurred). If the event did have an effect, one would expect the distribution of observations after the event to differ from those before. Moreover, it is advantageous to utilize the power of time series in removing any possible seasonal effect on the variables. It offers a useful means of preventing an uncontrollable event or events from influencing the results of this study.

Assumptions involved in the time series model are: (1) that there is a linear relationship between the dependent and the independent variable(s); (2) that the values of the variables are normally distributed; and (3) that time is the independent variable in ordinary least-square time series regression; it follows then that the error terms of consecutive observations be correlated. However, ordinary least-square regression requires an assumption that the error terms associated with each time series observation be independent, that is, not the function of any event involved in the model.[7]

For this study, conventional methods of ordinary least-squares may not be appropriate because of the fundamental assumption of independence error terms. Hence, there may be possible biases or violations of this fundamental assumption which may amount to producing different results. However, it is important to note that the regression equation in ordinary least squares is not biased, since the primary concern is with the statistical significance of the parameters. In essence, it means that the use of standard deviation of parameter estimates to make decisions may become problematic because of the biases whenever the error terms are correlated (as in time series). Normally, the F or t-statistics are used to test the significance of time series changes. If the bias in the estimate of the standard deviation is downward, the coefficient will be "enlarged" and the impact effect may appear impressively different from the actual effect. This study has therefore employed the F statistic to determine the relationship among the variables (see below). This procedure further helps in testing the study hypotheses.

Whether or not the ordinary least-square regression estimates of time series parameters are biased is determined by the estimates of the significance tests. The ideal method of overcoming this problem is the use of autoregressive integrated moving average models (ARIMA), or the associated modelling techniques developed by Box and Jenkins (1976). These techniques were designed to correct biases in the estimates of the error in a time series analysis. However, ARIMA models are not suited for this study because it is difficult to use the ARIMA modeling procedure with fewer than fifty to one hundred observations.

Nevertheless, Cook and Campbell (1979) suggest that if the number of time series observations is small and the errors are correlated, measures of multiple analysis of variance (MANOVA) or ANOVA may be most suitable for evaluating the significance of an impact effect.[8] This suggestion seems appropriate for this impact study in that the number of observations is small for the period 1964 to 1984. Because the number of observations is small and the error terms may be correlated, then the appropriate analytical technique was the analysis of variance (ANOVA).

The adoption of the ANOVA model in this study could not have completely overcome the violation of a basic assumption in ordinary least-square regression analysis, which is that the error terms be independent. It also follows that the value of dependent variables selected for one value of independent variable does not depend on the value selected for another independent variable. Since the impact data under study is of a time series character, the element of structural dependency among the variables cannot be ruled out. However, in the ANOVA model, this violation should not constitute a serious threat to the methodology. In a similar impact study, in which the number of observations was small and the Box and Jenkins technique was inappropriate, F. W. Hoole (1978) pointed out that when he conducted checks on the error terms for an autoregressive scheme, he detected no significant problem of autocorrelated error (that is, testing the independence of regression disturbances).[9] He reported that the estimates of regression coefficients, which were used to provide estimates of the trends, were consistent even when the error terms were autocorrelated. The ANOVA model may not offer complete solutions to all problems, but on the whole it appears to be an adequate model for this study.

The ordinary least-square regression model also assumes linearity, that the disturbance terms should have zero mean and that the variance of the errors will be the same, except for possible autoregression due to the time series nature of the data. On the whole, the regression model estimates should be unbiased, efficient, and consistent.

Research design

Social scientists are concerned with understanding the factors influencing changes over time. To this end, considerable progress has been made in developing indicators for evaluating the social well-being of a community or a nation through the application of aggregate data analysis. The aggregate statistics used for this study assess the changes in dependent variables (socioeconomic indicators such as the provision of roads, housing, water, electricity (power), health, and education, and the social costs characterized by levels of pollution) over the period 1964 to 1984 as a result of the impact of the oil industry on the oil producing areas.

The application of time series design is suited here in that there is an observable pattern of oil production trend and it is characterized by continuous effect for the entire period. However, there is a remarkably sharp rise in production level after 1974, which signifies a growth of the Nigerian oil industry. Thus, the design of this quasi-experimental study is of a special type because there is no specific point of intervention. The impact of the independent variable influenced each period of observation from 1964 to 1984.

The design can be diagrammed:

$$OX1\ OX2\ OX3\ OX4\ OX5\ OX6\ OX7\ OX8\ OX9\ \ldots\ OXn$$

where X is the independent variable or the explanatory variable, O is the observation, and n is the total number of periods observed. In this case the number of observations should equal twenty (from 1964 to 1984). Before 1974, oil was less significant in the Nigerian economy and after 1974, oil became a highly significant sector of the Nigerian economy.

Hypotheses

For the purpose of measurability and test-effectiveness, these three major hypotheses were proposed.

H^{1a} The indigenous population in the oil producing areas will benefit in each of the ecological factors tested.

H^{1b} The indigenous population in the oil producing areas will not benefit in the ecological factors tested.

H^{2a} The indigenous population in the non-oil producing area will benefit in each of the ecological factors tested.

H^{2b} The indigenous population in the non-oil producing areas will not benefit in each of the ecological factors tested.

H^{3a} The indigenous population in the oil producing areas will benefit more than those in non-oil producing areas (in the ecological factors measured).

H^{3b} The indigenous population in the oil producing areas will not benefit more than the indigenous population in the non-oil producing areas.

The three hypotheses were tested for six social indicators (education, health, housing, power, roads, and water) for both the oil producing areas and the non-oil producing areas. The null hypotheses were tested in operationalizing the study. The 5 percent level of significance served as the criterion for acceptance or rejection of each of the null hypotheses:

1. H^1 Oil production has made a significant difference in education.

    H^0 There is no difference.

2. H^1 Oil production has made a significant difference in health.

    H^0 There is no difference.

3. H^1 Oil production has made a significant difference in housing.

    H^0 There is no difference.

4. H^1 Oil production has made a significant difference in power (electricity) supply.

   H^0 There is no difference.

5. H^1 Oil production has made a significant difference in road infrastructure.

   H^0 There is no difference.

6. H^1 Oil production has made a significant difference in water supply.

   H^0 There is no difference.

The above hypotheses were tested for each of the following time periods: 1964–84, 1964–67, 1968–75, 1976–84, and 1975–80 (the oil boom years).

Selected data sources

The ideal data needed for this study should be comprised of all relevant social and economic service indicators (the dependent variables) in addition to comprehensive records of environmental changes such as pollution and reduction of the ecosystem. It would also be ideal if one could obtain measurable values of the actual independent variables, "the impact activities," rather than estimates drawn from levels of oil output. As ideal records are yet unobtainable, we must rely on the data that are available. Therefore, the data sources collected for this study are the dependent variables: social and economic service indicators (specifically, education, health, housing, power, roads, and water), environmental changes characterized by pollution, and social costs to the oil producing areas. These records were retrieved from publications of the Federal Office of Statistics, the Central Bank of Nigeria, federal and state government ministries of information, and the Nigerian National Petroleum Corporation. Although there are no comprehensive oil industry records on compensation, it is estimated to be 1 percent of each year's revenue from the federal revenue-sharing formula in which compensation of 1 percent is accorded   as a provision for the amelioration of ecological problems.[10]

Moreover, the actual impact values cannot be measured in terms of all geophysical activities (movement of equipment, road construction, earth clearing, digging, drilling, etc.), and the concomitant impact on the oil communities. Nevertheless, one would assume that the number of barrels produced per day is a function of the degree of extractive activities. Oil production records are available from 1958 to date. The oil production represents the independent variable observed over the years 1964 to 1984.

THEORY AND ANALYSIS

This study covered the twenty-year period from 1964 to 1984. The period was chosen because (1) there is a clear indication of Nigeria's economic transition from an agricultural-based economy to an oil-reliance economy; and (2) the nation experienced a rapid take-off in the growth of the oil industry, which resulted in overall national (and regional) development. Moreover, the period is marked by times of oil boom to oil burst. The study sought to identify whether changes in the selected socioeconomic indicators or the dependent variables over the period 1964 to 1984 have made a difference for the oil producing communities and the Nigerian nation. One can assume that the processes governing the interaction between the variables could be predictive of certain socioeconomic and ecological changes; if changes in the variables occurred during the period, what measurable effect did those changes have on the communities of the oil producing areas?

Given the oil production data from 1964 to 1984, there are observable differences in the pattern of oil production before and after the growth of the Nigerian oil industry. It is conceivable that these differences could effect changes in the dependent variables over the time period studied.

Since the analysis of variance model (ANOVA) is adopted for this study, the relevant statistical equation used is :

$$Y = A + BX + E \tag{1}$$

where A is an intercept, B is a parameter, X is the independent variable or oil production each year, E is the standard error term, and Y is the set of dependent socioeconomic variables. The analysis of variance is used to determine the magnitude of oil impact, resulting in an attempt to establish the proportionate degree of change among the variables over the period 1964 to 1984. Since the oil benefits or spillovers are spread nationally and regionally, the regression process covered both the federal government and each of the previous and current regional political divisions in the country (see Appendix, Tables A.1 to A.10).

Since this study seeks to test the relationship between the impact of oil production and socioeconomic activities, the following assumptions are made: first, that there is a relationship between the trend in oil production and the level of changes in socioeconomic activities in Nigeria; and second, that the changes in the socioeconomic activities in oil producing areas and the changes in non-oil producing areas will be significantly different.

For the purpose of enhancing effective testing and data analysis, the following four levels of analytical procedure are followed:

1. The impact of oil production on socioeconomic activities will be measured.

2. The impact of oil production on the producing areas will be measured. Such measurement will facilitate: (a) an understanding of the degree of direct influence on local socioeconomic activities; and (b) an understanding of the social costs to oil producing areas in terms of pollution, spillage and other oil related mishaps which may be correlated to trends in the level of production.

3. The degree of influence of oil production on non-producing areas will be measured. This measurement is an attempt to give an estimate of the intangible benefits that nonproducing areas are indirectly receiving through federal government sources. It is a reasonable attempt to justify the indirect benefits that nonproducing areas enjoy. Here, it is imperative to note that, in general, oil areas only yield their benefits through the influence of the federal government. In the case of dual government systems such as Nigeria's, the non-oil producing areas share in benefits derived from the oil resource (although not at the same level) through the federal revenue-sharing policy.

4. It is feasible that the use of analysis of variance will help to determine the measure of total impact and relative impact on the selected variables.

As indicated earlier, the F-statistic will be employed to test the relationship between the dependent variable and the explanatory variables. It is assumed that there is a linear relationship between the independent variable (oil production) and the dependent variable Y — the social indicators. The F-statistic permits us to test the significance of the R^2 statistic. It measures the proportion of variation in the dependent variable Y, explained by the regression equation. In essence, it measures the goodness of fit. The F-statistic allows us to accept the alternative hypothesis if the F-statistic is significantly different from zero. We can then conclude that the explanatory variables do explain the variation of the dependent variable Y about its mean (Pindyck and Rubenfeld 1981).[11]

Generally, the ordinary least-square model is used to derive the expression for R^2 and the F-statistic. Assume that the dependent variable Y can be expressed as

$$Y = B^1 + B^2X^2 + B^3X^3 \ldots + B^kX^k + E \qquad (2)$$

where B^1 is the intercept

$B^2, B^3, \ldots B^k$ are parameters

$X^2, X^3, \ldots X^k$ are explanatory variables

E is an error term/standard error.

Then the difference between Y and its mean may be written as:

$$Y_i - \bar{Y} = (Y_i - \hat{Y}_i) + \hat{Y}_i - \bar{Y} \tag{3}$$

where Y is the number of observations, $\bar{Y}$ is the mean and $\hat{Y}$ is residual.

Squaring both sides of the equation we obtain

$$\Sigma(Y_i - \bar{Y})^2 = \Sigma(Y_i - \hat{Y}_i)^2 + \Sigma(\hat{Y}_i - \bar{Y})^2 \tag{4}$$

where $\Sigma(Y_i - \bar{Y})^2$ = total variation of Y or total sum of squares (TSS)

$\Sigma(Y_i - \hat{Y}_i)^2$ = residual variations or residual sum of squares (ESS)

$\Sigma(\hat{Y}_i - \bar{Y})^2$ = Explained variation or regression sum of squares (RSS)

$$TSS = ESS + RSS \tag{5}$$

Dividing both sides of the equation by TSS gives

$$1 = \frac{ESS}{TSS} + \frac{RSS}{TSS} \tag{6}$$

The coefficient of determination (R^2) is the proportion of total variation in Y, the dependent variable, explained by the regression of Y on X. Thus

$$R^2 = \frac{RSS}{TSS} = 1 - \frac{ESS}{TSS} \tag{7}$$

Y_i is the dependent variable and X_i is the independent variable. We can express the variables as measured deviations from their means, thus

$$Y_i = Y_i - \bar{Y} \qquad X_i = X_i - \bar{X} \tag{8}$$

The predicted value of Y_i can be expressed as follows:

$$\hat{Y}_i = \hat{\beta} X_i \tag{9}$$

It then follows that each dependent variable observation can be written:

$$Y_i = \hat{Y}_i + \hat{\varepsilon}_i \tag{10}$$

where $\hat{\varepsilon}_i$ is a residual. Then

$$\Sigma Y_i^2 = \Sigma \hat{Y}_i^2 + \Sigma \hat{\varepsilon}_i^2$$
$$= \hat{\beta}^2 \Sigma X_i^2 + \Sigma \hat{\varepsilon}_i^2 \tag{11}$$

Therefore, it can be shown that

$$R^2 = \frac{RSS}{TSS} = \frac{\Sigma \hat{Y}_i^2}{\Sigma Y_i^2} \tag{12}$$

$$= \hat{\beta}^2 \frac{\Sigma X_i^2}{\Sigma Y_i^2}$$

$$R^2 = 1 - \frac{\Sigma \hat{e}_i^2}{\Sigma Y_i^2}$$

The subscript of F is used to denote the number of degrees of freedom. The value of the F-statistic will be zero only when the explained variance is zero. A low value may be an indication of a weak relationship between the dependent variable and the independent variable. A high F-value shows a strong linear relationship.

The use of the F-test is useful in its effectiveness in testing the joint hypothesis that if the parameters $B_2 = B_3 = \ldots B_k = 0$, then it can be shown that

$$F_{k-1,n-k} = \frac{R^2}{1 - R^2} \frac{N - k}{K - 1} \tag{13}$$

where the F-statistic with $k - 1$ and $n - k$ degrees of freedom allows for testing the hypothesis that none of the independent variables helps to explain the variation of dependent variables about its mean.[12]

Following from the generalized least-square model and the F-statistic, we can demonstrate the relationship between the production of oil X (the independent variable) and expenditures on the dependent variable Y. As noted above, the dependent variable is a set of socioeconomic indicators: specifically, education, health, housing, power, roads and water. We can now write an expression for the relationship between X and Y.

$$Y = f(o,u) \tag{14}$$

According to equation (14), the government expenditures on Y, a set of social indicators of well-being, is a function of oil production (o) and of (u), the other factors not included in the model or an error term by assumption.

Alternatively, we can express the linear relationship between X and Y with respect to each social indicator (i.e., education, health, housing, power, roads and water). It may be expressed as follows:

$$E^i = a + b_i o_i + u_i \qquad (15)$$

where

E^i = educational expenditure in the i-th year ($i = 1, 2, \ldots n$, representing 1964–84).

o_i = oil production in the i-th year

a = a constant

b_i = a regression coefficient

u = an error term

The expenditures on the social indicators for all governments were entered into the computer from the raw data (see Appendix). The analyses procedure was aided by the SPSSX computer program. The impact of overall oil production on the social indicators for the period 1964–84 and each of the periods are tabulated (see Chapter 6). Note, however, that the tables show distinct impact levels between oil producing areas (states) and non-oil producing states.

Table 5.1

Expenditures on Socioeconomic Development, Non-Oil Producing Areas/States (million naira)

Period	Areas/States	Education	Health	Housing	Power	Roads	Water
1964-1984		2,880,175	1,714,363	1,183,939	549,586	2,198,307	1,498,610
1964-1967	Western Nigeria	10,302	1,058	12,878	1,000	6,228	2,233
	Northern Nigeria	70,712	32,964	17,302	1,200	17,556	4,080
Subtotal		81,014	34,022	30,180	2,200	23,784	6,313
	Western State	33,683	40,716	15,011	850	20,525	21,214
	Lagos State	22,775	68,252	21,216	40	11,729	13,630
	East Central State	94,744	28,303	3,141	2,400	4,100	4,265
	North Central State	31,056	23,551	44,966	166	3,546	7,720
1968-1975	Northwestern State	19,382	28,937	35,320	1,797	5,254	6,563
	Northeastern State	26,350	38,693	79,411	520	4,489	8,517
	Benue-Plateau	17,368	14,500	30,546	168	9,068	13,896
	Kano State	22,068	36,759	40,374	380	7,284	5,276
	Kwara State	7,024	25,272	34,479	420	6,636	35,386
Subtotal		284,450	304,983	304,464	6,741	72,631	116,467
	Kaduna	94,230	54,592	32,180	27,688	49,931	43,294
	Niger	228,514	165,928	83,700	30,726	173,266	84,603
	Sokoto	158,300	35,766	90,961	32,564	122,945	99,778
	Benue	201,324	80,550	200,000	28,000	310,291	146,940
	Plateau	226,205	256,821	30,800	39,000	203,223	124,788
	Bauchi	284,546	204,330	170,831	123,240	167,526	76,923
1976-1984	Borno	112,934	51,728	18,206	49,036	218,574	138,210
	Gongola	157,543	32,711	30,755	39,210	185,288	129,236
	Kano	199,126	120,412	48,008	46,913	201,860	143,020
	Kwara	43,832	41,315	22,784	26,843	125,041	65,492
	Anambra	83,973	32,777	12,029	48,490	67,286	87,459
	Oyo	405,315	123,612	79,106	27,528	159,658	161,517
	Ogun	241,198	98,314	16,951	20,947	78,844	23,602
	Lagos	77,671	76,502	12,984	460	38,159	50,968
Subtotal		2,514,711	1,375,358	849,295	540,645	2,101,892	1,375,830
Total		2,880,175	1,714,363	1,183,939	549,586	2,198,307	1,498,610

Source: Compiled by the author.

Notes:
1964–67   Northern Nigeria, Western Nigeria

1968–75   N. Central, N.W. State, N.E. State, Benue Plateau, Kwara, East Central State, Western State, and Kano State

1976–84   Kaduna, Bauchi, Kano, Bornu, Niger, Kwara, Sokoto, Benue, Plateau, Gongola, Anambra, Oyo, Lagos, and Ogun.

Table 5.2

Expenditures on Socioeconomic Development, Oil Producing Areas/States

Period	Oil production in millions of barrels/day	Education	Health	Housing	Power	Roads	Water
				(million naira)			
1964–84	28,123.8	643,432	453,264	442,207	271,089	56,751	373,002
1964–67	Eastern region	72,214	18,822	16,124	780	14,614	4,080
	Midwestern region	3,046	918	6,480	500	3,836	3,296
Subtotal	1128.5	75,260	19,740	22,604	980	18,450	7,376
1968–75	Rivers State	14,097	15,279	104,604	400	5,878	4,000
	Midwestern State	15,574	9,695	55,222	4,749	17,543	6,093
	Southeastern State	8,943	12,601	2,063	200	3,073	3,533
Subtotal	11,208.3	38,614	37,575	161,889	5,349	26,494	13,626
1976–84	Cross Rivers	51,796	22,743	12,915	44,762	51,997	36,919
	Rivers State	58,714	32,111	29,211	39,976	41,104	29,218
	Imo	129,254	193,278	127,631	109,195	121,928	147,144
	Ondo	235,234	107,057	35,557	37,387	259,391	123,606
	Bendel	54,560	41,030	32,200	33,440	48,387	15,113
Subtotal	15,787.0	529,558	395,949	237,514	264,760	522,807	352,000
Total	28,123.8	643,432	453,264	442,207	271,089	56,751	373,002

Source: Compiled by the author.

Notes: 1964-67   Eastern region and Midwestern region
1968-75   Rivers, Bendel, and Cross River
1976-84   Rivers, Bendel, Cross River, Imo, and Ondo States

Statistical procedure

An analysis of variance was employed to determine relative impact levels. As stated earlier, the F-test was employed to determine the degree of impact, and statistically significant differences were found between oil producing areas and non-oil producing areas in the overall impact for the period 1964–84. The researcher would conclude that there is a strong relationship between the trend in oil production and changes in socioeconomic activities in Nigeria (see Tables 5.1 and 5.2), and also that the spillover benefits in terms of social and economic development are more significant in non-oil producing areas than in oil producing areas.

NOTES

1. S. Bunker, *Extractive Economies: The Underdevelopment of the Amazon* (Urbana, IL: University of Illinois Press, 1985).

2. J. Thompson and A. Blevins, "Attitudes Toward Energy Development in the Northern Great Plains," *Rural Sociology* 48, no. 1 (Spring, 1983): 149.

3. G. Anders et al., "The Economics of Mineral Extraction," *Southern Economic Journal* 48, no. 4 (1982): 1142.

4. L. Leistritz and R. Chase, "Socioeconomic Impact Assessment of On Shore Petroleum Development: A Conceptual Consideration and Case Study." Paper presented at the Second International Conference on Oil and Environment, Halifax, Nova Scotia, August 16-19, 1982.

5. S. Murdock and L. Leistritz, *Socioeconomic Impact of Resource Development: Methods of Assessment* (Boulder, CO: Westview Press, 1981).

6. Organization for Economic Cooperation and Development, "Social Assessment Technology: Review of Selected Studies," *OECD Report* (Paris, 1978), 10.

7. T. D. Cook and D. Campbell, *Quasi Experimentation and Design and Analysis Issues for Field Settings* (Chicago: Rand McNally, 1979), 207.

8. Ibid., 235.

9. W. F. Hoole, *Evaluation: Research and Development Activities* (Beverly Hills, CA: Sage Publications, 1978), 66.

10. Central Bank of Nigeria, *Report* (Lagos, Nigeria: Central Bank Publications, 1981).

11. R. S. Pindyck and D. L. Rubenfeld, *Econometric Models and Economic Forecast* (New York: McGraw Hill, 1981), 77-82

12. Ibid., 64-67, 78-82.

6

Findings

The empirical data and other information pertaining to this study were analyzed both statistically and descriptively. The findings are presented in this chapter. The major concern of the proposed hypothesis was to test the relationship between trends in oil production and changes in social and economic activities in the country, and to ascertain what measurable effect the industry had on oil producing states (areas).

STATISTICAL ANALYSIS

The impact of oil on the social indicators (education, health, housing, power, roads, and water) is shown in three ways. The first is the overall impact (Table 6.1), second, the impact on the oil producing states (areas) (Table 6.2) and finally, the impact on non-oil producing states (Table 6.3). The analysis of variance technique was applied in testing each hypothesis with the 0.05 percent level of significance and the F-test serving as the standard for statistical conclusion. The results of the analysis are presented below.

IMPACT OF OIL PRODUCTION ON THE SELECTED SOCIAL INDICATORS

Overall impact of oil production on education, health, housing, power, roads, and water

An evaluation of the data in Table 6.1 reveals that the overall impact of oil on education, health, power, roads and water was not significant prior to the growth of the oil industry. But a separate examination of each period shows that the development of health, housing, roads, and water infrastructures were significant for the period 1968–75, 1976–84 and during the oil boom period 1975–80. Notably, the development of education, roads and water were not necessarily highly significant. However, all the socioeconomic development variables shown were reasonably significant for the entire period 1964–84 but one cannot attribute the result to any single period or political administration. It is interesting to note that road development during oil growth through oil boom and burst is not highly significant; this could be attributed to the concentration of road infrastructural development within the urban metropoles. Empirically, road development in selected urban locations such as Lagos is impressive, but in rural areas, the development of roads has been minimal. This may be a prime factor in the major disparities that still exist between urban and rural areas. The same could be said for disparities in education, power supply, housing, and water supply. The illiteracy level remains high, and there are still no adequate institutions to meet the educational needs of the growing population. These findings are consistent with the condition of social indicators discussed in Chapter 1.

Table 6.1

The Overall Impact of Oil Production

PERIOD	DF	SUM OF SQUARES	F. VALUE	SIGNIFICANT F	R.
Education					
1964–84	1	2.14967	6.53129*	0.01190	0.23182
1964–67	1	0.00967	0.02784	0.86780	0.01556
1968–75	1	0.72679	2.12804	0.14740	0.13479
1976–84	1	0.91136	2.68126	0.10430	0.15094
1975–80 (Boom)	1	0.23181	0.67034	0.41460	0.07613
Health					
1964–84	1	5.85766	19.72938*	0.00000	0.38367
1964–67	1	0.46638	1.35667	0.24650	0.10798
1968–75	1	0.72674	4.11986*	0.04470	0.18597
1976–84	1	2.55761	7.85540*	0.00590	0.25286
1975–80 (Boom)	1	2.57273	7.90504*	0.00580	0.25361
Housing					
1964–84	1	9.85252	37.58322*	0.00000	0.49630
1964–67	1	1.75749	5.28499*	0.02330	0.20961
1968–75	1	2.60211	8.00161*	0.00550	0.25505
1976–84	1	3.54749	11.19160*	0.00110	0.29780
1975–80 (Boom)	1	3.50546	11.04624*	0.00120	0.29603
Power					
1964–84	1	0.92596	2.72522	0.10515	0.15215
1964–67	1	0.59294	1.73036	0.19100	0.12175
1968–75	1	0.56672	1.65274	0.20120	0.11903
1976–84	1	0.07932	0.22849	0.63360	0.09453
1975–80 (Boom)	1	0.24041	0.69535	0.40610	0.07753
Roads					
1964–84	1	3.63109	12.95522*	0.00050	0.31820
1964–67	1	1.24914	4.15008*	0.04390	0.18630
1968–75	1	1.58285	5.30990*	0.02300	0.21009
1976–84	1	0.71713	2.34649	0.12830	0.14141
1975–80 (Boom)	1	0.95096	3.13242	0.07940	0.16284
Water					
1964–84	1	2.76262	22.99085*	0.00000	0.40818
1964–67	1	0.44047	3.13830	0.07910	0.16299
1968–75	1	0.89372	6.53155*	0.01180	0.23216
1976–84	1	0.88446	6.47985*	0.01220	0.23096
1975–80 (Boom)	1	0.83908	6.12971*	0.01470	0.22495

Source: Compiled by the author.

Note: *Significant at 5 percent level.

Impact of oil production on education, health, housing, power, roads, and water in oil producing areas (states)

With respect to the impact of oil on the social and economic development of the producing states (areas) as characterized by changes in the social indicators, the data in Table 6.2 reveal that the selected social indicators show no sign of reasonable significance at any period. This could support the theory that under the dual government system, oil areas simply yield their benefits through the influence of the federal government. It also appears to support the notion that oil areas suffer doubly due to the existing socioeconomic disparities; poor conditions are only exacerbated by the activities of the oil industry. The statistical inference seems to affirm that the worsened situation exists due to the lack of essential social infrastructure. One can now reasonably assert that oil wealth does not bring about development in the producing area. Evidently, the disproportionate investment in Nigeria's social and economic infrastructures has done the utmost disservice to the oil areas. The oil areas continually suffer from environmental pollution, the displacement of the people from their land, food shortages, and unemployment. There seems to be a strong and direct correlation between the intensity of oil production in an area and the relative negativity of its impacts there, as well as the area's social and economic underdevelopment. In spite of this, the federal government and the oil industry have not deemed it necessary to establish comprehensive social planning for the special needs of the oil areas. It seems to the author that state and local governments do not have the resources to handle the problems of the oil industry; their revenue allocations are inadequate to improve the social development of their area and combat the extraneous social problems precipitated by the oil industry. The federal government should exercise its sovereign rights to seek the cooperation of the oil industry in finding a lasting solution.

Table 6.2

The Impact of Oil on Producing Areas

PERIOD	DF	SUM OF SQUARES	F. VALUE	SIGNIFICANT F	R.
EDUCATION					
1964–84	1	0.02993	0.07505	0.7864	0.05471
1964–67	1	0.14283	0.36224	0.5527	0.11951
1968–75	1	0.16221	0.41220	0.5267	0.12736
1976–84	1	0.68085	1.82648	0.1886	0.26093
1975–80 (Boom)	1	0.36665	0.95152	0.3387	0.19148
HEALTH					
1964–84	1	0.47726	1.25294	0.2736	0.21846
1964–67	1	0.00226	0.00565	0.9407	0.01503
1968–75	1	0.35983	0.93316	0.3433	0.18969
1976–84	1	0.20079	0.51227	0.4808	0.14170
1975–80 (Boom)	1	0.03195	0.08014	0.7794	0.05653
HOUSING					
1964–84	1	0.53206	0.40489	0.2471	0.23066
1964–67	1	0.34081	0.88209	0.3566	0.18461
1968–75	1	0.38808	0.74156	0.3973	0.16973
1976–84	1	0.00454	0.01136	0.9160	0.02132
1975–80 (Boom)	1	0.11431	0.28908	0.5956	0.10692
POWER					
1964–84	1	0.01892	0.04739	0.8294	0.04350
1964–67	1	0.16254	0.41307	0.5263	0.12749
1968–75	1	0.08382	0.21132	0.6497	0.09155
1976–84	1	0.05935	0.14926	0.7025	0.07704
1975–80 (Boom)	1	0.00758	0.01895	0.8916	0.02752
ROADS					
1964–84	1	0.26793	1.30330	0.2644	0.22260
1964–67	1	0.06716	0.31442	0.5800	0.11145
1964–67	1	0.17508	0.83654	0.1750	0.17994
1976–84	1	0.01033	0.04786	0.8286	0.04371
1975–80 (Boom)	1	0.00758	0.01895	0.8916	0.02961
WATER					
1964–84	1	0.12305	0.77857	0.3860	0.17379
1964–67	1	0.02568	0.15858	0.6938	0.07939
1968–75	1	0.08787	0.55109	0.4648	0.14686
1976–84	1	0.00015	0.00091	0.9762	0.00603
1975–80 (Boom)	1	0.01999	0.12325	0.7285	0.07004

Source: Compiled by the author.

Impact of oil production on education, health, housing, power, roads, and water in non-oil producing areas (states)

The statistical data also reveal the impact of oil production on the non-oil producing states (Table 6.3). The statistical readings show some relative similarity between non-oil producing states and oil producing states in that prior to the growth of the oil industry, both groups show that the development of the social infrastructures were statistically less significant. However, for the periods of oil growth through boom and burst, the non-oil producing states have significantly enjoyed derived benefits from oil, showing relatively high levels of significance for housing, health, roads, water, and education. Power, however, was less significant, similar to oil producing areas; this situation reveals the inadequacies of rural electrification and power supply as a national problem.

Although non-oil producing states show relatively strong levels of significance on social benefits, one cannot conclude that people in non-oil producing rural areas are better off. The spillover benefits to non-oil producing states are evident, yet distribution in those states is not devoid of disparities; urban growth and rural neglect are national problems. Still, it is indicated that non-oil producing areas enjoyed spillover benefits through federal revenue-sharing formulae. It should be noted here that very minimal consideration is given to ameliorating the social cost to the oil producing areas under the provision of the revenue-sharing formulae. This is not the fault of the nonproducing areas, but rather the result of an ineffective national distribution policy, which requires revision in order to meet its intended objectives of a balanced economy and equal benefits for all. Our findings have indicated that there is a statistically significant difference between the impact of the oil industry on oil producing states and its impact on non-oil producing states with respect to changes in the selected socioeconomic variables.

Table 6.3

The Impact of Oil on Nonproducing Areas

PERIOD	DF	SUM OF SQUARES	F. VALUE	SIGNIFICANT F	R.
EDUCATION					
1964–84	1	2.34760	7.47091*	0.00076	0.27974
1964–67	1	0.06861	0.20178	0.65440	0.04782
1968–75	1	0.59659	1.78551	0.18490	0.14102
1976–84	1	1.24607	3.81354*	0.05400	0.20380
1975–80 (Boom)	1	0.30609	0.90713	0.34350	0.10101
HEALTH					
1964–84	1	5.69890	20.63680*	0.00000	0.43585
1964–67	1	0.53248	1.59017	0.21060	0.13323
1968–75	1	1.08254	3.29434*	0.07290	0.18996
1978–84	1	3.10100	10.14521*	0.00200	0.32151
1975–80 (Boom)	1	3.09419	10.12006*	0.00200	0.32115
HOUSING					
1964–84	1	9.95040	43.67342*	0.00000	0.57592
1964–67	1	1.47917	4.56392*	0.03540	0.22205
1968–75	1	2.52902	8.10141*	0.00550	0.29035
1978–84	1	4.41578	15.18863*	0.00020	0.38366
1975–80 (Boom)	1	4.30204	14.73340*	0.00020	0.37870
POWER					
1964–84	1	1.19585	3.65346*	0.05920	0.19905
1964–67	1	0.46283	1.37891	0.24350	0.12421
1968–75	1	1.10380	3.36149*	0.07010	0.19182
1976–84	1	0.09018	0.26533	0.60780	0.05483
1975–80 (Boom)	1	0.29500	0.87392	0.35240	0.09916
ROADS					
1964–84	1	4.20509	14.34577*	0.00030	0.37439
1964–67	1	0.98081	2.97429	0.08810	0.18081
1968–75	1	1.16631	3.55956*	0.06250	0.19717
1976–84	1	1.62666	5.04510*	0.02720	0.23286
1975–80 (Boom)	1	1.92121	6.02115	0.01610	0.25306
WATER					
1964–84	1	2.90022	26.58960*	0.00000	0.48168
1964–67	1	0.41786	3.04349*	0.08460	0.18284
1968–75	1	0.85061	6.42553*	0.01300	0.26086
1976–84	1	1.19332	9.28762*	0.0030 0	0.30898
1975–80 (Boom)	1	1.10801	8.55908*	0.00440	0.29773

Source: Compiled by the author.
Note: *Significant at 5 percent level.

7

Summary of Findings and Implications for Social and Economic Policy

It is not surprising to the researcher that this study was unable to refute the hypothesis that there is a correlation between the trend of oil production and changes in socioeconomic activities in the country based on the statistical evidence derived from the data.

Based on the results of the statistical analysis of this study, the following conclusions were drawn:

1. Non-oil producing areas (states) gain more socioeconomic benefits from oil resource than do oil producing areas.

2. The source of imbalance can be linked to the federal government's distribution pattern of social and economic infrastructures in the country. The imbalance can be further attributed to the structural inequities inherent in federal revenue-sharing formulae. According to B. E. Okogu (1986)

   on the public finance front, the present revenue allocation formula which gives some 65% of the federally collected revenue to the central government should be revised with a view to giving a greater share to the states. This is important because their activities bear a more direct relation to the day to day lives of Nigerians. . . . Nigeria has moved from the extreme of the derivation principle to one where the oil producing areas are not getting enough assistance to cope with the ecological effects of oil production.[1]

Finally, the trend in oil production is correlated to increased social cost to the oil producing areas by way of spills and other forms of pollution. Ezimora Chike contends that

Nigeria recorded 784 oil spills between 1976 and 1980. Apart from health hazards, these spills led to the loss of 1,336,875 barrels of oil to the national economy. In 1981 alone there were 233 incidents of oil spills leading to a loss of 22,840 barrels. The records do not necessarily reveal the exact number of spills. Many oil companies do not report spills which they consider as minor. In other words, the volumes of oil reported spilled are at best approximations of the actual numbers."[2]

Additionally, *Oil Spill Bulletin* reported that according to "data collected by the Nigeria National Petroleum Corporation, there was a total of 1581 oil spills during the thirteen-year period, the mean number of spills per annum is 124, of barrels per spill 1,062. The spill figures range from 150 to 630,405 barrels."[3]

Pollution data seem to show a correlation between intense oil production and the increasing number of spill incidents (Table 7.1). In addition to the record of spill incidents, other forms of pollution are observed daily. Nigerian oil industry flares away about 78 percent of its natural gas. Yinka Omorogbe (1987) asserts that studies have shown that the gas flaring has badly polluted the areas surrounding the flares.[4]

Nigeria has the largest deposit of natural gas in Africa, with proven reserves estimated at 2,400 million cubic meters. The Niger Delta basin holds most of the natural gas deposit.[5] Nigeria has the potential for developing and controlling its oil and gas exploration, but still depends on foreign concessionaries. The oil concessionaries find it cheaper to flare away the gas, although the technology to reinject the gas back into the soil does exist. A study of the Iranian oil industry (Abghari 1982)[6] revealed that concessionaries were not keenly interested in natural gas for a number of reasons, among them the fear of expropriation and nationalization. In addition, oil was considered cheaper to handle and was readily marketable. Thus concessionaries, faced with fixed-term leases, preferred to concentrate their efforts on oil extraction. Therefore natural gas was flared; in spite of the increased pollution to the surrounding areas, their choice was

Table 7.1

Production and Pollution Distribution by State[a]

	1964	1965	1966	1967	1968	1969	1970	1971
PRODUCTION*								
River (1)	25,965	52,657	80,787	61,763	27,511	104,519	5,740	8,114
Bendel (2)	18,127	36,761	56,398	43,117	19,206	72,966	4,007	5,664
Cross River (3)	2,303	4,670	7,164	5,477	2,440	9,269	509	720
Imo (4)	2,254	4,570	7,011	5,361	2,388	9,071	498	704
Ondo (5)	196	397	610	47	208	789	43	61
POLLUTION**								
Rivers (6)	—	—	—	—	—	—	79.5	8,009
# OF SPILLS								
Rivers (7)	—	—	—	—	—	—	0.53	7.42
POLLUTION**								
Bendel (8)	—	—	—	—	—	—	55.50	5,591
# OF SPILLS								
Bendel (9)	—	—	—	—	—	—	.37	5.2
POLLUTION**								
Cross River (10)	—	—	—	—	—	—	7.05	710
# OF SPILLS								
Cross River (11)	—	—	—	—	—	—	.047	0.66
POLLUTION**								
Imo (12)	—	—	—	—	—	—	6.90	695
# OF SPILLS								
Imo (13)	—	—	—	—	—	—	.046	.64

Table 7.1 (cont.)

	1972	1973	1974	1975	1976	1977	1978	1979
PRODUCTION*								
Rivers (1)	9,625	10,902	11,946	9,466	11,008	11,114	10,112	12,195
Bendel (2)	6,719	7,611	8,340	6,608	7,685	7,759	7,060	8,514
Cross River (3)	854	967	1,059	839	976	986	897	1,082
Imo (4)	835	946	1,037	821	955	965	878	1,059
Ondo (5)	73	82	90	71	83	84	76	92
POLLUTION**								
Rivers (6)	27,237	50,657	34,828	30,133	10,612	16,506	51,543	334,115
# OF SPILLS								
Rivers (7)	22	31	56	628	67.8	55.1	82	83
POLLUTION**								
Bendel (8)	19,014	35,365	2,4314	21,036	7,409	11,523	35,982	233,250
# OF SPILLS								
Bendel (9)	15.2	23	38.9	47.4	38.5	57	58.1	89.2
POLLUTION**								
Cross River (10)	2,415	4,492	3,089	2,672	941	1,464	4,571	29,629
# OF SPILLS								
Cross River (11)	1.93	2.71	4.94	6.01	4.9	7.24	7.5	11.33
POLLUTION**								
Imo (12)	2,364	4,397	3,023	2,615	921	1,433	4,474	28,998
# OF SPILLS								
Imo (13)	1.88	2.71	4.8	5.9	5.9	7.24	7.22	11.09
POLLUTION**								
Ondo (14)	–	–	–	–	20	20	20	20
# OF SPILLS								
Ondo (15)	–	–	–	–	.6	.6	.6	.6

Table 7.1 (cont.)

	1980	1981	1982	1983	1984
PRODUCTION					
Rivers (1)	10,945	7,579	6,832	6,548	6,890
Bendel (2)	7,641	5,291	4,769	4,571	4,810
Cross Roads (3)	971	672	606	581	611
Imo (4)	950	658	393	568	598
Ondo (5)	83	57	52	49	52
POLLUTION**					
Rivers (6)	311,668	12,105	18,272	3,180	2,900
# OF SPILLS					
Rivers (7)	128	124	115	56	58
POLLUTION**					
Bendel (8)	206,480	8,451	12,756	–	–
# OF SPILLS					
Bendel (9)	89.2	86.2	79.9	–	–
POLLUTION**					
Cross River (10)	26,228	1,074	1,620	–	–
# OF SPILLS					
Cross River (11)	11.33	10.95	10.2	–	–
POLLUTION**					
Imo (12)	25,670	1,051	1,586	2,500	900
# OF SPILLS					
Imo (13)	11.09	10.72	9.94	3	2
POLLUTION**					
Ondo (14)	20	–	–	–	–
# OF SPILLS					
Ondo (15)	0.6	–	–	–	–

Table 7.1 (cont.)

Sources: Derived estimates by the author from the following sources:
Production distribution (estimates) by state is based on data
provided by Ayodele Sesan in *Socioeconomic Planning Science,*
Vol. 19, no. 5, Table 4 (1985): 299, and P. Olayiwola's data in
*Petroleum and Structural change in a Developing Country: The Case
of Nigeria,* (New York: Praeger, 1984), Table 7.3, p. 107.
Pollution data estimates: statistic of spills in Nigeria (state distribution of oil spills 1976–80), Ayodele Sesan, ibid., Table 6, p. 300,
and Proceedings of the 1983 International Seminar (NNPC), Table 1,
p. 94.
1983–84 data are derived from "National Oil Contingency Plan"
by Major O. Aduloju, paper presented on the Petroleum Industry
and the Nigerian Environment, Kaduna, Nigeria, November 10-14,
1985, Table 6, p. 4.

Notes: [a] The oil production and pollution distribution derived estimates are
based on the assumption that there is correlation between intensity
of production and incidents of pollution. The derived estimates
show that about 59 percent of the pollution occurred in Rivers State,
33 percent in Bendel, 4.12 percent in Cross River, another 4.01 percent in Imo State, and 0.33 percent in Ondo State. All other states:
Production and pollution data not available.

*Production figures are in millions of barrels per day per year.

**Pollution in quantity spilled (barrels).

toward economy. In 1973, however, when the Iranian government took over the management of its oil industry, the flaring of gas by concessionaries fell. The government of Iran took steps to produce natural gas for alternative domestic use and also entered into specific agreements to export the gas to Europe and the Soviet Union. Thus, the pollution caused by flaring gas was minimized.

Nigeria should similarly embark on gas production, through joint ventures or outright ownership. A stepping-stone to such a policy has already begun: Nigeria has embarked on the development of a liquefied natural gas (LNG) plant in Bonny Rivers State. It is a joint venture with Shell Gas and Agip Company wherein the government has a 60 percent equity interest, Shell Gas 20 percent, and Agip 10 percent. The production of LNG is aimed at European markets and is expected to begin in 1995. This is an encouraging move in the right direction in identifying alternative uses of gas. It also makes economic sense, considering the fact that Nigeria's crude oil stock could be depleted by the year 2018, given the 1988 rate of consumption. Gas exports could become Nigeria's main foreign exchange in the twenty-first century as energy experts estimate that the country's gas reserves could last for 100 years.[7] Such a new gas policy will not only identify alternative domestic uses but will also be an added export commodity to external markets abroad. The pollution problem may not be completely eliminated, but it will be a step forward in reducing pollution in the affected areas.

The growth of the oil industry has precipitated tremendous social costs to the oil producing areas. The disruptive effect of oil extraction has caused serious ecological imbalances, ravaging plants and economic crops. As such,

monetary compensations cannot be a close substitute to what environmental disruption takes from the communities of the oil fields. Instead of direct cash payments which are subject to immediate pressure, it might be better to invest the money in a supervised and coordinated community development program, especially when the compensation is for damage to community owned property.

. . . This would take the form of developing rural community industry, agricultural revolution, providing social services such as improving rural water supply, health, education and other infrastructures.[8]

Since federal revenue sharing is not based on the derivative principle, the percentage allotted for ecological damage should be increased to at least 25 percent in order to help solve the immense ecological problems of oil areas. Considering the fact that pollution constitutes a threat to human health and welfare, the need to set up a comprehensive mitigation policy should be the priority for both the government and the oil companies. A comprehensive mitigation policy will require an interdisciplinary approach to research, involving physical, natural, and social scientists. For instance, social scientists would research the politics of revenue allocation and the derivation principle and its implication for mineral producing areas. It will also be highly useful for both the oil industry and oil area residents if a specific study on the psychosocial impact of pollution and other disruptive effects of oil industry on the indigenous population is undertaken. A research scheme for the oil producing areas should be an ongoing process to assess the complexities involved in oil industry operations, particularly employing socioeconomic impact assessments before and after oil activities. The research scheme will serve as an information bank and will assist in responding effectively to the problems of the oil areas. It will also be a useful resource center in providing the appropriate information for policy planning and implementation.

DISCUSSION

Implications for social and economic policy

The intensive extraction of oil to meet external demand has caused immense damage to the socioeconomic environment of the host communities. The extractive activities do not take into serious consideration the ecological factors on which the inhabitants depend. This has often led to food shortages because of a decline of arable land, environmental decay, and the ultimate displacement of the indigenous people's mode of survival. Consequently, the native inhabitants tend to become vulnerable to the social, economic, and political power of the extractive industries and their producer states, which in turn leads to the generation of dualism, with structural inequalities and economic dependency. Meanwhile, no comprehensive social planning is undertaken to minimize the adverse effects of the extractive activities on indigenous people. The mere existence of extractive industry to boost export receipts for a producer government in the third world does not necessarily cause overall development. In most cases, the revenue generated will be just enough to pay for external debts. Extractive industry, therefore, benefits foreign nations more frequently than the native population. Nigeria is not an exception. For example, the nation exported billions of dollars worth of oil within five years (1980–85), but its debt service ratio increased from 10 percent in 1980 to 19 percent in 1985. Nigeria's foreign debt has increased to nearly $22 billion and was expected to rise to $31 billion by 1989.[9]

This situation has resulted in a domestic crisis for Nigeria in terms of economic dislocation, massive unemployment, retrenchments, food shortages, and political instability. The nation was left with only one alternative: to approach the International Monetary Fund (IMF) for rescue —with lots of strings attached. However, the cost and style of living of the Nigerian people has been tremendously changed. They migrated to the nearest urban centers in search of jobs under the prevailing high unemployment. Needless to say, the state of perpetual dependency and the social disorders that plague Nigeria are a result of its existing economic crisis.

An added dimension to the problem is the application of technologies that are inappropriate and inadequate for developing countries. It is not in the best interest of the imported technologies to encourage indigenous development; rather they foster increasing dependency. In Nigeria, as elsewhere in the third world, oil industry is capital intensive and calls for exceptional skills to work in the oil fields. But the growth of the oil economy has displaced the indigenous agricultural economy in which most rural residents had been employed. P. Maitra (1986) also noted this pattern of displacement:

The importation of technology has meant high economic growth. Traditional exports of raw materials are losing markets in developed economies because of the increasing sophistication of technology in those economies, and in the process, underdeveloped economies are facing a serious resource crisis despite the fact that they have enormous supplies of these resources (including labor of their own which they cannot put to use as sophisticated technology does not need them)."[10]

In sum, the transfer of technology or capital from developed to underdeveloped countries has the effect of creating: (1) a high growth rate and sophistication in the industrial sector; and (2) a persistent dualistic structure and reduced demand for native labor. The result of this transfer is unemployment, stagnation, and continued poverty.

For example, Benjamin and Devarajan (1985) in a World Bank study of oil revenues and economic policy in Cameroon revealed that the distribution of benefits across different classes of workers was quite skewed in favor of skilled urban workers. Although real wages increased throughout the economy, the gap between rural and urban wages widened to enforce structural imbalances. In addition, the poor social infrastructure and low level of education remained obstacles to development.[11]

The scenario of mixed economic activities that can result from the foreign quest for raw materials poses a serious problem in planning for social change. Under ideal conditions, what is needed for any nation's development is not merely agricultural productivity, but the overall enhancement of the indigenous people's quality of life by means of the provision of health, social and economic infrastructures. In addition, a planned mitigation policy combined with a community impact agreement is desirable, offering the oil industry, the government, and community leaders a means of responding effectively to growing pollution problems and other negative byproducts of oil mining. To reiterate, there is a dire need for the oil industry and the producer government to cooperate and plan with the people of the mineral areas to revive and preserve their biological and ecological heritage. For this reason, the following plan of action is proposed.

A FRAMEWORK FOR BREAKING THE BARRIERS TO DEVELOPMENT OF MINERAL PRODUCING AREAS

Any research may be useful in providing new forms of enlightenment about the subject matter, but it would not be of real value without proposing specific ideas as solutions to the problems discussed. For this reason, the author has put forward a number of recommendations. The recommendations might be a useful set of tools to be incorporated into social policy planning and administration designed for mineral producing areas.

The following set of recommendations contain specific illustrations or examples where necessary. This study and many others have shown that ordinary people are often the victims of disruptive economic expansion who are denied a means of improving their social and economic circumstances. A good government is not one that protects the interest of only privileged or favored interest groups, but one that seeks and protects the general welfare of all its people. The federal government that permits the exploration and exploitation of minerals in exchange for royalty benefits should also have the power to alleviate the problems that exploitation will bring. Some of the recommendations of this researcher are:

1. The government should use its sovereign power to strengthen the preventive and safety requirements for all drilling activities. The government must require all mineral extracting firms to adopt state-of-the-art technology that would eliminate (or at least minimize) damage to the environment and its inhabitants.

2. The government should have the power to change the terms of liability and provide only short-term leasing conditions, but give limited tax credit to firms with up-to-date, preventive equipment. An insurance against pollution should be a mandatory requirement. It should also be required under any lease term that all firms engaged in mineral extraction provide the necessary social infrastructure before drilling commences, if the short-term or long-term presence of the extracting firm will negatively affect the normal life of the people. The author is aware of the issue of assessing the national benefit against the community's concerns and well-being. One method of evaluation would require that all social and economic costs attributed to oil and extractive activities be charged to the firm engaged in that development. Alternatively, a surcharge in the form of taxes could be placed on all unintended flows and pollution. Another method would be to renegotiate leases to cover the social cost as a means of compensating victims of pollution. Peter Nijkamp (1977) contends that energy extraction has catastrophical effects; hence, firms that cause damage to the oil areas should be obliged to pay for it through adequate compensation.[12]

3. One of the worst features of the Nigerian oil industry is the increased social cost to the oil producing areas by way of pollution. The government and the oil firms should cooperate in deriving an enforceable contingency plan that would minimize the level of oil pollution. The contingency plan might have a penalty provision requiring that companies that are ill equipped or have a record of excessive pollution be terminated from their lease contracts. Furthermore, a means of facilitating legal action against polluters should be established. The government obviously possesses the power to enforce its laws. According to an OECD report (1977), catastrophic oil spill incidents could be substantially reduced simply by more careful attention by operators and adherence to good safety practices. Agencies were encouraged to enforce regulations strictly.[13] A. E. K. Nash et al. (1977) point out that the United States federal government stepped in when Chevron Oil violated the law. Chevron and its eight partners had to pay a $2.3 million fine in settlement of the suit brought against them.[14]

The government of Nigeria should adopt similar plans rather than remaining aloof to collect taxes and share profits, and have the problem of compensation solved by the parties involved.

Should the need occur, the government should be able to get involved and take direct control, because in most cases, a large segment of the oil mishap victims are illiterate and uneducated; they face difficulties in pressing their rightful demands in an effective way. The current situation allows oil companies and unscrupulous persons to take advantage of their vulnerability.

As a precondition for fostering need-based distributive justice, this plan would require the planned establishment of social and economic infrastructures specific to mineral producing areas.

The criteria for just distribution and community social development should embrace a social welfare policy that can help promote development with increased equity. Such a policy would aid in the development of human resources, including the strengthening of family life, and would help people learn to improve their own lives as they contribute to national development. Growing out of these concerns, social welfare objectives strive to enhance the well-being of people by raising their level of living, by ensuring social justice and a more equitable distribution of national wealth, and by enhancing the opportunity of the people to develop to their fullest in terms of health, education, and participation as contributing citizens.[15] It includes the full participation and mobilization of the population at all levels (national as well as local), a constant and steady improvement in the material and spiritual well-being of all members of society, improvements in living and working conditions, and a comprehensive development of education, health, and culture on the basis of a dynamic and well-balanced economic growth.[16] It is also extended to emphasize an equitable distribution of income and wealth, and the realization of far-reaching socioeconomic changes, including industrialization and the development of the state sector in industry, progressive agrarian reforms, cooperation in agriculture, and so on. Thus, the integrative approach to development maintains that any national development strategy must include a committed effort to satisfy the basic needs of the masses. Basic needs are defined to include food, shelter, clothing, and access to essential public services.[17] These in turn are related to a series of policies — income distribution, rural development, employment creation, popular participation, and so on — designed to be of immediate benefit to the deprived inhabitants. Socioeconomic infrastructure is, then, defined as the amount of capital invested in roads, waterways and other forms of transportation, communication, water supplies, financial institutions, electricity, health and sanitation services, and educational and cultural facilities.[18]

The author believes that any effective integrative socioeconomic development approach should have an "organized system of social relationships that permits individuals to develop their abilities and promote their well-being (in harmony with the needs of the community)."[19]

The first need-based development strategy should be the revival of agriculture. The Nigerian experience of the impact of the oil boom on agriculture may have some semblance to the Iranian experience during the oil boom of the 1970s in that the oil boom had depressing effects on the rural economy. The oil boom precipitated an outflow of the agricultural workforce to the urban areas due to wage differentials. Hassan Hakiman (1988) contends that the rapidly rising wages sparked off by development induced a greater participation of urban labor, to the detriment of participation in agricultural production. The rural residents and agricultural workers were drawn into non-farm employment in urban areas, and as a result, the commitment to agriculture declined.

In Nigeria, the oil boom, which culminated in the building of expensive material infrastructure in the urban areas and a neglected agricultural sector, simply reinforced the rural–urban divide. There was an impressive growth in urban areas while the rural areas faced stagnation and decay. A study of oil and inequality in rural Nigeria was done by P. Collier (1983), who demonstrated that the rural population suffered during the oil-financed consumption bonanza of the 1970s.[20]

The rapid export of oil actually reinforced income reduction in rural areas; naively, one would have expected rural income to have risen. Faced with these conditions, the rural workforce had little choice but to migrate to urban areas, believing them to be economically favorable, only to find themselves drawn into the vicissitudes of a cash-based economy. They found the cities saturated with unemployed workers who had been displaced from the subsistence sector, and without the absorption capacity to utilize them. The result was continued unemployment.

The Green Revolution, which would have improved the rural agricultural economy, was not well directed to encourage employment for rural residents and foster self-reliance in food supply. Instead, it served more of the interest groups within and abroad. Thus, in a developing country such as Nigeria, which lacks the proper technological mix to generate adequate employment, growth has followed an uneven profile. The growth has been urban rather than rural; it has been much too oriented to the modern sector, without enough regard for the traditional; it has been industrial rather than agricultural; it has been large scale and capital intensive instead of small scale and labor intensive; and the benefits have generally gone to the foreign investors and the indigenous upper classes who influence policy.[21] Wayne Nafziger (1988) has shown that inequality in Africa among the political elites, proletariat, peasants, and rural poor is linked to the colonial legacy and the contemporary global economic system of imbalances, and that the policies of the ruling elite have exacerbated discrepancies within African society.[22]

The author recommends policy changes to reflect a shift in goals from output maximization to poverty reduction through: (1) the production of affordable goods and services consumed by the poor; (2) the creation of employment opportunities in the rural economy with the appropriate technological mix in the non-oil sector; and (3) the provision of essential public services in education, health, housing, power, water, and so on. This will go a long way in inducing a self-reliant economy. It is only then that real development can begin.

The oil industry's displacement of the traditional agrobased economy has created food shortages and malnutrition. The researcher recommends that oil drilling in specific arable lands be stopped unless adequate technological measures are employed to protect the environment, particularly food systems, since land is very limited in the oil producing areas. The agricultural revival of the area can be effective if there is cooperation between the government, the private sector, and the people. It is also important that the appropriate technology is provided and local labor force participation is encouraged. The agricultural development of the area will be more effective if allied activities such as transportation and marketing facilities are developed, along with well-coordinated economic, social and public services. Bar-El et al. (1987) asserts that the development of rural people will depend on both farm and non-farm factors.[23] Therefore strategists should focus on processes rather than on products by recognizing that land, labor, water, and technology alone do not lead to balanced agricultural and regional development; the incorporation of such variables as markets, towns, service industries, financial institutions, and organizations is also required. Together, they have a major impact on regional development. It should be noted, however, that citizen participation is very important to the successful implementation of this plan.

The conventional wisdom of third world development is based on the inflow of capital and technology, economic growth, and the enhancement of per capita income. These may be necessary, but are not sufficient in themselves to create balanced development. An alternative route to the attainment of equality is through participation.[24] The participatory approach would require a change from the cascade approach to development planning through grassroots-based development planning. This would entail planning with the people of the mineral producing areas by directing investment toward them and formulating with them policies to improve the distribution of benefits and employment opportunities in their communities by supporting infrastructures (roads, waterways, power, water, educational and health facilities, etc.) that will induce self-reliance and minimize problems of migration and dependency. According to Wolfgang Balabkins,

during the first ten years of independence, Nigeria's output of food production grew at a higher rate than the population increase, and the country had no difficulty in feeding itself. With the onset of the oil boom in the early 1970s, Nigerian agriculture went into a steep decline. Millions of peasants abandoned their plots and left for the big towns in the hope that petro-dollars would be closer to their reach than on the farm. They were hoping to get well-paying jobs, schools for their children, decent housing, potable water nearby, and better medical care. What they often learned after leaving their farms was that they had exchanged rural poverty for urban misery.[25]

Any strategy toward development should therefore foster self-reliant communities and thus minimize exploitation and excessive differentiation in wealth, income, and power. This development approach is akin to the Ujaama concept,[26] not because of its efficiency but in the pragmatic usefulness of the model.

This approach could conceivably eliminate the problem of food shortages and other basic social needs. For example, the Nigerian Green Revolution, which was aimed at increasing food production, did not yield the expected results; instead, it generated huge profits for special interest groups within Nigeria and abroad. According to Yusufu Usman (1982), when General Obasanjo launched operation "Feed The Nation" in May 1976 under the banner of the Green Revolution, over two billion naira was spent:[27] "Most of the money was spent abroad, ostensibly for the purchase of machinery, equipment and fertilizers. In addition, trends in food imports also rose rapidly." Nigeria's food import bills during the oil boom 1975 through 1981 were as follows:

Year	Payment for Food Imports (in naira)
1975	306.8 million
1976	404.1 million
1977	783.4 million
1978	1.09 billion
1989	818.8 million
1980	1.16 billion
1981	1.86 billion

Any industrial development that does not take into account the means to attain self-sufficiency in food production may prove to be counterproductive. Ex-president Kwame Nkrumah pointed out that

the urgent need to plan industrial development on a continental scale must not, however, blind us to the equally important need to do the same for agriculture, fishing, and forestry. . . . African states are importing larger amounts of food than ever before from abroad. This trend must be stopped by a carefully planned expansion of our own agriculture. As an industry, there can be specialization so that each region or state concentrates on producing the agricultural products for which it is best suited.[28]

Though no country can be totally self sufficient, excessive external dependency should not be encouraged.

Nigeria's Green Revolution program was aimed at increasing agricultural output by 4 percent per year through 1985, but this aspiration was not achieved. The increase in agriculture was barely 1 percent per year and the increased demand for food encouraged the importation of food items from abroad. Nigeria's total agricultural imports during 1981 alone were estimated at well over $3 billion, 75 percent of which was food. The United States supplied roughly 18 percent, or $544 million worth of products, representing a 56 percent increase over 1980 exports. The Nigerian grain imports bill from the United States alone consisted of wheat valued at $225 million, rice at $233 million, soybeans at $3.3 million, and corn at $41 million (see Table 7.2).[29] Nigeria budgeted $13 billion for agriculture, but a sizeable part of this was swallowed by foreign food imports. This not only caused the rapid decline of external reserves but perpetuated the problem of food shortages and attendant social and economic crises (Table 7.3). According to Paul Collier (1988), the recent oil slump has severely reduced individual incomes in Nigeria, and this decline in living standards may threaten food security for some vulnerable social groups. However, during the oil boom of the 1970s, food production declined while the relative price of food increased, inducing concern for food security. It follows that the oil boom contributed to food insecurity by enabling the government to bid labor away from the food sector. Conversely then, the oil slump of the 1980s, although it has lowered incomes, may actually create an increase in food production.[30]

Table 7.2

Nigeria: Grain Imports from the United States, 1977-82
(in 1000 Metric Tons)

Year	Rice	Corn	Wheat/Wheat Flour
1977	413	25	1020
1978	560	75	1300
1979	240	40	1350
1980	400	175	1400
1981	650	300	1600
1982	600	400	1700

Source: U.S. Department of Agriculture, *Sub-Saharan Africa,* Economic Research Service Supplement to WAS-27 1981/82, 14-15.U.S. Department of Agriculture 1981–82.

The chairman of Global 2000 and former president of the United States, Jimmy Carter, has suggested that world leaders should recognize and appreciate the fact that problems associated with increasing food production can be solved, and that these leaders should be personally involved in order to enhance

Table 7.3

Nigeria: Estimated Food Deficits and Surplus
(thousands for selected periods)

Commodity	1975	1980	1985
Maize	-170.890	-299.978	-524.499
Millet	-552.626	-1,050.674	-1,789.904
Sorghum	-1,018.412	-1,912.695	-3,184.886
Rice	+199.255	+383.026	+821.942
Wheat	-143.152	-190.720	-273.354
Yams	-2,402.988	-4,260.937	-6,716.327
Cassava	-995.720	-1,716.889	-2,908.528
Potatoes (Sweet)	-20.988	-31.024	-52.582
Potatoes (Irish)	-2.812	-4.201	-6.555
Cocoyams	-34.592	-97.626	-206.293
Plantains	-165.570	-286.496	-288.588
Ground Nuts	+52.333	+3.448	+64.240
Cow Peas	+6.979	+59.921	+106.087
Soyabeans	+16.237	+25.931	+37.699

Source: Federal Ministry of Statistics, Agricultural Division (Lagos, Nigeria: 1985).

prospects for success. He argues that the Green Revolution in India, Pakistan, and Africa is a hopeful sign that food insecurity need not be permanent. He added that small-scale farming could be the key to the permanent success of food programs. He further suggested that food production be integrated with health, education, and other aspects of national life.[31] Hence, a drastic restructuring of social development through the people's participation could offer a better means to attain equitable distribution of economic benefits and social justice.

THE NEED FOR COMMUNITY IMPACT MONITORING SYSTEMS

One of the issues raised in the problem statement of the study was the question of whether it would be necessary for the oil producing areas to continually bear the brunt of Nigeria's development and the mining interests of the multinational firms without mitigation. Part of the problem of the oil producing areas may be linked to the lack of a community impact monitoring system. In developing countries, where the state of environmental awareness and regulatory policies are either relaxed or ineffective, multinational companies feel encouraged to take undue advantage. However, in developed nations, where environmental awareness and community empowerment are quite strong, they are less likely to do so. For instance, in 1987 a Key West community in Florida fought to prevent drilling in that area.[32] The community preferred the preservation of environmental integrity to perceived oil benefits. In another example, the *Christian Science Monitor* reported that when oil spills threatened the wildlife and pristine beauty of Antarctica, Greenpeace protested to stop any mineral mining in the region.[33]

Above all, the role of the government as a regulatory agency to enforce protection of its citizens is effective in developed economies. For example, the U.S. congressional committee on merchant marine and fisheries took steps to protect its citizens and the environment during the Monongahela River oil spill in Floreffe, Pennsylvania. On May 26, 1988, the House committee conducted a hearing on the impact of the oil spill on the environment and the lives of those in the area, and designed a policy to protect the nation's environmental resources now and in the future.[34] In contrast, the developing countries' community empowerment and environmental awareness are seriously lacking. Hence, the multinational companies have either exported or created toxic hazards in third world environments without abatement. According to Michael Edelstein (1987), an examination of issues on toxic exposure suggests that the wastes have been transferred from highly developed countries to less developed countries (LDCs).

[T]he growing exposure of citizens in LDCs to toxic materials reflects . . . the relocation of heavy industries and other hazardous activities to less regulated environments. The failure of industrialized nations to extend protective regulatory restrictions . . . and outright toxic wastes for disposal in LDCs. . . . While catastrophes of the scope of Bhopal and Chernobyl are fortunately not common events, the susceptibility of the third world population to ongoing toxic hazards is proven.[35]

F. E. Osai Sai (1988) contends that:

Most developing countries do not have any suitable method for handling . . . disasters . . . due primarily to the lack of logistics, absense of technical knowhow, and poverty. Planning for emergencies posed by . . . [toxic wastes and other forms of pollution] directed at them by the industrial nations is unthinkable. . . .

The industrialization cycle starts with the raw materials which are processed through many intermediate steps to give products and services. The cycle remains open until the wastes and by-products are safely contained in the ecosystem. It is not closed by a mere geographical shifting of the problem base. It is not just sufficient to address global environmental problems such as depletion of the ozone layer . . . , acid rain caused by fossil fuelled plants, the greenhouse effect, and what have you; and yet by design or default espouse the annihilation of the people and the destruction of the ecosystem in the third world.

Unfortunately, for the people of the third world, particularly in African nations, the exploitation cycle is complete and closed. It started with the removal of the valuable natural resources tagged as raw materials which are processed and used in the developed nations. The wastes have been returned, and the resultant health and environmental problems we have to face.[36]

According to O. L. Spash and Ralph C. d'Arge (1990), there exists a worst case situation on the long-term effects of global warming, the greenhouse effect, and other forms of pollution. The findings from their research predict that those nations in developed economies which are contributing to the bulk of global pollution are the nations which will benefit most. The richer nations will become relatively richer and the poorer nations will become even more impoverished and will be made worse off in the long run.[37] The reason is that wealthier nations of the Northern Hemisphere are better equipped technologically to deal effectively with the greenhouse problems. The great north-south dichotomy will be reinforced and conditions in developing countries will be made worse unless the wealthier nations will negotiate not to harm the third world nations for their own gain, even though the third world nations could not stop them from doing so. This negotiation is necessitated by ethical considerations and the interdependent nature of the world community.

The Canadian Action Plan and initiative for sustainable development in cooperation with some developing countries is encouraging. The Canadian international experience has recognized that the differences in culture, governmental capability, public awareness, planning traditions, resource bases, and other factors would necessitate custom made approaches for each country.[38]

It is further noted that the approaches tried with success in the developed world may not be possible or desirable in developing nations. The developed world often opts for environmental quality at the cost of developmental momentum. Developing nations cannot afford that luxury. They can sustain neither environmental quality without development nor development without environmental quality. Only the more difficult challenge of sustainable development—implementing development while maintaining and enhancing environmental quality—will meet their needs.[39]

In developed economies such as the United States, governments have been able to enact laws to punish offenders when public harm has been created by the unlawful disposal of toxic waste. In the United States, the Environmental Protection Agency quickly comes to the rescue. The governments in both developing and developed countries should cooperate to enforce criminal prosecution of any corporate offender in what is essentially and environmentally a global community. A corporate entity that evinces reckless disregard for human life should be viewed as a criminal offender and not a practitioner of normal business conduct.[40] There should be universally recognized criminal sanctions applicable to all persons, natural and juristic, with the ability to damage and destroy the existence of human beings or the entire ecosystem. When human lives are put at risk for the sake of corporate profits, we must move to deter the crimes rather than merely compensate for them (if indeed that is even possible). It is perhaps the only way to abate the apparent corporate homicide in the third world.

Nigeria has long been known to produce strategic minerals, from the heydays of coal, iron ore, columbite, and tin through the oil boom, yet environmental laws are either weak or nonexistent, despite the problems of pollution and the disruption of the nation's ecosystem. The problems of environmental pollution and lack of physical planning are attributable to four basic factors:

1. uncontrollable natural factors such as the climatic impact on soil, water, air and vegetational equilibria (including the advancing desert)

2. inadequate social and political attitudes and behavior toward the environment. There is no effective education and awareness about a wide range of environmental issues

3. unregulated or improperly regulated economic growth, particularly in the oil industry and other areas of the industrial sector

4. inadequate public policy responses (considered to be a major culprit).[41]

Nigeria needs to take a close look at its environmental policy and establish adequate programs and responses to environmental concerns. The government, through its public policy, should prioritize environmental pollution as a threat to the health and security of Nigerians.

The government needs to draft and enact appropriate laws to regulate the activities of individuals, corporate bodies, and communities with regard to their impact on the quality of the environment and the elements within. This will involve: (1) delineating appropriate jurisdictional boundaries to facilitate effective monitoring, evaluation, and enhancement of the state of the environment and elements within it, as influenced by all pertinent factors; (2) designing appropriate institutional frameworks to facilitate an efficient and effective performance of environmental regulatory and management functions; (3) the establishment of adequate planning systems to ensure that environmental resources will be utilized in an optimally efficient way and to promote public enlightenment about the consequences of environmental pollution and the virtues of environmental cleanliness.[42] African states, and Nigeria in particular, must undertake measures to ensure the optimal exploitation of natural resources, which must necessarily be conditioned by ecological limitations. Therefore, the government as a regulatory body must seek to ensure an ecologically sustainable economic development through proper environmental management.

THE ESTABLISHMENT OF FORMAL SOCIOECONOMIC MONITORING SYSTEMS

The oil producing areas of Nigeria have for many years experienced the adverse effects of the oil industry without the benefit of an adequate mitigation policy. Current policy toward the oil areas offers no hope and requires change. Such change should include the establishment of comprehensive community impact monitoring systems, the purpose of which would be to provide a comprehensive data base for timely decisions and action. According to Leistritz and Chase (1984), the criteria for a monitoring system should include: (1) the procedures for refor-mulating (updating) impact projections; (2) data collection scope; and (3) reporting procedures and formats.[43] In addition, the monitoring systems should take into account the special circumstances of the oil areas, particularly with regard to the indicator to be monitored. Policymakers agree that the factors monitored should include traditional economic growth and de-cline, changes in population, housing, social services, level of pollution, health care systems, education, and land tenure. A comprehensive impact monitoring system would be most effec-tive if citizens were made a part of the decision-making process, particularly regarding the influence of technology on social change. The participation of citizens can fulfill three basic func-tions:

1. the decision-making process

2. making the information available to the public through education

3. offering a means of collaborative decision-making that brings together the oil industry, government, and the citizens as partners in that process and in the sharing of responsibilities.[44]

This in turn will minimize the negative impacts of oil on the citizens because their rights and interests will be respected and protected. The rights and privileges of all parties involved in the energy development process should be wholly integrated into all phases of mineral resource development.

THE ESTABLISHMENT OF A FORMAL COMMUNITY IMPACT AGREEMENT WITH THE OIL COMPANIES

In addition to a monitoring system, there should be a community impact agreement with the firms in the oil industry. The objective of this agreement would be to protect the in-digenous population from impact-related costs and also to protect the industry from unsubstantiated claims for compensation.[45] The lack of a community impact agreement may be a major factor in the number of community uprisings against oil companies because of their failure to compensate perceived or actual damages. For instance, on July 6, 1987, the people of the Iko Abasi Local Council Area of the Cross River State, while protesting the neglect and pollution of their water by the Shell Petroleum Development Company, clashed with law enforcement agents, which resulted in property damage valued at thousands of naira to both the oil company and community. When a community's livelihood is destroyed by oil pollution and there is no swift response to ameliorate the situation, it is conceivable that people will react adversely to induce a remedy.

In Nigeria, compensation for ecological disturbances comes under Part 4, Sections 18 and 19 of the Oil Pipeline Act of 1956 as modified by the 1965 Act and the Land Use Decree of 1978, which stipulates that compensation is not only payable for physical damage done to buildings, cash crops, or other property of a landowner/holder, but also for any damage caused by oil pollution. However, there is laxity in the enforcement of this act, and it lacks legislative clarity in terms of the liabilities of oil companies for these damages. Even the Inspectorate Division of the state-owned Nigerian National Petroleum Corporation (NNPC) lacks the legal empowerment to compel a defaulting oil company to provide compensation for damages arising from oil-related mishaps.[46]

The lack of an effective mode of compensation remains a problem, but in the event of oil pollution or other disturbances to individual or community property, estate surveyors or valuers are employed to assess the extent of damage and determine a fair compensation. In the absence of the expertise of the estate assessor, it is possible to settle the issue by the mutual agreement of the claimant and the oil company responsible for the pollution, with the Inspectorate Division of the NNPC acting as mediator. Given the complexities and disruptive nature of oil exploration, the establishment of a fair and adequate method of compensation should be a priority as a means of meeting the emergency needs and concerns of the mineral producing areas.

The establishment of an impact agreement should reduce the problems of perceived neglect and inadequate compensation that have often led to confrontation and the destruction of mutual property. The community impact agreement should include provisions for the terms of negotiation, financial agreements, monitoring, and arbitration. The affected communities will then know that they are not shouldering an unfair burden and that their social costs will be compensated. However, the effectiveness of such a strategy will depend on recognizing the influencing factors of interorganizational coordination.

THE NEED FOR A PERMANENT RELIEF PROGRAM

An agency for crisis management, as well as a relief program, should be established with the aim of responding quickly and effectively to victims of pollution. Currently, there is no planned response or relief program in the event of oil-related mishaps. Instead, relief is often administered on an ad hoc basis. The establishment of a permanent relief program will greatly enhance the ability of the government, the oil industry, and concerned relief teams to respond effectively to oil-related disasters.

Ad hoc relief schemes are no doubt well intentioned, but they provide an ineffective means of administering to serious problems associated with oil disasters. A standing relief plan will require the establishment of appropriate infrastructures to ensure adequate water supply, food, medicine, shelter, and availability of relevant technical equipment. The efficient management of oil disasters will also require interorganizational coordination between the government, the companies, and the local leaders in determining: (1) the characteristics of disaster agents; (2) the organizing structure in the communities of the oil

area; (3) demographic and ecological factors; (4) the preparedness of the emergency systems and communication; (5) the resources available; and (6) the interorganizational properties and
experience.[47.] For this reason, the establishment of a national
task force would be necessary. This task force would be composed of representatives from the oil industry, the government,
and the communities, and its purpose would be to research and
continually supply information about local conditions in mineral
producing areas.

A meaningful planning strategy for the mineral producing
areas would require the provision of adequate infrastructures,
therefore the existing program for the development of rural
infrastructures should be expanded to incorporate the special
needs of the mineral producing areas. The task force, as a result
of its research, would be able to advise the Directorate of Rural
Infrastructure on these special needs, and on specific socioeconomic and environmental planning strategies that would be
most likely to meet those needs.

The government of Nigeria's Oyo State has a special benefit
plan as a part of its mineral resources development strategy for
producing areas:

To ensure that the people of the state derive maximum benefit from the
exploitation of these resources, this administration has adopted guidelines
which include allocation of 10 percent equity participation to the state government on mineral resources development venture[s] and an undertaking by the
mining companies to provide social and economic benefits for the area to be
affected by their operations.[48]

This is an important policy element that had been lacking
between the oil producing states and oil companies. The worthy
example shown by Oyo state should be made integral to all
mineral interests in producing areas.

NOTES

1. B. E. Okogu, "The Outlook for Nigerian Oil: 1985–2000," *African Review* (December 1986):22.

2. Ezimora Chike, "Human Factor: Main Cause of Oil Spillage?" *The Guardian*, November 5, 1983, 4.

3. *Oil Spill Bulletin* (Aberdeen, United Kingdom), December 1983, 4.

4. Yinka Omorogbe, "The Legal Framework for Production of Petroleum in Nigeria," *Journal of Energy and Natural Resources Law* 5, no. 4 (1987).

5. Paul Hackett, "Nigeria: Economy," in *Africa South of the Sahara, 1990,* 19th ed. (London: Europa Publications, 1989): 775.

6. M. H. Abghari, "A Property Rights Application in Utilization of Natural Resources: The Case of Iran's Natural Gas" (doctoral dissertation, University of Georgia, 1982).

7. *West Africa,* March 28, 1988, 561.

8. O. Ogbonna, "The Geographic Consequences of Petroleum in Nigeria with Special Reference to Rivers State," (doctoral dissertation, University of California, 1979), 267.

9. "Nigeria's Economic Problems," *African Heritage* magazine (September/October 1987): 7.

10. Priyatosh Maitra, *Population Technology and Development* (London: Gower Publication, 1986), 76-77.

11. N. C. Benjamin and S. Devarajan, *Oil Revenues and Economic Policy in Cameroon: Results from Computable General Equilibrium Model,* World Bank Staff Working Paper no. 745 (Washington, DC: World Bank, 1985).

12. Peter Nijkamp, *Theory and Application of Environmental Economics* (New York: North Holland Press, 1977), 41.

13. *OECD Report* (Paris: OECD, 1977), 23.

14. A. E. K. Nash, et al., *Oil Pollution and Public Interest* (Berkeley: University of California, Institute of Governmental Studies, 1977), 24.

15. United Nations, *Poverty and Self-Reliance: A Social Welfare Perspective,* (New York: United Nations Publications no. E921V-1, 1982), 13.

16. See United Nations Commission for Social Development, *Report on the 26th Session* (New York: United Nations Economic and Social Council, no. E/CN.5/582, 1979).

17. For detailed information, see Sidney Dell, "Basic Needs or Comprehensive Development: Should the UNDP Have a Development Strategy?" *World Development* 9: 291–308. Also see the United Nations Committee for Development Planning, *Report on the 6th Session* (January 5-15,1970) Document no. /4776, para. 14, and *Employment Growth and Basic Needs: A One World Problem* (Geneva: International Labor Office, 1976), 31-33.

18. *Economic Development in the Third World* (New York: Longman Publishers, 1985), 382.

19. Harold L. Wilensky and Charles N. Lebeaux, *Industrial Society and Social Welfare* (New York: Free Press, 1967), 139.

20. P. Collier, "Oil and Inequalities in Nigeria," in *Social Impact Assessment and Management,* F. Larry Leistritz and Brenda Ekstrom, eds. (New York: Garland Publication, 1986), 33-34.

21. Hassan Hakiman. "The Impact of the 1970s Oil Boom on Iran Agriculture," *Journal of Peasant Studies* 15 (January 1988): 218-37.

22. Wayne Nafziger, *Inequality in Africa* (New York: Cambridge University Press, 1988).

23. Raphael Bar-El et al, *Patterns of Change in Developing Rural Regions* (Boulder, CO: Westview Press, 1987), 10-21, 61.

24. E. M. Rogers et al, *Social Change in Rural Societies,* 3rd edn. (Englewood Cliffs, NJ: Prentice Hall, 1988), 360.

25. N. W. Balabkins, "Factors Which Have Influenced Nigerian Industrial Development," *Rivisita Internationale Di Scienze Economiche e Commerciali* 35 (January 1988): 34.

26. John R. Hay et al., "Self Reliance and the Ujaama Concept: The Case of Tanzania," in *Sociology of National Development Theories and Issues in Third World Urbanization,* R.

Hay and J. Abuloghod, eds. (New York: Methuen Press, 1977), 366.

27. Yusufu B. Usman, "Behind the Oil Smokescreen," *Nigeria Standard* newspaper, May 7, 1982, 11.

28. Kwame Nkrumah, past president of Ghana, *Neocolonialism: The Last Stage of Imperialism,* (London: Thomas Nelson and Sons, Ltd., 1965): 1-2.

29. U.S. Department of Agriculture, *Sub-Saharan Africa,* Economic Research Service Supplement to WAS-27 1981/82, 14-15.

30. Paul Collier, "Oil Shocks and Food Security in Nigeria," *International Labor Review* (November-December 1988): 76.

31. "Workshop Reviews Global 2000 Activities," *Ghana Today* 1, no. 6 (1989), pp. 4-5.

32. *Atlanta Constitution,* May 24, 1987, 31A.

33. David Clark Scott, "Antarctic Oil Spill Adds Fresh Fuel to Anti-Mining Campaign,"*Christian Science Monitor,* February 8, 1989, 1.

34. *Public Affairs Information Systems* 75, no. 6 (March 1989): 30.

35. Michael Edelstein *A Framework for Examining Psychosocial Impacts of Toxic Exposure in Less Developed Countries* (unpublished manuscript, School of Social Sciences and Human Services and the Institute for Environmental Studies, Ramapo College of New Jersey, 1987).

36. Franklin E. Osai Sai, "Environmental Implications of Toxic Wastes and Dumping in Underdeveloped Countries" (paper presented at the Institute of International Studies, Berkeley, California, October 19, 1988), p. 14.

37. O. L. Spash and Ralph C. d'Arge, "Economic Strategies for Mitigating the Impacts of Climate Change on Future Generations" (paper presented at the 65th annual WEA International Conference, San Diego, California, June 29 - July 3, 1990), pp. 13-20.

38. "Action Plan for Sustainable Development of Indonesia's Marine and Coastal Resources," *Canada/Indonesia Medium-Term Planning Support Project* (Vancouver, British Columbia: Canada Department of the Environment), 229.

39. Ibid.

40. Louis M. Barbone, "The Corporation's Liability in Criminal Law: Systematic and Procedural Policy Choices Constituting a Reckless Disregard for Human Life," *Criminal Justice Quarterly* 9, no. 3 (Fall 1985): 38.

41. A. G. Onibokun, *Environmental Pollution in Nigeria. Guidelines for Action* (Ibadan, Nigeria: Nigerian Institute of Social and Economic Research, 1986), 1-5.

42. Ibid.

43. L. Leistritz and R. Chase, "Socioeconomic Impact Monitoring Systems: Review and Evaluation," *Journal of Environmental Management* 15 (1982).

44. Manfred Redelfs, "Citizens' Participation in Technology Assessment Practice at the Congressional Office of Technology Assessment," *Impact Assessment Bulletin* 6, no. 1 (1988), 55.

45. Community Impact Monitoring Program (Township of Atikokan and Ontario Hydro), *Final Report,* 1985:2.

46. Godwin Uduehi, "Compensation for Ecological Disturbances and Personal Losses," *NAPETCOR Quarterly* (1986): 5-7.

47. Y. Yamamoto, "Interorganizational Coordination in Crisis: A Study of Disaster in Japan" (doctoral dissertation, Ohio State University, 1985), 322.

48. "Oyo State: Turning the Industrial Wheel," *The African Guardian,* Vol. 5, no. 35 (September 10, 1990), 24.

8

The Future of Oil and the Producing Areas

In our every deliberation, we must
consider the impact of our decisions on
the next seven generations.

The Great Law of the Six Nations
Iroquois Confederacy

Oil has drastically influenced the internationalization of Nigeria's economy. Therefore any prognostic approach to the future of oil and the producing areas must necessarily consider the politics of oil on the international scene. It is the behavior of the participants in the oil market (consumers and producers alike) that influences the oil policies of a particular state, and Nigeria, being an influential member of OPEC, cannot possibly act in isolation. Nigeria's oil policies may have a direct bearing on OPEC power. They will also depend on the state of the world economy, geopolitical conditions, the influence of non-OPEC competitors in the world oil market, and the respective energy policies of oil consuming nations.

These conditions and other unforeseen factors could impact on the oil market. However, the future of oil and the producing areas may be affected by two broad major factors: first, world geopolitical conditions, and second, the state of the world economy. If history repeats itself, the experiences of the past may well be replicated over the decades ahead. It is important that each factor be analyzed separately.

World geopolitical conditions are at best precariously balanced, given the unresolved political problems of the Middle East. This area is highly dominant in the world oil market and is proven to hold a major share of global oil reserves. Historically, the interruptions to oil flow have been linked to specific political imbalances or to regional crises in the area. For instance, as early as 1951, a major strike closed what was then the world's largest refinery (500,000 bbl/day) in Abadan (Iran) during Mohammed Mossadegh's regime. The incident was a culmination of the Anglo-Iranian crisis. As a result, Iranian crude output of 700,000 bbl/day, which was roughly 6 percent of the world's total production, was shut down. The multinational oil corporations, in cooperation with their home governments, quickly blocked the movement and sale of Iranian oil in response to nationalization. Further crises ensued. In July 1956, the Suez Canal was nationalized by Colonel Nasser of Egypt and the Suez–Sinai War had begun. The roles of the two superpowers, Britain and France, influenced the closing of the Suez Canal in 1956 through 1957, which prevented the passage of Persian Gulf oil to markets in Europe.

Some of the many notable crises that have interrupted oil flow are: the Six Day War in 1967 between Israel and its Arab neighbors, which resulted in a reduction of oil production by Arab states; the Nigerian Civil War (1967–70), which, although occurring outside the Middle East, was still disruptive; the outbreak of the Yom Kippur War in October 1973; the 1973 oil embargo by Arab producers against the United States, which resulted in a severe energy crisis; and the Iran–Iraq War and the threat to the Strait of Hormuz. The effect of these events demonstrates the delicacy of geopolitical conditions, the vulnerability of the region to crisis, and the use of oil as a weapon or a target for disruption. The state of hostility that continues to exist in the region signals the possibility that further disruptions to the flow of oil remain imminent.

The Middle East is a crisis-prone and highly unstable area, the hotbed of world geopolitics; however, it also has a high concentration of oil reserves and productive capacity. Therefore, "the growing political, economic and religious divisions of this region, its repeated military conflicts and its vulnerability to big power intervention have heightened the anxieties about oil supply interruptions and oil price instability."[1] This is especially true when oil is used by the Gulf states as a weapon in political disputes.[2]

How did these crises impact on Nigerian oil? From the onset, crises over the Suez Canal and the disruptive effect on oil flow heightened the need for more oil exploration efforts outside the Middle East. Consequently, major discoveries were made in Africa — Algeria (1958), Nigeria (1958), and Libya (1959). Thus Nigeria was drawn into the oil picture in 1958, when commercial production began in Oloibiri in the country's Niger Delta Basin. From there, Nigeria evolved into a world-class oil producer. During the Middle East crises of the 1970s, and particularly during the period of the Arab oil embargo and the Iran–Iraq War, Nigeria became one of the major oil suppliers to the industrialized world, and its revenues increased substantially. The crises proved to have unintended spillover benefits for Nigeria.

Previous writers on the subject of oil in the global economy have also acknowledged the fact that Nigeria benefited from the crises of the Middle East. According to R. D. Walton (1977), the Six Day War and Arab–Israeli War strengthened Nigeria's position in the world oil market.[3] In this regard, Peter Odell (1970) also noted that "the closure of the Suez Canal in 1967 and [again in] 1974 altered the relative abilities of different countries . . . to compete in the world [oil] market, and particularly worked to the advantage of Venezuela, Libya and Nigeria, whose oil does not have to go through the Canal to reach Europe."[4] The Middle East is notably crisis-prone. If the crises continue into the decades ahead, there is a strong likelihood that Nigeria will again benefit from the chronically disruptive circumstances of the Middle East.

THE ESSENTIALITY OF OIL IN THE WORLD ECONOMY

The future of oil and the producing areas in Nigeria will also depend on the relative importance of oil in the global economy. Oil and global trade relationships (especially between industrialized nations and developing countries) will greatly influence the Nigerian position in world economy in terms of its market performance and revenues, which in turn will have an overall impact on its social and economic development. The position of oil in international trade relationships may be classified according to the following consumer–producer behavioral order:

1. industrialized oil consuming and producing nations, such as the United States

2. industrialized oil consumer-exporter nations, such as Norway, the United States, and Canada

3. oil producers that are developing countries and members of OPEC

4. oil producers that are developing countries but not members of OPEC, such as Mexico, Trinidad and Tobago, Cameroon, and Malaysia

5. oil producers within the Communist bloc, such as China and the Soviet Union

6. oil consuming-producing nations with high potentials for developing alternative energy resources, such as the United States, Soviet Union, Britain, and Canada

Each category is analyzed with respect to its own influence on the world oil market. The analyses include the historical and contemporary behavior of oil producing and consuming nations, with the presupposition that past experience will offer clues for future performance. It is the author's view that each category of producer or consumer will behave differently in the international oil market.

INDUSTRIALIZED OIL CONSUMING AND PRODUCING COUNTRIES

One country, such as the United States, can make a significant impact on the world oil market. The United States is a major buyer of oil from OPEC and non-OPEC producers. It is also a major player in the world geopolitical scene.

The OPEC pricing system influences the demand and supply of oil. The United States may or may not cooperate with OPEC. The United States would cooperate with OPEC if non-cooperation were expected negatively affect its domestic economy, particularly in oil dependent states like Texas and Oklahoma. For instance, the price collapse of 1986 caused some oil companies to retrench their capital investments, and many highly skilled laborers lost employment. Thus, in the United States, those states that were highly dependent on oil income suffered a severe depression, which unleashed an oil lobby for political intervention at the national level.[5] The United States has already been extensively explored, and production levels are declining; it is unlikely that any major new discoveries will be made in the future. It is also true that costs of production are higher in the United States and the demand for foreign oil could therefore increase, unless cheaper alternative energy resources are successfully developed.

The United States, however, may not want to entrust its energy needs to an international cartel like OPEC because, historically, the United States has been one of the main victims of oil embargoes and other forms of disruption. The United States suffered economic losses during the Arab embargoes of 1946, 1957, 1967, and 1973–74, as well as during the production disruption created by the Nigerian Civil War, the Iranian Revolution, the Iran–Iraq war, the conflicts in the Strait of Harmouz, and the Iraqi-Kuwait conflict (or the Gulf Crisis, 1990). The spillover effects of the events in the Middle East are not wholly separate from the behavior of certain member states in OPEC.

The United States could respond by stockpiling oil as a safeguard against the economic consequences of oil disruption, and to secure its energy security position.[6] It could then take further steps to reduce demand for imported oil by imposing tariffs on it, should such a move be deemed beneficial. This policy could jeopardize the market power of oil exporting countries, since the United States is seen as a major consumer. The United States could utilize its technological prowess to improve management and utilization of energy resources through conservation measures and the development of alternative energy sources to sustain its needs. The United States is an influential member of the International Energy Agency (IEA), which was established in 1974. The main objective of the IEA was to bring oil prices down and, according to Jafar M. Saad (1988), the IEA was responsible, through the governments of its member countries and oil companies, for the price upheaval witnessed in 1979. Its objective was to destroy OPEC as a major economic power so that it could not threaten the inequitable structure of economic and political relations between the developed economies and developing ones.[7] If this strategy were to continue, it would result in confrontation, rather than cooperation, with OPEC. However, the United States, as a superpower, may wish to avoid a permanent confrontational strategy with OPEC, and instead seek avenues for cooperation in the interest of market stability. Given the interdependencies between the oil producing and consuming countries, it is worthwhile for both to share the responsibility of maintaining market stability at all times. Munkirs and Knoedler (1988) contend that the solution rests primarily with the United States. The United States is still the strongest economic unit in the world. It must reassert its leadership in establishing a mechanism to stabilize the supply and demand of all strategic commodities. The organizational mechanism created must be able to protect the individual self-interests of the industrial producing, consuming, and developing countries, as well as their collective self-interest.[8]

In essence, protecting the interest of OPEC is vital not only to the stability of the oil market, but also to sustaining the international economic and geopolitical relationships within the world community of nations.

INDUSTRIALIZED OIL CONSUMER-EXPORTER NATIONS

Another influential group in the world oil market is the set of industrialized oil consumer-exporter nations exemplified by the United Kingdom, Canada, and Norway. Some of these countries are likely to cooperate fully with the rest of the industrialized world in taking advantage of OPEC weaknesses, or to maintain some degree of cooperation with OPEC, especially when OPEC's pricing policy is in their best interest. For example, in the 1970s, when OPEC was in command of the oil market, both Norway and Canada acted like members. The two countries were privileged de facto members of OPEC, in that they benefited from OPEC's policies and did not deviate from the organization's price directives. Such behavior is inconsistent with conventional expectations regarding new entrants into a cartelized market. Norway was accorded official observer status at OPEC meetings.[9]

In contrast, during the period of price collapse in the 1980s, those countries took a different turn. They did not adhere to OPEC's quota system to reduce the supply of oil, an initiative to stabilize prices. Instead, Norway, Canada, and Britain took advantage of OPEC's new strategy of production cutbacks and increased their respective outputs, only to flood the oil market and induce a further decline in prices. Their behavior is consistent with the policies of the IEA, in which most of the consumer exporter nations hold membership. These policies and those of the United States seek to maintain the energy security and economic stability of the industrialized nations.

The oil production effort of Norway, Canada, and Britain did undercut OPEC when market conditions slackened. Norway and Britain in particular increased their production to an astonishing 571 percent, while total OPEC production declined to almost 50 percent. This behavior did not encourage market stability. These countries should seek to cooperate with, rather than confront OPEC, considering their relatively low number of reserves. The life expectancies of crude oil reserves at 1987 levels of production are less than six years for Britain and thirty-nine years for Norway, relative to OPEC's combined oil reserve life expectancy of 108 years.[10] Production costs, as well, are higher for these countries. As F. J. Al-Chalabi points out:

The vulnerability of the North Sea oil producers to any price war stems from the very high production costs of their oil fields. North Sea oil production is the most expensive in the world. In the U.K., it is estimated that the per-barrel cost of production from the oil fields amounts to US$10; for new fields, $18; and for the most recent fields, $30. By contrast, OPEC oil, especially in the Middle East, is very cheap, the cost of production not exceeding, at most, $2 per barrel.[11]

The OPEC potential for control of world oil is still high; hence it is reasonable that the defense and restoration of oil price structure, now and in the future, should be a collective responsibility of all oil producing countries in both the developed and developing world.

OIL CONSUMING AND NONPRODUCING DEVELOPING COUNTRIES

This group of countries, which includes Bangladesh, Liberia, Ethiopia, Ghana, Mali, Niger, Haiti, Burma, Tanzania,

Costa Rica, Kenya, Peru, Chile, Argentina, Zambia, and Zimbabwe, does not have a significant influence on the international oil market, but they play an important part in world demand for oil. They constitute no threat to OPEC or to the industrialized world. These countries are not only poor and disadvantaged but debt-ridden, depending largely upon the export of primary commodities to foster economic and social development. Unlike OPEC, however, they do not hold a strong bargaining position in the world market, and unlike industrialized countries, they lack alternative energy resources and technological prowess, and must therefore rely heavily on oil for their industrial growth. Higher oil prices, then, coupled with an excessive burden of foreign debt, stifle the potential of most developing countries for steady growth and development. They have a large number of human reserves but economic growth is slow due to a decline in demand for their primary goods. Rising oil prices worsen their prospect for growth and development unless they receive special assistance from OPEC and non-OPEC oil producing countries and foreign aid from the industrialized world. There is, however, a growing number of industrialized developing countries such as Taiwan, South Korea, Singapore, and Thailand who can withstand to a certain degree a rise in oil prices because of their increasing economic and technological advantage over the rest of the developing world. Cuba, for example, enjoys its advantageous position as a result of the economic and technical support and the oil subsidies that it receives from the Soviet Union.

If the industrialized world experiences a recessionary economy along with higher oil prices and interest rates, measures would be taken by developed economies to cut back on imports from debtor nations. Consequently, these third world nations face a continual struggle for economic survival, with the hard choice of meeting debt payments or opting to default. The perennial problems of debtor nations may be reflected in the Holy Bible's book of Proverbs, chapter 22, verses 2, 7, and 16, which states, "The rich and the poor meet together. The Lord is the maker of them all. . . . The rich rules over the poor and the borrower is servant to the lender. . . . He that oppresseth the poor to increase his riches, and he that giveth to the rich, shall surely come to want."

The macroeconomic instability of the world is exacerbated by the unstable oil market. Consequently, oil consuming and nonproducing developing countries remain vulnerable to externalities associated with the erratic behavior of oil producing and consuming countries.

OIL PRODUCERS: DEVELOPING COUNTRIES AND OPEC MEMBERS

The oil producing developing countries that belong to the Organization of Petroleum Exporting Countries are most influential in the world oil market. OPEC is the successor cartel to the Seven Sisters cartel of oil companies, and is determined to play an active role in the international oil industry. Its policy objectives as stated in its Declaratory Statement are: that hydrocarbon resources in member countries are one of the principal sources of their revenues and foreign exchange earnings; that these resources are limited and exhaustible; that all countries have an inalienable right to exercise permanent sovereignty over their natural resources in the interest of their national development; and that with respect to crude oil prices, the posted or tax reference price that serves as the basis for assessing the per barrel government take shall be determined by the government. OPEC, then, is a union of sovereign governments who are determined to increase their bargaining power to influence and control the direction of the world oil market through their efforts:

- to keep oil competitive with other energy sources through production and pricing policies;
- to protect the per barrel purchasing power of oil export revenue;

Table 8.1

OPEC and non-OPEC (non-Communist world) Production, 1973–88 (mbd)

| | Production | | |
	OPEC	non-OPEC	Total
1973	30.99	14.9	45.89
1974	30.73	14.46	45.19
1975	27.16	14.26	41.42
1976	30.74	14.40	45.14
1977	31.25	15.36	46.61
1978	29.81	16.57	46.35
1979	30.93	17.70	48.63
1980	26.88	18.36	45.24
1981	22.60	18.84	41.44
1982	18.99	20.09	39.08
1983	16.99	20.88	37.87
1984	16.35	22.20	38.55
1985	14.45	23.05	38.50
1986	18.33	22.63	40.96
1987	17.70	22.60	n/a
1988	17.00	22.50	n/a

Source: OECD, IEA.

- to maintain the intrinsic value of oil, both as a non-renewable resource and as a raw material for other uses of petroleum;

- to take cognizance of the impact of oil prices on the world economy and, especially with the efforts of the developing countries, to establish a new international economic order;

- to regulate oil production in order to secure an equilibrium between supply and demand in the market.[12]

OPEC attempts to control oil production and pricing by the use of quotas. Historically, there has been a connection between production quotas and market shares on the international oil scene. The origin of OPEC's quota system is well summarized by Fadhil J. Al-Chalabi:

Table 8.2

Distribution of the Loss of Revenue among OPEC Members 1985–86 ($ million)

| | | Income in | | % |
	1985	1986	1987	change
Algeria	9,170	3,760	8,000	-12.7
Ecuador	1,927	983	1,350	-29.9
Gabon	1,668	848	950	-43.0
Indonesia	9,083	5,451	6,144	-32.3
Iran	13,115	6,600	9,200	-29.8
Iraq	11,380	6,980	11,300	—
Kuwait	9,729	6,200	7,800	-19.8
Libya	10,520	4,700	5,600	-46.7
Nigeria	12,338	6,300	6,900	-44.0
Qatar	3,355	1,460	2,100	-37.4
Saudi Arabia	25,936	21,190	21,500	-17.2
UAE	13,395	5,890	8,800	-34.3
Venezuela	10,325	6,713	7,200	-30.2
Total OPEC	131,967	67,073	96,844	-26.6

Source: OPEC Review

[A]ll OPEC agreements on production since 1982 have been more or less influenced by market share. In setting the pattern for distribution of total production into national quotas, we can but recall the Achnacarry Agreement among the major international oil companies in the late 1920s, referred to usually as "As Is." This restored the oil price structure after the ravaging price war among the oil companies. The "As Is" agreement was essentially based on the shares which the companies held immediately prior to the agreement, which remained essentially unaffected by the price war. The qualification of "As Is" simply meant that the status quo was being preserved without change.

In OPEC, however, such a concept may not always lead to rational and optimal sharing in the world market, as the companies' historical market sharing cannot be compared with that of OPEC Member Countries. The huge levels of market share enjoyed by some major oil companies, such as British Petroleum and Exxon (formerly Standard Oil of New Jersey), mainly reflected the fact that these two companies had access to much wider reserves than other companies like Texaco or Compagnie Francaise de Petrole. The history of the intercompany struggle clearly indicates that it was access to crude ownership that determined the strength of the company—i.e., in the status quo at that time, the market situation of each company more or less reflected its access to the crude.

The situation in OPEC is different, however, in some cases contrasting with that of the companies. We have already mentioned the disparity that existed among Member Countries in terms of the reserves/output ratio, and the fact that, in some low-reserve Countries, the rate of reserve depletion is much higher than in others with large reserves but a low depletion rate. The case of Kuwait can once more help illustrate this situation. If we apply to Kuwait the same reserves/output ratio as for Indonesia, its production share would be 14.3 mb/d, which the OPEC ceiling would naturally be unable to support. Because of the strength of its economy and its small population, Kuwait chose to produce much less. Furthermore, OPEC consists of sovereign Countries with a great variety of population levels, economic structures, financial requirements, levels of development, etc. Unlike the companies whose primary objective is to maximize profits, OPEC's production policies are geared to socioeconomic requirements, so that Countries with low reserves push for a proportionately higher share than those with high reserves, whose financial requirements are usually less pressing.[13]

To OPEC, the retention of the quota system is a means to influence the production and pricing of oil resources to benefit its members. It is also a means to improve its credibility as a powerful cartel. The basic rationale of OPEC as a cartel is not different from other developing countries' view, which emphasizes the risky dependent nature of the sale of raw materials for foreign exchange, and that a disruptive change in world demand for their raw material could seriously jeopardize each nation's balance of payment. It is further argued that the nature of extractive industry constitutes a systematic depletion of the valuable national assets of the host country, while leaving little of enduring value. Moreover, in the short run, these raw materials or primary goods are subject to uncontrollable fluctuations, and in the long run they are exhaustible.[14]

OPEC's efforts to control the world oil market in order to attain its objectives were remarkably effective from the 1970s through the early 1980s. Total OPEC revenue increased from $8 billion in 1970 to $276 billion in 1980.[15] But soon the demand for oil began to decline, from 52 mbd in 1979 to a low of 45.6 mbd in 1983, which led to the eventual decline in prices in 1986. Subsequently, OPEC revenues fell to a low of $79 billion in 1986 and were about $96 billion in 1987. The price upheaval adversely affected OPEC's ability to maintain its power and the unity of its membership. The international petroleum industry is highly vulnerable to shocks, since it is influenced by both economic and political forces.

The thirteen OPEC member countries are Algeria, Ecuador, Gabon, Indonesia, Iran, Iraq, Kuwait, Libya, Nigeria, Qatar, Saudi Arabia, United Arab Emirates (Abu Dhabi, Dubai, and Sharjah), and Venezuela. OPEC as a group holds 79 percent of oil reserves and 61 percent of proven natural gas reserves in the non-Communist world. Saudi Arabia holds over 168 billion barrels or 30 percent of the proven oil reserves in the non-Communist world.

The population of OPEC member countries grew rapidly at an average annual rate of nearly 2.8 percent from 1960 to 1975. According to the United Nations' medium variant and most likely projection, their population will increase on average at a rate of nearly 2.7 percent annually from 1975 to 2000. Thus by the year 2000 the population of OPEC countries is projected to be just over 560 million.[16]

OPEC member countries are faced with the problems typical of developing countries. A. Hassan Taher (1982) posits that the attitudes of the thirteen OPEC member countries and the relative extent of their dependence on petroleum production differ greatly according to the circumstances unique to each country. Iran, Indonesia, Nigeria, Algeria, and Venezuela have relatively large populations and need high oil revenues to support economic development programs. In contrast, Saudi Arabia, United Arab Emirates, and Kuwait with relatively small populations have been producing at levels well in excess of domestic revenue needs in order to satisfy the international market demand.[17] As a result, these countries have accumulated temporary financial surpluses beyond their domestic absorptive capacity. The projection of the real value of these financial assets against inflation and currency depreciation is a serious problem. These differences may explain why certain OPEC members produce beyond their quota, and the rationale for cheating.

The problem of cheating, or non-quota adherence, was partly responsible for the Iraqi-Kuwait conflict. It was reported on August 3, 1990 that Iraq's president, Saddam Hussein, ordered a military action against Kuwait, and the Iraqis invaded that country. Iraq's incursion into Kuwait is believed to have been a move to punish Kuwait for perceived insubordination.[18] Part of the rationale for the invasion is that Kuwait overproduced oil, surpassing its quota enough to depress oil prices. The Iraqi-Kuwait conflict sent new shock waves into the world oil market, precipitating an immediate increase in oil prices. The severity of Iraq's action had regional and international implications and was serious enough to generate global concern.

J. Munkirs (1988) contends that the petroleum production process, given our current storehouse of technologically based knowledge, tends toward creating surpluses, and that surpluses in a strategic commodity tend to generate collectively contrived scarcity or, if you will, collective action to stabilize supply and demand.[19] The oil price instability of the 1980s eroded OPEC power and the cartel lost revenues. The organization took steps to combat price instability through production cutbacks and a quotas system, but the non-OPEC producing countries undermined the organization's position in the world market, and the OPEC market share fell drastically. In the late 1980s, OPEC as a whole produced only 40 percent of the world's total oil supplies, whereas it had accounted for 64 percent of those supplies in 1979. However, OPEC holds nearly 83 percent of the words's proven recoverable reserves. In 1986 775 billion barrels were concentrated in its member countries, and the Gulf region held most of the reserve.[20] Given this proven reserve advantage, the revitalization of OPEC power in the future is highly possible, especially given a scenario of increased demand for oil.

According to OPEC President Rilwanu Lukman, the rise in demand for oil began again in 1988 and, barring economic recession, the growth will continue. The projected figures for OPEC production order through the year 2000 are as follows: 17-21 mbd for 1990, 19-24 mbd for 1995, and 21-28 mbd for the year 2000, given OPEC's position as a residual supplier and others presumed to be supplying at maximum capacity.[21] If the essentiality of oil is maintained and there is continued growth in demand, oil will boom again at about the turn of the century and OPEC could regain its power and market share. For instance, according to the U.S. Department of Energy, if the price of oil is kept at $15 per barrel up to 1990, and then increased to $23, it could rise to $28 by 1995. The low-price scenario suggests that world oil consumption could reach 53 mbd in 1995, relative to 46.5 mbd in 1985, an increase of 6.6 mbd. Increased demand is also predicted by Gaadalli Al Fatti, head of the OPEC Secretariat, who estimated that world demand will increase from 47.9 million barrels per day in 1987 to 51.0-53.1 in the year 2000.[22] The regionally projected demands are 3.0-3.5 mbd in North America, about 0.5 mbd in the Pacific region, 1.5 mbd in Western Europe, about 2.0 mbd in non-OPEC developing countries, and about 0.8 mbd in OPEC countries.[23] This could be an indicator of future energy cycles. There is a strong likelihood that OPEC pricing policies will play a major role in determining the future structure of the world oil market.

According to Ibrahim Youssef (1984), political upheavals in Indonesia, Iran and Nigeria

since 1960 have brought military and militant regimes to power that, for a while, upset the balance of forces inside OPEC. But in the end, the new regimes fell in line with OPEC's communal interest. Whenever it approaches a precipice, OPEC has shown enough common sense to step back. The political competition among member countries notwithstanding—including four years of war between Iran and Iraq—OPEC still adheres to the common goal of maximizing the value of its energy resources. That purpose takes precedence over every other concern. The fact that OPEC stuck together for 24 years is in itself a marvel. It is the best argument for OPEC's survival. As Indonesia's oil minister constantly reminds everyone, OPEC's 13 members are all in the same boat: "We sink or swim together." All OPEC members know this is true. That is why when cheating gets out of hand and OPEC seems to be on the verge of losing all control over oil prices, its members always manage to fall back in line. OPEC most likely will survive as an organization. The new OPEC that will emerge from the great crisis that began in the 1980s will be a more moderate organization, dominated by Saudi Arabia and bent on making oil prices the subject of fewer surprises and more dependability for consumers.[24]

Reflecting on the prospects for the development of oil producing countries in an interdependent world, A. H. Taher quotes Fadhil J. Al-Chalabi:

Although oil producing countries differ in economic and social structures, it is nevertheless, fair to estimate that the time horizon needed for achieving such structural changes in their economies will be generally longer than that envisaged for the energy transition. If the latter is made at a much faster rate than the former, development prospects in the oil producing countries could be compromised before an adequate level of economic structural change has been realized. Consequently, there should be a balance between the pace of economic and social development in the oil producing countries and the pace of transition in the western countries towards a lesser dependence on imported oil. The faster the rate of development, the greater are the incentives for the oil producing countries to cooperate with the consuming countries in smoothly accelerating the energy transition.[25]

Taher goes on to say:

If the state of the world economy outside OPEC countries is relatively unhealthy, the oil exporters themselves will be unable to develop satisfactorily in either a quantitative or qualitative sense, however the objectives of human endeavor might be defined. Oil exporting countries need to use the unique opportunities they have been blessed with in the form of oil and gas reserves to put in place an economic and social infrastructure during the next generation which is capable of surviving and advancing as their reserves of hydrocarbons are depleted. This can only be done in an interdependent world.[26]

OIL PRODUCERS: DEVELOPING COUNTRIES THAT ARE NON-OPEC MEMBERS

As exemplified by Mexico, Trinidad and Tobago, Malaysia, Cameroon, Oman, Egypt, and Angola, the membership in this group is a set of developing countries that moderately influence the world oil market. They earn spillover benefits from OPEC pricing policies and threaten no serious confrontation with OPEC. Although oil production in this category of producers increased to about 134 percent in 1986, they cooperated with OPEC to stabilize oil prices when market conditions became unfavorable. This group of oil producers is most likely to accept OPEC's principles of cooperation rather than seek confrontation.

OIL PRODUCERS: COMMUNIST BLOC NATIONS

Communist bloc oil producers are potential new entrants into the competitive world oil market. They are likely to increase their oil production and sell to Western consumers in exchange for western currencies and for the purchase of technologies to foster development in their "reformed" economies.

The increased participation of the Soviet Union or China could create a new international economic order specific to the oil market. The new entrants from the Communist bloc can flood the oil market to reduce OPEC power and control unless they join OPEC or cooperate with OPEC for geopolitical reasons. According to Carrol Bogert (1990), the trans-Ural region of Tyumen in the USSR has oil reserves richer than Saudi Arabia. If the area gains a certain degree of autonomy from Moscow, the Tyumens could sell their oil themselves. The trans-Ural region's oil output has an estimated worth of $37 million per year.[27]

Also, Ginger Szala (1986) contends that the Soviet Union is the world's largest oil producer.[28] It produces more than 12 million barrels per day, or more than 21 percent of the world's oil. The thirteen members of OPEC have a combined production of 30 percent of the world's oil, of which Saudi Arabia holds 9 percent. The United States is the second-largest producer and also a major consumer. It produces about 18 percent of the world's output.

The above statistics show that the Soviet Union has high potential to control the world oil market. It could be the detriment of OPEC if it increases production to compete in this world market, exchanging its oil for Western currencies and technologies in an effort to develop its newly reformed society. However, this scenario is wholly unlikely, because the Soviet Union would want to cooperate with OPEC for geopolitical reasons. It also has a special interest in the developing countries. For instance, the Soviet Union had an accord with Iran to cut production by 100,000 barrels per day. This agreement, though involving relatively small numbers, shows that the spirit of cooperation exists. An added factor is that both the Soviet Union and China are world-class superpowers and as such they would not encourage rapidly increased production of depletable and nonrenewable resources like oil just to satisfy the western appetite for them or to gain short-term economic benefits. Considering the long-term strategic and military significance of oil to both superpowers, it is supposed that this rationale would curtail oil production for either China or the Soviet Union except for possible periodic increases in the production and sale of oil for developmental needs. It is conceivable then to reason that if oil production is curtailed by the Communist bloc nations, and if they cooperate with OPEC, then OPEC is likely to maintain its strength and cohesiveness, and its ability to exercise its power as a cartel over the world oil market.

The combined role of Communist bloc of nations in the world oil market has been very marginal, yet they are highly influential on the world geopolitical scene. There are, however, records of Soviet oil exports to the West, and China is encouraging expanded development of its petroleum industry; it has exported a limited amount of crude oil to friendly countries for foreign exchange. China is a supporter of OPEC, but the Soviet Union was among the notable exceptions of non-OPEC oil producers who did not quite cooperate with OPEC.[29] However, the Soviets watched as OPEC's fortune soared from $11,023 billion in 1971 to $92,449 billion in 1975. When it reached $275,028 billion in 1980, the lucrative nature of OPEC power lured even the Soviet Union, and they once nursed the ambition of going cartel with OPEC.[30] In general, however, members of this producer bloc are likely to be sympathetic to the economic and geopolitical interests of OPEC member states.

OIL CONSUMERS IN DEVELOPED ECONOMIES WITH HIGH POTENTIALS FOR DEVELOPING ALTERNATIVE ENERGY SOURCES

The cycle of OPEC dependency could be broken if a close substitute to oil is discovered or technologically produced, displacing oil as an essential commodity. For example, the industrial revolution brought coal into prominence as the chief source of energy until 1950, when oil displaced it. Since then, the world coal consumption has declined, rendering coal a less essential commodity. This could also happen with oil. In addition, oil has an essential role to play in military preparedness. Therefore the military demand for oil is high and there is a close relationship between NATO and the International Energy Agency. Oil's essential role in war and strategic planning for the energy security of future emergencies has forced NATO and the IEA to undertake the development of synthetically derived petroleum fuels from coal, sand, and oil shales to induce self-sufficiency and for military purposes.[31] This would in effect set the stage for the demise of OPEC's power. The displacement of oil is, however, unlikely to occur unless a safer source of energy is discovered.

All of the circumstances discussed could have some measure of influence on the world energy scene; however, one cannot be too certain about the direction of the world energy outlook. The level of uncertainties may rest on the price of oil and OPEC's responses to changing times ahead in the world energy market.

EXTERNAL INFLUENCE ON NIGERIA'S ENERGY POLICY

Nigeria has been an influential member of OPEC since its inception. The behavior of the Nigerian state in the future may well be a response to international conditions, which could be favorable or unfavorable. Its activities could well be identified with OPEC's responses to changes in the world energy market. It is assumed here that past experience offers a clue to future performance, and that it is possible that the Nigerian experience and position will repeat itself. However, Nigeria's reaction to the international oil scene could be conditioned by prices, reserve base, level of production, and the status of its economy. Furthermore, Nigerian performance will depend also on the degree of OPEC's strength. For instance, the OPEC-induced favorable price developments of the 1970s resulted in increased revenue to Nigeria (from under $1 billion in 1970 to $25.3 billion in 1980). In contrast, during the market collapse of the 1980s, Nigerian production in 1983 was conditioned by OPEC's quota allocation and averaged 1.3 mbd. Its average export declined to about 1 mbd in the 1980s, as compared with 2 mbd in the 1970s. The quota system, coupled with the price collapse, resulted in the decline of Nigeria's oil revenue to $7.2 billion in 1987, a 70 percent drop from 1980. At the peak of the global oil market crisis in 1986, revenue had fallen to $6.2 billion. The sharp drop in oil prices, together with an external debt burden of over $20 billion, created social and economic problems for Nigeria. The foreign exchange earnings from oil that had funded the impressive development plans in the 1970s could not be replicated in the 1980s due to the oil market slump.

Therefore, if past experiences are repeated, the Nigerian market share and performance may well be dependent on substantial OPEC market power. Robert Erc, a petroleum consultant, estimated that oil prices will increase from $18 per barrel in 1988 to $27 per barrel in 1994. From 1992 the price could increase at an annual rate of $2 per barrel and hit $25 in 1993, eventually climbing to the $27 per barrel mark by 1994.[32] But according to a research report by R. A. Marshalla and Dule Neshitt (1986), future world oil prices under maximum cartel power are projected to increase as shown in Table 8.3.

Table 8.3
Projected World Oil Prices, 1992–2022

Year	Maximum Cartel (1983 $bbl)
1992	38.11
1997	40.37
2002	42.22
2012	46.63
2022	50.63

Source: The Energy Journal (January 1986): 17.[33]

A maximum exercise of cartel power could lead to an 80 percent increase in world oil prices. Under this scenario, Nigerian projected oil production is estimated at between 1,500 and 1,745 bbl/day by 1990 and between 1,745 and 2,800 bbl/day by the year 2000. The country's levels of production will be constrained, however, by the discipline of the demand for OPEC oil, which is estimated to grow at a rate of 5.3 percent a year for the next fifteen years. Oil revenues are expected to range from $6 to $13 billion in 1990 and by the year 2000, they could range from $21 to $52 billion.[34] It is assumed here that Nigeria might

Table 8.4

Nigeria: Actual and Projected Status of Debt
(in million U.S. dollars)

	Debt	Debt Disbursements	Long-term Debt Service
1970	567	56	96
1971	651	106	94
1972	732	147	95
1973	1,205	67	229
1974	1,274	92	192
1975	1,143	104	270
1976	906	91	400
1977	3,146	89	138
1978	5,091	1,471	149
1979	6,235	962	393
1980	8,855	3,759	772
1981	12,018	7,167	1,302
1982	12,815	5,779	1,705
1983	18,422	5,611	2,144
1984	18,435	4,068	3,462
1985	19,324	3,265	4,039
1986	23,164	3,423	1,740
1987	30,039	3,488	983
1988	30,718	4,102	1,984
Projected			
1989	—	—	6,082
1990	—	—	5,271
1991	—	—	3,642
1992	—	—	3,710
1993	—	—	3,847
1994	—	—	3,474
1995	—	—	2,495
1996	—	—	1,930
1997	—	—	1,366
1998	—	—	908

Sources: *World Debt Tables 1989* and *World Debt Tables 1990*, World Bank, Washington, DC.

diversify its export base, but projections indicate that between 80 and 90 percent of total export earnings will be derived from oil exports through 1995.[35] The improved revenue for Nigeria could materialize earlier than expected driven by the Gulf Crisis (the Iraqi-Kuwait conflict) of 1990, which may have triggered another "oil boom" for oil producing countries whose oil does not have to pass through the Persian Gulf. History could repeat itself. The Gulf Crisis may have unintended spillover benefits for Nigeria and other oil producers outside the Middle East. The 1990 crisis has induced a rapid increase in the per barrel cost of oil, which could once again work to the advantage of Nigeria in improving its revenue position.

Although Nigeria's projected revenue base might seem encouraging, if the country continues to depend on foreign markets without diversification or foreign asset investment, the earnings from oil will once again be spent on debt service, at the expense of much-needed development programs. Unless measures are taken to avert this, the country will experience further cycles of economic depression and austerity. Yusufu Bala Usman states the case quite strongly:

At the rate things are going Nigeria shall continue to repay external debts with larger and larger portions of its foreign exchange earnings for another one hundred years or more! This is not an exaggeration. . . . The Rolling Plan and the Perspective Plan, set up as they are to continue along the path of SAP [Structural Adjustment Program], shall further entrench the fiscal system established by SAP and continue with the escalation of the debt burden and subjugate our economy to the eternal repayment of external debts.

What makes this situation very grave is that right now, in this first year of the 1990s, after all the "economic diplomacy" and the "successful" reschedulings — meaning the postponement of the repayment of the principal—the Federal Government alone is allocating 42 percent of its total expenditure of N39.7 billion largely to pay interest on external debt. This massive amount of N16.8 billion is equivalent to the whole of the 1990 allocation to the twenty-one state governments and half of the total allocation to the local governments from the Federation Account!

As the decade of the 1990s advances, and the rolling plans roll along, all geared to debt repayment, what proportion of our resources are going to be sunk into this cesspool of debt repayment? For, by the mid-1990s, the repayment of the principal would have started and the debt strangulation of our economy shall have taken it back to a position which is no different from the worst form of early colonial plunder. For, the raw commodities we shall be producing for export shall be entirely used to repay these debts with the whole system sustained by violent repression.[36]

Nigeria has not effectively utilized its oil exports to sustain balanced growth in all sectors of its domestic economy. According to Ira Sohn (1987), with 97 percent of Nigeria's exports concentrated in oil, between 10 and 23 percent of export receipts in 1990 are likely to be needed for interest payment. However, if oil prices improve by the year 2000, the interest payment claim on export earnings could range from 3 to 14 percent.[37] Naturally, it follows that Nigeria must seek a balance between servicing external debt to avoid default and promoting the processes that will induce sustainable economic growth and development. The hard choice will depend on effective planning and management, with the aim of fostering better performance in the future.

PROSPECTS FOR THE FUTURE DEVELOPMENT OF OIL PRODUCING AREAS

The complex interrelationships among the various economic and geopolitical forces could directly or indirectly impact on Nigeria's oil producing areas through its energy policies and the direction of its economy. The prospects for the development of the oil areas depends on the future state of development planning in Nigeria and the future structure of revenue sharing within the country's dualistic government system. In the past, the oil producing areas have often lagged behind in development, partly due to the fact that wealth derived from the oil resource was not shared according to the derivative principle, but was based instead on population. This practice weakened the fiscal capacity of the producing states, since all state budgets depend on allocation from the federal pool. Moreover, the meager 1.5 percent allotted to mineral producing areas for the amelioration of ecological disturbances was inadequate to combat the real social cost to the host communities. The oil industry and government established neither a comprehensive mitigation policy nor effective social planning for the affected communities. Hence, for the most part, inhabitants of the oil producing areas were made victims, rather than benefactors, of the oil resource derived from their land.

Prospects for the development of oil producing areas would require drastic policy changes. The oil industry and the government would need to incorporate the special needs of the inhabitants into all phases of the resource development. One of those needs is for a human settlement approach to planned mitigation policy. Another is the issue of compensation, which has not been effectively addressed. The oil industry and the government should share the responsibility of establishing a means of fair and effective compensation planning and administration, with full compensation for the social costs to host communities as the primary objective. Compensation to communities for risk should be seen as the logical extension of compensation for social and economic impacts; hence, the objective of compensating a community for real cost or perceived risk is consistent with the moral principle of distributive justice[38] Distributive justice is a means to operationalize fairness and to ensure that all parties in the exchange relationship will benefit proportionately from the oil resource.

Thus, measures of a comprehensive mitigation policy should remain an integral part of balanced social and economic development, with the specific needs and interests of the people at heart. Nigeria should seek to emulate the worthy exemplars of oil policy in China and Malaysia. The Chinese government was concerned about the effects of petroleum development on indigenous minority groups in its eastern producing areas, in terms of physical and cultural pollution and its impact on the traditional economy. The Chinese government took steps to provide training programs for the people and to protect the rights and interests of its minority population, including the avoidance of moral and spiritual pollution of the people due to the foreign presence in their environment. The Malaysian example indicates that, despite the oil producing states ceding all oil rights to the federal government, they still received half of the oil royalties and federal allocation for development projects. To ensure that the people fully benefit from oil, the derived revenues were used to develop the agricultural sector (an important aspect that Nigeria neglected for years). This practice favored an increase in overall development in the Malaysian economy.

The Malaysian oil royalty and its federal allocation plan can serve as a model for oil producing states in Nigeria, which could cooperate to demand structural changes in the federal revenue-sharing plan to increase their fiscal capacity. The recommended changes in the federal revenue-sharing plan, as reported by the Political Bureau, represent a step forward in achieving an efficient revenue allocation system. It will also be helpful if limited autonomy is granted to oil producing states and local governments that will allow them to impose a special mineral tax on oil companies, with particular reference to pollution and other negative externalities. This tax could provide a reliable source of funds that would enable the producing states to tackle their ecological problems.

Nigeria's quest for social and economic development is unlikely to get far without becoming a part of the global industrial expansion and resource utilization, but its progressive effort has left a sizeable segment of its citizens worse off. The elites have enjoyed most of the benefits derived from oil wealth while the rural masses have been its victims. Nigeria's economic progress has had little or no effect in alleviating the lot of ordinary people and has little implication for future betterment unless the suggested policy changes are undertaken. A drastic policy change might require a sort of "domestic Marshall Plan" to help the impoverished and emaciated rural masses in the mineral producing areas and nonproducing areas alike. The aid plan should be extended to include agriculture and food development, afforestation, erosion control, the dredging of nonnavigable waterways, and development of better rural infrastructure in order to make the living conditions of the people more tolerable. It is a better way to transform oil profits into the development of needy areas, and a good way to vitalize intercommunity or regional trade through increased commodity movement between areas. The government and the oil industry can jointly embark on a special oil-fueled aid plan to improve the social and economic conditions of the mineral producing areas. Oil—"black gold"—has been responsible for the social and economic transformation of the country since the 1970s. The essentiality of oil as a strategic mineral is not in dispute, hence, balancing the developmental and human needs in the producing areas must be integral to the mineral interest.

Conservation of the environment is a requirement for the well-being of succeeding generations. A good mix of conservation measures, coupled with socially responsible behavior by the oil industry, could safeguard the future of oil and its producing areas. The oil industry and the government should cooperate to encourage an ecologically sustainable development, one that meets the goals of the present without compromising the ability of future generations to meet their own needs.[39] The extraction of oil takes place mostly in economically backward areas, and the indigenous voice is hardly considered in the extractive process. Oil-based developing countries such as Nigeria export about 82 percent of their oil production. This rate constitutes roughly 80 percent of their total exports. The significance of oil in the development and growth of these economies and need for a planned extraction policy should thus be clear. Such a plan, while allowing for realistic growth and development, should typically consider overall coherence, absorptive capacity, and conservation measures. The literature on the exhaustion of nonrenewable resources suggests that long-run extraction and export of a resource stock cannot continue indefinitely at an accelerated rate (Parhizgari 1987).[40]

Nigeria's economic future should not wholly rely on one strategic mineral resource that is subject to external demand and price instability. Rather, diversification of the entire economic base should be encouraged, especially in agriculture. A continued reliance on oil alone cannot guarantee sustained economic growth. According to Alan Gelb (1988), much of the potential benefit of the oil windfalls has been dissipated, and oil producers may actually end up worse off despite revenue gains. Gelb proposes that developing countries need to look to their economic management and its attendant political factors for successful economic development and that the reliance on natural resources alone is not enough.[41] Therefore a heavy dependence on oil or any other primary product as an export item introduces an instability of external origin. This view would affirm that the mere existence of an extractive industry to boost the export receipts of a developing country does not necessarily bring about sustainable development in that country. Instead, problems of social strife, economic instability, and environmental decay are created.

Historically, since oil became a valuable energy resource, it has been vulnerable to shocks, characterized by fluctuations in production and price. This character is not only influenced by the laws of supply and demand in classical economics, but also by the international political and economic relationships within the world community of nations. Just as stringent governmental regulatory policies and environmental activists in developed nations are protecting their environment for posterity, it is not advisable for the developing society to encourage the depletion of resources and environmental degradation in exchange for ephemeral economic benefits without adequate protection to ensure the survival of succeeding generations. Social planning for the mineral areas should also include a heritage trust fund. The purpose of a heritage fund is to save for the future and diversify the economy, with the aim of improving the quality of life of the people.[42] In the last two decades, oil extractive activities increased to 300 percent in developing countries, as compared with only 10 percent in developed countries. There exists the danger of mortgaging the environment for a desolate future, that is, exchanging long-term environmental quality for short-term ephemeral benefits.

No nation should sacrifice its valuable resources for the sake of short-term monetary benefits. By extracting oil without regard to the side effects or the quality of citizens' health and longevity, the nation does not improve either its social or its economic sectors; instead, a declining trend will be onset. Those who may feel that the problems of oil producing areas are not in their backyard, and who may feel a safe distance from the oil communities, should be reminded that Nigeria is an entity within one environment; a decay in part will ultimately affect the rest of the nation. The fate of the mineral producing communities should be a concern for all. When ordinary people and their environment become victims of disruptive economic expansion without adequate protection or provision of alternative means to improve their social and economic circumstances, they will remain vulnerable. Therefore, the need to broaden the social responsibility and performance of the oil industry in order to maintain economic progress with environmental balance should be a matter of compulsion.

The essence of systemic balance is also reflected in the inspirational Islamic thoughts on a balanced system of economic security: Wealth must be earned properly, without abuse, and wealth should be used for the betterment of the needy. Reflecting on a systemic view, Mohammed Siqqi wrote, "As a small thorn to any part, [a] thorn in any part of [the] human body pricks one spot but pains the whole to restlessness. Similarly, the needy pricked and pinched by the thorn hunger destroy the peace of the whole humanity."[43]

Over the years, the oil industry's activities have threatened the host community's food systems and the rest of the ecology on which the inhabitants depend. The result has been the precipitation of food shortages and ecological deterioration. These enlightened thoughts from Islam affirm the fact that a problem in one part of the system ultimately affects the whole; hence our social system or nation (and, ultimately, our entire planet) may be viewed as "one body." The ecclesiastical view of systems theory is also reflected in the teachings of *Alhadis* (the Islamic Holy Book) which reads: "There is a piece of flesh in the body, when it is sound, the body is sound, and when it is unsound, the whole body becomes unsound. Behold it is the heart."[44]

Similarly, the inspirational words of the Holy Bible reflect the unity and diversity in one body. The Apostle Paul wrote:

But now indeed there are many members, yet one body. And the eye cannot say to the hand, I have no need of you; nor again the head to the feet, I have no need of you. No, much rather, those members of the body which seem to be weaker are necessary.

And those members of the body which we think to be less honorable, on those we bestow greater honor, and our unpresentable parts have greater modesty. But, God composed the body, having given greater honor to that part which lacks it;

That there should be no schism in the body, but that members should have the same care for one another. And if one member suffers, all the members suffer with it or if one member is honored, all the members rejoice with it.[45]

The ecclesiastical thoughts on systems clearly reflect that the parts could not be separate from the whole, so it behooves us not only to be partakers of derived benefits from the natural resource, but also partakers of the negative externalities suffered by the producing areas. Thus it is imperative that all parties involved in the mineral resource development (that is, the oil companies, the government, and the citizens) should cooperate to foster socially responsible economic behavior through caring for the people and the entire ecosystem. A Christian stewardship creed expresses that ideology:

We believe in God, Creator of the world; and in Jesus Christ the redeemer of creation. We believe in the Holy Spirit, through whom we acknowledge God's gifts, and we repent of our sin in misusing these gifts to idolatrous ends.

We, as stewards, affirm the goodness of life. We rejoice in accepting the abundance with which God has endowed the earth. We commit ourselves to participate in God's redemptive intention for the world: that all people should be able to live in peace and to enjoy the days of their lives free from hunger, disease, hopelessness and oppression.

As stewards, we commit ourselves to love and justice among persons and nations in the equitable distribution of income and wealth. We affirm the ownership of property as a trust from God. We acknowledge the responsibility to share the abundance of creation. We regard the conditions created by poverty to be demeaning to the human spirit.

As stewards, we insist on the efficient management of human and natural resources in the production of the goods and services needed by the human community. We insist on conserving resources in order to sustain permanently the fruitfulness of the earth. . . .

As stewards, we acknowledge the necessity of civil government. We encourage all people to participate in the activities of responsible citizenship.

We believe that Christian stewardship is a joyful response to God's gifts; it is a spiritual understanding of the practical and economic aspects of all of life.[46]

The impact of the oil industry has precipitated negative changes within the Nigerian ecological system. These negative changes, if left unabated, could result in serious adverse ecological consequences for the entire nation. It would be erroneous to think that only the oil producing areas will suffer from the adverse effects. The negative consequences would be very much like a contagious disease that could spread to the rest of the system. Therefore, it would behoove the government, oil industry, and concerned citizens to work together to avert any threat to the existence of their unique system. Nigeria could learn from the Amazonian experience, in which the impact of extractive activities established a local dominant class that created a mode of extraction that exploited the indigenous population and nature such that neither could fully recover. The dominant class organized various modes of extraction in response to global market opportunities, but the rates of exchange for their exports were so unequal that the cycles of extraction and trade ultimately impoverished not only the physical and human environments, but also the dominant classes that depended on them (Bunker 1985).[47] Furthermore, the extractive industry is not cost effective if the earned currency from oil extraction is swallowed by foreign investors with little or no regard for the host communities. We should all be reminded that, irrespective of the wave of change in the international commodity market at any given time, the nature of conservancy, overall socioeconomic development, and the citizens' welfare are our constant and everlasting concern.

NOTES

1. Henry R. Linden, "World Oil — An Essay on its Spectacular 120-year Rise (1859-1979), Recent Decline, and Uncertain Future," *Journal of Energy Systems and Policy* 11, no. 2 (1987–88): 256.

2. Raymond Vernon, *The Oil Crisis* (New York: W. W. Norton, 1976), 229.

3. Richard J. Walton, *The Power of Oil* (New York: Seabury Press, 1977), 139.

4. Peter R. Odell, *Oil and World Power: Background to the Oil Crisis* (Middlesex, England: Penguin Books, 1970), 168.

5. Rilwanu Lukman, "The Energy Outlook: Possible Strategies for Oil Producers and Consumers," *OPEC Bulletin* (September 1988): 7.

6. Jafar M. Saad, "OPEC Oil Production and Pricing Polices," *OPEC Bulletin* (April 1988): 12.

7. George Horwich and David Leo Weimer, *Responding to International Oil Crises* (Washington, DC: American Enterprise Institute for Policy Research, 1984): 69.

8. J. R. Munkirs and J. T. Knoedler, "Petroleum Producing and Consuming Countries," *Journal of Economic Issues* 22, no. 1 (March 1988): 17.

9. Nazli Chouri, *International Politics of Energy Interdependence* (Lexington, MA: D. C. Heath, 1986), 43.

10. Rilwanu Lukman, "The Energy Outlook," 7.

11. Fadhil J. Al-Chalabi, *OPEC at the Crossroads: Past Critique and Future Vision* (Exeter, Great Britain: Pergamon Press, 1989),16.

12. Jafar M. Saad, "OPEC Oil Production," 12-15.

13. Fadhil J. Al-Chalabi, *OPEC at the Crossroads,* 34.

14. Peter Wright et al, "The Developing World to 1990: Trends and Implications for Multinational Business," *Long-Range Planning,* Vol. 15, no. 4 (1982): 190.

15. Rilwanu Lukman, "OPEC President Stresses Need to Restore Oil Market Certainty," *OPEC Bulletin* (November/December 1988): 6.

16. A. H. Taher, "Basic Problems and Policy Options," *Energy: A Global Outlook* (New York: Pergamon Press, 1982), 55.

17. A. H. Taher, "OPEC Developing Countries' Energy Situation," *Energy: A Global Outlook* (New York: Pergamon Press, 1982), 154.

18. Gerald Butt, "Iraqi Invasion Sparks Troubled World Response," *The Christian Science Monitor* (August 3, 1990):1.

19. J. Munkirs and J. Knoedler, "Petroleum Producing and Consuming Countries," 17.

20. Fadhil J. Al-Chalabi, "World Market in the 1990s," *OPEC Review* (Autumn 1988): 233.

21. Rilwanu Lukman, "The Energy Outlook," 5-8.

22. Gaadalli Al Fatti, "Security of Oil Supply and Demand," *OPEC Bulletin* (February 1989): 16.

23. Subroto, "Present Dynamics and Future Prospects for the Oil Market," *OPEC Bulletin* (February 1989): 9-10.

24. Ibrahim Youssef, *The Future of OPEC* (Washington, DC: Middle East Institute, 1984).

25. Fadhil J. Al-Chalabi, "Problems of World Energy Transition: A Producer's Point of View" (presentation at a seminar on development theory and cooperation sponsored by OAPEC, Rome, Italy, April 1981), as quoted in A. H. Taher's "The Case for Effective Cooperation," in *Energy: A Global Outlook* (New York: Pergamon Press, 1982), 155.

26. A. H. Taher, "OPEC Developing Countries Energy Situation" in *Energy: A Global Outlook* (New York: Pergamon Press, 1982), 155.

27. Carrol Bogart, "Autarky: A New Challenge. A Special Report on the Soviet Union," *Newsweek* (June 4, 1990): 23.

28. Ginger Szala, "Energy: Where the Players Stand," *Futures: The Magazine of Commodities and Options* 15, no. 10 (October 1986): 44.

29. Rilwanu Lukman, "The Energy Outlook," 5.

30. "OPEC: A Bloom and Burst Saga," *Development Outlook,* Vol. 1, no. 3 (August 1986): 15.

31. Tom Cutler, "Oil's Essential Role in War and Strategic Planning for Energy Security," *Petroleum Economist* (London: 1989).

32. Robertson Erc, "Oil Prices to Reach $27 by 1994," *OPEC Bulletin* (March 1988): 46.

33. Prices are assumed to be at a 2 percent interest rate.

34. Ira Sohn, "External Debt and Oil Prices: Some Prospects for Oil Exporting Developing Countries," *Energy Policy* (October 1987): 408-13.

35. Rilwanu Lukman, "Nigeria's Outlook on International Cooperation for a Stable Oil Market," *OPEC Bulletin* (October 1988): 3.

36. Yusufu Bala Usman, "The 1990 Budget and Our Future," *Nigeria Homenews* (January 25-31, 1990): 4.

37. Ira Sohn, "External Debt," 418-19.

38. Raymond Baril, "Community Impact Management: Models for Compensation," paper presented at the Annual Conference of the Canadian Nuclear Society, Montreal, Quebec, June 1983.

39. M. Redcliff, "Sustainable Development: Exploring the Contradictions," *Journal of Development Studies* 25, no. 1 (October 1988): 127.

40. Ali M. Parhizgari, "Optimum Depletion of Oil Resources in a Developing Country," *Energy Journal* 8, no. 3 (July 1987): 32.

41. Alan Gelb, *Oil Windfalls: Blessing or Curse?* (New York: Oxford University Press, World Bank Publication, 1988).

42. Alberta Heritage Savings Trust Fund, *Annual Report 1986-1987* (Edmonton, Alberta, 1986), 4.

43. Mohammed Siqqi, *Economic Security in Islam* (Lahore, Pakistan: Kazi Publications, 1939), 24.

44. *Alhadis*, vol. 2, in Alhaj Maulaka F. Karim, *The Book House,* (Lahore, Pakistan, 1939), Chapter 18, p. 256.

45. *Holy Bible,* Corinthians 1:12 (New York: Thomas Nelson, 1982), 1122.

46. United Methodist Church, *The Book of Resolution of the United Methodist Church* (Nashville: United Methodist Publishing House, 1988), 35.

47. Stephen Bunker, *Extractive Economies: The Underdevelopment of the Amazon* (Urbana, IL: University of Illinois Press, 1985).

Appendix

Table A.1

Nigeria: Federal Government Expenditures
by Social Service Category, 1964–84 (in million naira)

	Education	Health	Housing	Power	Roads
1964	14,498	22,428	22,062	1,064	9,448
1965	14,064	25,930	28,752	1,064	13,368
1966	15,536	31,064	19,914	1,065	18,932
1967	15,872	30,476	11,444	1,065	19,836
1968	18,452	29,918	5,942	1,065	19,438
1969	18,420	26,190	3,274	1,065	13,174
1970	18,580	2,050	26	1,133	1,392
1971	3,494	976	584	1,133	1,397
1972	3,307	2,838	239	1,133	1,393
1973	5,655	2,448	1,824	1,133	1,393
1974	12,469	5,062	2,116	1,133	1,395
1975	25,438	22,000	2,352	1,335	1,693
1976	11,162	22,700	2,205	2,406	3,986
1977	24,831	22,703	2,299	3,333	8,986
1978	39,470	11,980	2,340	2,332	10,310
1979	36,040	13,244	1,967	3,861	1,063
1980	36,043	18,341	2,080	5,400	1,083
1981	4,900	2,400	3,184	4,800	1,358
1982	4,900	2,400	3,184	4,800	1,358
1983	4,900	2,400	3,184	4,800	1,358
1984	4,900	2,400	3,184	4,800	1,358

Sources: 1. Analyses of government accounts 1958, 1978, and 1977 from the Federal Office of Statistics, Lagos, Nigeria 1979: Table 2, p. 2; Table 22, p. 39; and Table 88, p. 105. Figures may be final consumption expenditures (1964–74). 2. *Economic and Social Statistics Bulletin,* Federal Office of Statistics, Lagos, Nigeria, 1985: Table 32, p. 31; Tables 34 and 35, pp. 33-35. Figures for 1981–84 are averages from the 1981–85 development plan.

Table A.2

Nigeria: Regional Expenditures by Social Service Category, 1964–75 (in million naira)

Name Of Agency	Measure	1964	1965	1966	1967
1. Govt. of	Education	14,412	15,654	17,252	23,394
Northern	Health	6,366	8,010	8,402	10,186
Nigeria	Housing	3,806	4,462	4,144	4,890
	Power	300	300	300	300
	Roads	3,000	2,376	4,498	7,682
	Water	1,020	1,020	1,020	1,020

1967 Administrative Changes

	Measure	1968	1969	1970	1971	1972	1973	1974	1975
1b. Govt.	Education	2,652	3,194	1,780	1,780	1,436	2,611	6,509	11,094
of North-	Health	1,774	982	1,220	1,561	2,199	4,151	5,652	6,012
Eastern	Housing	843	467	1,242	4,574	10,115	5,273	7,294	15,158
Nigeria	Power	60	60	—	—	—	—	—	46
	Roads	1,424	102	352	352	352	352	352	260
	Water	—	—	1506	1506	1506	1506	1506	190
2. North	Education	2,652	3,194	1,092	1,092	1,620	2,438	3,622	3,672
Western	Health	1,774	1,472	1,472	2,126	2,633	2,852	6,667	9,941
State	Housing	,843	,467	2,270	5,232	1,033	12,006	4,257	9,192
Govt.	Power	60	60	—	—	—	—	—	1,677
	Roads	1,424	102	662	662	662	662	662	418
	Water	225	225	225	172	172	172	172	5,200
3. Benue	Education	2,652	3,194	954	852	1,735	2,086	2,086	3,809
Plateau	Health	1,774	1,402	1,402	1,466	2,154	614	614	5,074
State	Housing	843	467	928	1,250	4,436	7,437	7,437	7,748
Govt.	Power	60	60	—	—	—	—	—	48
	Roads	1,424	102	1,402	1,402	1,402	1,402	1,402	532
	Water	225	225	866	866	866	866	866	9,116
4. North	Education	2,652	3,194	954	852	1,735	2,086	2,086	3,809
Eastern	Health	1,774	1,594	2,244	3,266	3,218	3,974	7,333	15,290
State	Housing	843	467	1,266	52,104	7,079	7,077	8,875	1,700
Govt.	Power	60	60	—	—	—	—	—	40
	Road	1,424	102	565	565	565	565	565	138
	Water	225	225	541	541	541	541	541	5,362
5. Kano	Education	2,652	3,194	1,358	1,674	2,164	2,658	2,386	5,982
State	Health	1,774	1,597	1,768	3,378	3,895	5,618	9,262	9,467
Govt.	Housing	843	467	6,340	11,148	10,918	7,765	1,498	1,395
	Power	60	60	—	—	—	—	—	260
	Roads	1,424	102	1,100	1,100	1,100	1,100	1,100	258
	Water	142	142	900	900	900	900	900	492

Table A.2 (cont.)

	Measure	1968	1969	1970	1971	1972	1973	1974	1975
6. Kwara	Education	2,652	3,194	1,052	1,282	1,552	1,263	1,213	4,816
State	Health	1,774	1,597	1,182	1,658	2,876	3,040	4,995	8,150
Govt.	Housing	843	467	1,980	5,224	5,147	3,904	9,025	7,889
	Power	60	60	–	–	–	–	–	300
	Roads	1,424	102	670	670	670	670	670	1,760
	Water	225	225	6,078	6,076	6,076	6,076	6,076	4,556

Sources: 1. *Analyses of Government Accounts, 1958-1977,* (Lagos, Nigeria: Federal Office of Statistics, 1979) Table 5, p. 5. 1b. Ibid. Table 36, p. 53. 2. Ibid. Table 38, p. 54. 3. Ibid. Table 29, p. 46. 4. Ibid. Table 37, p. 54. 5. Ibid. Table 32, p. 49. 6. Ibid. Table 33, p. 50.

Notes: Figures may be final consumption expenditures or average capital expenditure estimate.

Figures for power, water, and roads are derived averages from public capital expenditure for 1970–74 and 1975–80 development plans. Third National Plan: Federal Ministry Planning 197, pp. 23, 349.

Figures for housing 1970–76 are estimated from *Analyses of Government Accounts,* Tables 77, 78, 81, 82, and 83.

Table A.3

Northern Nigeria: Regional Expenditures by Social Service Category, 1976–84 (in million naira)

Administrative Agency	Measure	1976	1977	1978	1979	1980	1981	1982	1983	1984
1. Kaduna State	Education	2,026	2,026	12,744	12,745	16,781	5,197	5,197	6,498	31,016
	Health	5,652	4,048	5,437	5,438	9,943	10,143	2,252	1,882	9,797
	Housing	5,739	5,739	5,740	5,740	3,456	1,233	1,233	1,600	1,700
	Power	2,440	2,440	2,440	2,442	2,500	4,288	4,288	5,085	1,765
	Roads	2,339	2,340	2,339	2,396	24,500	2,836	2,836	5,085	5,260
	Water	1,679	1,680	9,015	9,015	2,063	4,615	4,615	5,310	5,302
2. Niger State	Education	19,409	19,409	11,065	27,423	27,423	35,170	35,170	35,180	18,265
	Health	10,457	10,457	10,609	25,650	25,650	26,650	26,650	26,650	3,155
	Housing	8,000	8,000	10,750	10,750	6,600	8,500	8,500	8,500	14,100
	Power	5,000	5,000	2,000	5,072	5,072	2,194	2,194	2,194	2,000
	Roads	26,847	26,848	11,240	14,083	14,083	23,845	23,845	23,845	8,630
	Water	23,100	23,100	10,399	10,398	3,989	3,989	3,989	3,989	1,650
3. Sokoto State	Education	3,355	3,711	27,449	24,290	28,551	32,128	13,598	17,402	7,816
	Health	1,233	1,989	2,499	2,622	6,717	8,670	6,798	3,194	2,044
	Housing	9,192	508	378	2,000	1,361	18,738	11,843	26,691	20,250
	Power	2,325	3,500	3,500	3,000	2,674	9,055	2,335	3,334	2,841
	Roads	7,722	5,995	9,337	15,002	18,642	32,431	16,747	13,494	4,175
	Water	7,557	2,463	12,206	12,339	13,188	9,083	5,643	6,164	31,135
4. Benue State	Education	15,708	15,708	15,708	15,708	15,708	30,696	30,696	30,696	30,696
	Health	7,030	7,030	7,030	7,030	7,030	11,350	11,350	11,350	11,350
	Housing	20,000	20,000	20,000	20,000	20,000	25,000	25,000	25,000	25,000
	Power	2,400	2,400	2,400	2,400	2,400	4,000	4,000	4,000	4,000
	Roads	23,991	23,991	23,991	23,991	23,991	47,584	47,584	47,584	47,584
	Water	9,116	9,116	9,116	9,116	9,116	25,340	25,340	25,340	25,340
5. Plateau State	Education	13,881	13,881	13,881	13,881	13,881	39,200	39,200	39,200	39,200
	Health	35,105	35,105	35,105	35,105	35,105	20,324	20,324	20,324	20,324
	Housing	2,000	2,000	2,000	2,000	2,000	5,200	5,200	5,200	5,200
	Power	3,000	3,000	3,000	3,000	3,000	6,000	6,000	6,000	6,000
	Roads	17,123	17,123	17,123	17,123	17,123	29,402	29,402	29,402	29,402
	Water	7,668	7,668	7,668	7,668	7,668	21,612	21,612	21,612	21,612
6. Bauchi State	Education	16,353	64,120	28,862	35,733	33,333	3,690	3,690	52,718	46,047
	Health	5,210	5,627	5,218	15,186	15,707	4,141	4,142	55,787	93,012
	Housing	1,166	1,167	8,750	1,000	1,000	68,000	68,000	7,748	14,000
	Power	2,000	2,000	3,080	3,080	3,080	5,000	5,000	10,000	9,000
	Roads	2,155	13,750	16,165	23,041	33,300	7,206	7,206	31,200	33,503
	Water	7,411	8,575	5,556	6,686	12,136	2,029	2,030	27,500	5,000
7. Borno State	Education	7,866	9,866	9,866	17,139	17,139	13,086	13,086	13,086	11,800
	Health	3,350	3,350	9,680	9,680	9,680	9,680	1,904	1,904	2,500
	Housing	1,000	1,000	1,500	1,500	1,500	1,502	1,502	1,502	7,200
	Power	2,000	2,000	4,612	4,612	4,612	10,000	10,000	10,000	12,000
	Roads	9,808	23,900	23,910	12,178	12,178	40,000	40,000	40,000	16,600
	Water	8,122	8,122	8,222	8,222	8,222	30,000	30,000	30,000	7,300
8. Gongola State	Education	1,611	2,566	8,315	1,054	1,360	58,380	58,380	12,939	12,938
	Health	4,930	1,065	1,185	2,668	4,231	2,174	2,405	4,053	10,000
	Housing	7,000	1,356	2,000	2,000	3,300	5,200	5,200	2,349	2,350
	Power	5,774	1,389	1,390	1,545	1,545	4,950	6,633	7,992	7,992
	Roads	11,387	11,387	13,884	13,885	13,150	30,774	30,774	23,320	36,726
	Water	2,227	2,228	19,167	5,694	4,274	1,732	25,430	25,429	43,055

243

Table A.3 (cont.)

Administrative Agency	measure	1976	1977	1978	1979	1980	1981	1982	1983	1984
9. Kano State	Education	5,982	9,492	9,491	9,491	39,327	39,337	71,420	6,360	8,226
	Health	9,262	9,463	9,467	9,470	14,800	14,793	24,912	10,145	18,100
	Housing	1,377	1,386	1,386	2,457	2,460	6,977	15,835	8,610	7,520
	Power	5,760	5,760	5,800	1,080	1,080	9,333	5,200	7,700	5,200
	Roads	4,686	7,158	2,602	2,604	2,604	32,906	54,000	42,900	52,400
	Water	2,556	2,556	4,473	4,473	4,500	2,462	48,000	38,000	36,000
10. Kwara State	Education	1,061	1,062	1,230	1,945	1,945	9,147	9,147	9,148	9,147
	Health	1,149	3,452	3,452	5,277	5,277	5,674	5,674	5,675	5,685
	Housing	7,880	2,603	2,008	1,760	1,760	1,690	1,690	1,692	1,692
	Power	3,000	3,000	3,000	3,000	3,000	2,960	2,961	2,961	2,961
	Roads	15,566	15,566	15,566	15,566	15,566	15,228	15,228	15,238	15,223
	Water	1,364	7,977	7,978	5,982	5,983	9,052	9,052	9,052	9,052

Sources: 1. Capital estimates of Kaduna State in *Analyses of Government Accounts* (Lagos, Nigeria: Federal Office of Statistics, 1979), Table 36, p. 53. 1b. Capital estimates of Kaduna: Ministry of Planning (Kaduna), *Expenditure Summary,* 1980, p. 351; 1984, p. 425. 2. Estimates of Niger State: Government of Nigeria, Ministry of Finance, *Minna,* 1977–78, p. 149; 1984, pp. 197-203. 3. Estimates of Sokoto State: *Government Summary Sectors,* 1977–78, p. 181; 1978–79, p. 187; and 1984, p. 195. 4. *Analyses of Government Accounts* (Lagos, Nigeria: Federal Office of Statistics, 1979), Table 89, p. 106; capital estimates of Benue (p. 194); and Plateau State governments (p. 206), Federal Office of Statistics, Lagos, 1985. 5. Ibid. 6. Estimates of the Bauchi State government: Minister of Planning, Bauchi, Nigeria, *Capital Estimates Summary by Subsector,* 1977–78, p. 133; and 1984, p. 202. 7. Capital estimates of Borno State (1984). Ministry of Economic Planning, Maduguri, 1977–78 and 1984, pp. 153, 401. 8. Capital estimates of Yola State government, 1984, p. 224. 9. Estimates of Kano State government: *Capital Expenditure Summary* (1983), 1981–1985 Plan, p. 264. 10. Estimates of Kwara State government: Illorin 1979–80, p. 166. Figures are averages for 1975–80 and 1981–85.

Table A.4

Eastern Nigeria: Regional Expenditures by Social Service Category, 1964–84 (in million naira)

Administrative Agency	Measure	1964	1965	1966	1967
Eastern	Education	13,104	17,474	19,040	22,596
Nigeria	Health	4,270	3,834	4,939	5,780
Regional	Housing	2,324	3,310	3,346	7,144
Government	Power	120	120	120	120
	Roads	2,920	2,726	2,496	6,472
	Water	1,020	1,020	1,020	1,020

Eastern Nigeria Administrative Changes in 1967

Name Of Agency	Measure	1968	1969	1970	1971	1972	1973	1974	1975	1976
1.Govt.	Education	—	—	—	19,746	19,710	19,744	23,183	7,236	7,254
of East	Health	—	—	—	4,552	5,408	6,220	6,559	5,564	9,596
Central	Housing	—	—	—	666	614	657	841	363	363
State	Power	—	—	—	—	—	—	—	2,400	2,400
	Roads	—	—	—	1,000	1,000	1,000	1,000	100	100
	Water	—	—	—	853	853	853	853	853	853
2. Govt.	Education	—	—	—	1,994	2,308	2,697	436	1,508	8,759
of South	Health	—	—	—	1,902	2,232	3,185	3,741	1,541	2,936
Eastern	Housing	—	—	—	294	372	456	538	403	3,000
State	Power	—	—	—	—	—	—	—	200	662
	Roads	—	—	—	74	346	752	219	1,682	5,105
	Water	—	—	—	408	408	408	408	1,901	1,901
3. Govt.	Education	—	—	—	192	32	2,053	10,532	1,288	2,556
of Rivers	Health	—	—	—	1,730	1,902	2,627	3,589	5,431	5,484
State	Housing	—	—	—	2,362	3,958	6,733	39,409	52,142	2,000
	Power	—	—	—	—	—	—	—	400	1,000
	Roads	—	—	—	488	734	660	2,568	1,428	10,130
	Water	—	—	—	620	620	620	620	1,520	1,520

Table A.4 (cont.)

Agency	Measure	1977	1978	1979	1980	1981	1982	1983	1984
4. Govt.	Education	19,141	21,447	10,172	11,314	3,624	3,624	3,624	7,400
of Anambra	Health	7,100	3,658	4,361	5,192	1,917	1,917	1,917	1,917
State	Housing	1,900	3,947	1,000	1,000	1,000	1,000	1,000	1,000
	Power	2,000	3,090	1,000	1,000	10,000	10,000	10,000	10,200
	Roads	18,199	14,296	9,059	4,595	4,361	4,361	4,361	8,004
	Water	16,799	14,830	7,000	10,100	25,345	25,345	25,345	25,345
5. Govt.	Education	10,436	1,390	1,431	16,120	3,415	3,415	3,415	3,415
of Cross	Health	3,598	3,098	3,195	4,450	1,299	1,299	1,299	1,299
River	Housing	1,600	585	1,000	2,250	1,120	1,120	1,120	1,120
State	Power	9,200	500	1,000	1,000	8,100	8,100	8,100	8,100
	Roads	8,620	8,318	6,000	6,450	4,376	4,376	4,376	4,376
	Water	1,901	7,107	6,150	8,600	2,450	2,450	2,450	2,450
6. Govt.	Education	2,168	11,290	11,290	4,540	4,540	4,540	4,540	13,250
of Rivers	Health	5,484	5,484	7,545	1,166	1,166	1,166	1,166	3,450
State	Housing	3,016	3,016	5,683	2,624	2,624	2,624	2,624	5,000
	Power	13,000	6,587	5,661	1,682	1,682	1,682	1,682	7,000
	Roads	1,034	1,040	1,040	1,040	4,380	4,380	4,380	13,680
	Water	1,520	1,520	1,520	1,520	14,340	14,340	14,340	14,340
7. Govt.	Education	5,801	29,839	12,245	5,451	5,451	24,304	38,350	4,186
of Imo	Health	14,883	62,821	14,030	33,897	25,150	24,200	7,660	5,839
State	Housing	4,460	3,000	3,000	7,533	5,457	8,500	18,000	1,000
	Power	2,000	2,000	3,000	6,755	6,801	58,200	24,139	5,100
	Roads	2,411	5,972	10,180	13,081	13,081	26,800	42,376	7,977
	Water	11,681	26,151	10,266	10,800	3,000	24,000	41,022	19,797

Sources: *Analysis of Government Accounts,* 1981-84 averaged. 1958/59 to 1977, Federal Office of Statistics, Lagos, Nigeria, 1979, Table 4, p. 4; Table 18, p. 27; Table 24, p. 41; Table 90, p. 107; Table 99, p. 116; and Table 100, p. 117. Capital estimates of Anambra State government, Enugu, Nigeria, 1979/80, 1980, pp. 202 and 1985, p. 173. Capital estimates of Cross River State government, Calabar, Nigeria, 1975/80, pp. 235 and 289. Capital estimates of Rivers State government, Port Harcourt, 1979/80 and 1984, pp. 353 and 393. Capital Estimates of Imo State government, 1978/79, 1979/80, and 1984, pp. 231, 274, and 275.

Notes: In 1976 the government of East Central State was renamed the government of Anambra State and the Government of South Eastern State was renamed the government of Cross River State. Imo State was created from East Central State in 1976. The government of Rivers State was not renamed.

Table A.5

Western Nigeria: Regional Expenditures by Social Service Category, 1964–84

Name of Agency	Measure	1964	1965	1966	1967	1968	1969
1. Govt.	Education	1,310	3,438	1,890	3,664	3,516	3,446
of Western	Health	188	248	394	228	572	1,068
Nigeria	Housing	346	5,414	5,042	2,076	3,454	3,570
	Power	250	250	250	250	250	250
	Roads	992	698	1,378	3,160	4,704	3,206
	Water	197	197	197	1,642	1,642	1,642

Name of Agency	Measure	1970	1971	1972	1973	1974	1975	1976
1. Govt.	Education	3,445	2,118	2,444	3,303	9,364	6,047	2,240
of Western	Health	1,068	4,702	5,770	6,199	8,427	12,910	1,180
Nigeria	Housing	3,570	368	374	776	1,040	1,859	660
(cont.)	Power	—	—	—	—	—	350	560
	Roads	2,103	2,103	2,103	2,103	2,103	2,100	2,100
	Water	2,886	2,886	2,886	2,886	2,886	3,500	3,500

Administrative Changes in Western Nigeria, 1976

New Name of Agency	Measure	1977	1978	1979	1980	1981	1982	1983	1984
2. Oyo	Education	3,693	7,038	5,315	5,315	95,802	95,802	95,802	95,802
State	Health	7,119	18,741	1,227	1,227	23,726	23,726	23,726	23,726
Govt.	Housing	3,256	3,256	4,187	4,187	16,000	16,000	16,000	16,000
	Power	190	190	2,732	2,732	5,374	5,374	5,374	5,374
	Roads	700	700	1,265	1,265	38,757	38,757	38,757	38,757
	Water	117	8,755	8,755	8,755	33,492	33,492	33,492	33,492
3. Ogun	Education	3,036	3,594	3,739	7,544	55,887	55,887	55,887	55,887
State	Health	4,073	7,838	5,879	6,195	18,484	18,484	18,484	18,484
Govt.	Housing	4,441	1,308	2,616	2,602	1,441	1,441	1,441	1,441
	Power	190	190	190	190	5,000	5,000	5,000	5,000
	Roads		850	13,082	1,500	3,000	14,928	14,928	14,928	14,928
	Water	1,500	1,683	1,296	9,615	2,086	2,085	2,085	2,085

Table A-5(cont.)

4.Ondo	Education	2,313	2,312	2,127	2,855	54,849	54,849	54,849	54,849
State	Health	2,243	2,243	2,243	17,003	20,733	20,733	20,733	20,733
Govt.	Housing	2,244	2,244	3,160	1,961	6,432	6,432	6,432	6,432
	Power	190	190	190	190	9,110	9,110	9,110	9,110
	Roads	3,694	3,694	3,694	5,225	60,596	60,596	60,596	60,596
	Water	117	117	4,735	4,735	28,184	28,184	28,184	28,184

Sources: 1. *Analyses of Government Accounts, 1958–77,* (Lagos, Nigeria: Federal Office of Statistics, 1979), Tables 3, 17, pp. 3, 23; and Table 101, p. 118. Capital expenditures first and second national development plans (Lagos, Nigeria: Federal Government Printers, 1962 and 1970), 13, 273. 2. Capital estimates of Oyo State, Ibadan, Nigeria, 1977–78, p. 12; 1977–80, p. 10; 1982, p. 11. Averages for 1981-84 are derived from 1981–85 Development Plans. 3. Ibid. Capital estimates of Ogun State government (Abeokuta), 1978–79 and 1979–80. Averages are estimated as in (2) above. 4. Capital estimates of Ondo State, Akure, Nigeria, 1979–80, 1980, pp. 12, 14. Average estimates for 1981–84 are derived as (2).

Table A.6

Midwestern Nigeria (Bendel State) and Lagos State: Expenditures by Social Service Category, 1964–84

Agency	Measure	1964	1965	1966	1967	1968	1969
Midwestern	Power	125	125	125	125	125	—
Nigeria	Roads	904	1,387	1,164	390	3,994	408
	Health	98	104	602	34	176	2,161
	Education	502	552	734	1,258	1,652	1,388
	Water	—	—	—	—	—	420
	Housing	652	2,076	1,440	2,313	2,848	2,848
Govt. of	Power	—	—	—	—	—	—
Lagos	Roads	—	—	—	—	254	372
State	Health	—	—	—	—	4,934	4,896
1967–84	Education	—	—	—	—	4,888	4,954
	Water	—	—	—	—	—	—
	Housing	—	—	—	—	—	38

Agency	Measure	1970	1971	1972	1973	1974	1975
Midwestern	Power	—	—	—	—	—	4,624
Nigeria	Roads	1,878	1,878	1,878	1,978	1,778	4,251
	Health	2,746	470	875	1,155	1,350	759
	Education	1,104	1,236	2,665	684	633	6,212
	Water	420	74	74	74	74	1,469
	Housing	5,060	7,878	7,920	9,629	11,410	7,629
Govt. of	Power	—	—	—	—	—	40
Lagos	Roads	144	142	234	554	558	9471
State	Health	6,620	8,372	8,812	9,998	8,052	16,568
1967–84	Education	758	860	1,272	2,030	3,947	4,006
	Water	870	870	870	870	870	9,280
	Housing	340	2,362	4,894	2,796	10,248	480

Agency	Measure	1976	1977	1978	1979
Bendel	Power	4,624	4,624	4,624	4,624
State of	Roads	4,251	4,251	4,251	4,251
Nigeria	Health	7,350	7,350	7,350	7,350
	Education	6,444	6,444	6,444	6,444
	Water	1,469	1,469	1,469	1,469
	Housing	5,240	5,240	5,240	5,240

Table A.6 (cont.)

Agency	Measure	1976	1977	1978	1979
Govt. of	Power	40	40	40	40
Lagos	Roads	6,679	6,679	6,679	6,679
State	Health	19,943	10,799	11,260	11,260
1967–84	Education	18,777	5,218	7,956	7,956
	Water	9,280	9,280	9,280	9,280
	Housing	480	480	480	480

Agency	Measure	1980	1981	1982	1983	1984
Bendel	Power	4,624	2,580	2,580	2,580	2,580
State of	Roads	4,251	6,783	6,783	6,783	6,783
Nigeria	Health	7,350	1,070	1,070	1,070	1,070
	Education	6,440	5,590	5,590	5,590	5,590
	Water	1,469	1,942	1,942	1,942	1,942
	Housing	5,240	1,500	1,500	1,500	1,500
Govt. of	Power	40	65	65	65	65
Lagos	Roads	6,679	1,191	1,191	1,191	1,191
State	Health	11,620	2,995	2,995	2,995	2,995
1967–84	Education	7,956	7,452	7,452	7,452	7,452
	Water	9,280	1,142	1,142	1,142	1,142
	Housing	480	2,646	2,646	2,646	2,646

Sources: 1. *Analyses of Government Accounts 1958 To 1977,* (Lagos, Nigeria: Federal Office of Statistics, 1979), Table 110, p. 127, Table 80, p. 97, Table 95, p. 112. 2. Capital expenditure, Federation of Nigeria First National Development Plan 1962–68 (Lagos, Nigeria: The Nigerian National Press, 1962), P. 13. 3. Figures for 1970–74, 1975–80, and 1981–84 are Averages estimated from sectoral distribution of public sector capital investment as recommended in the Second, Third, and Fourth National Development Plans. See P. Olayiwola, *Petroleum And Structural Change* (New York: Praeger, 1987), Table 8.2, p. 145. 4. Summary of capital estimates 1979–80 and 1981–85, Bendel State government, Benin City, Nigeria, pp. 443, 1044. 5. Ibid., Tables 21, 26, 79, pp. 37 And 43; Table 94, p. 111. 6. Lagos State capital estimates (average estimates from Total Allocation Plan 1975–80, 1981–85), pp. 80 and 293.

Table A.7a

Nigeria: Oil Production and Producing Areas

Name of field, discovery date	Depth, ft.	No. of wells Producing	No. of wells Total	1986 average b/d	Production Cumulative to Dec 31, 1986 bbl	*API gravity
AGIP-PHILLIPS						
Akri, 1977	9,600-10,600	6	11	8,465	59,065,599	41.8
Akri West, 1975	9,900-10,200	–	2	–	482,258	31.4
Ashaka, 1968	9,700-12,000	1	1	429	2,128,652	36.7
Beniku, 1974	12,000	1	2	360	3,309,326	29.7
Ebegoro, 1976	11,500-12,000	7	9	8,885	56,328,995	35.7
Ebocha, 1965	8,000-10,900	10	16	7,794	105,779,769	36.2
Idu, 1973	7,750-10,700	–	10	–	23,862,581	28.0
Kwale, 1968	10,000-11,500	3	4	1,154	3,095,572	41.5
M'Bede, 1966	7,300-9,400	11	14	14,984	152,227,985	41.6
Obama, 1975	11,600-14,300	11	8	17,643	86,517,279	40.8
Obiafu, 1973	9,300-12,200	13	17	11,991	75,575,425	43.9
Obrikom, 1973	8,000-10,000	7	12	6,173	52,019,234	41.5
Odugri, 1972	12,500	1	2	730	9,434,454	40.2
Ogbogene, 1976	10,000	–	2	–	3,302,763	37.0
Ogbogene W., 1981	13,000	–	1	–	353,135	56.2
Okpai, 1968	10,000-12,000	8	8	3,832	16,139,904	44.3
Omoku W., 1975	11,500	1	1	634	4,716,282	27.4
Oshi, 1974	9,600-11,300	15	11	10,529	59,744,703	37.7
Tebidaba, 1975	10,300-13,300	13	10	19,277	105,788,553	34.7
Umuoru, 1975	14,100	3	4	1,974	3,698,886	42.2
Agwe, 1977	10,800	–	1	–	1,998,132	47.9
Clough Creek, 1977	10,000-12,400	11	9	9,519	16,890,585	35.6
Beniboye N.	9,000-10,000	9	9	8,513	5,233,810	33.9
Taylor Creek, 1985	13,724	–	–	–	–	–

Table A.7a (cont.)

Name of field, discovery date	Depth, ft.	No. of wells Producing	No. of wells Total	Production 1986 average b/d	Production Cumulative to Dec 31, 1986 bbl	*API gravity
PHILLIPS						
CHEVRON						
Gilli-Gilli, 1967	7,600-14,000	2	2	1,036	2,956,448	46.7
Abiteye, 1970	5,750-9,400	12	19	10,264	59,300,936	39.7
*Delta, 1965	5,600-9,500	22	27	18,889	157,813,222	37.3
*Delta South, 1965	7,100-10,179	18	27	25,807	26,336,514	38.4
*Isan, 1970	5,900-9,000	4	11	2,307	41,381,423	40.4
Makaraba	7,100-12,005	12	26	23,811	78,212,263	27.7
*Malu, 1969	4,800-6,300	12	18	16,864	91,734,394	40.4
*Mefa, 1965	8,570-12,030	4	5	5,516	15,533,842	38.1
*Meji, 1965	5,200-10,900	19	22	17,723	139,025,576	31.9
*Meren, 1965	5,000-7,500	28	51	59,359	453,033,041	31.9
*Okan, 1964	5,500-9,245	36	67	37,026	416,770,100	38.1
*Parabe/Eko, 1968	4,500-8,200	11	23	6,702	96,307,191	40.4
Utonana, 1971	7,400-9,165	2	5	640	7,660,783	20.4
*W. Isan, 1971	7,825-10,229	4	9	3,028	33,221,198	40.4
Yorla South	1,389-12,635	–	2	–	834,040	41.0
Jisike, 1975	6,300-7,600	3	4	2,261	5,138,087	41.1
Robertkiri, 1964	11,484-13,190	5	12	5,398	5,280,997	40.2
*Tapa, 1978	8,150-10,842	10	10	11,527	243,737,794	39.5
AMLAND						
Izombe-Ossu, 1974	9,500	15	15	12,409	46,855,328	41.0
*Akam, 1980	6,700	9	9	9,331	11,651,481	35.2
*Adanga, 1980	5,600-7,300	8	8	15,739	5,804,731	35.0
ELF						
Aghgo, 1972	–	15	22	3,815	21,313,918	24.8
Okpoko, 1967	–	10	24	10,203	26,873,488	24.8
Obodo-Jatumi, 1966	–	22	25	11,251	56,679,802	24.8
Upamini, 1965	–	11	18	2,443	14,178,237	24.8
Obagi, 1964	–	70	77	54,576	334,488,915	24.5
Erema, 1972	–	4	5	3,851	7,863,600	24.6
MOBIL						
*Adua, 1967	6,970	4	5	8,493	40,238,557	30.3
*Asabo, 1966	5,600	8	14	14,747	151,393,607	32.4

		Production				
Name of field, discovery date	Depth, ft.	No. of wells		1986 average b/d	Cumulative to Dec 31, 1986 bbl	*API gravity
		Producing	Total			
*Ekpe, 1966	8,200	5	17	5,867	182,909,275	30.3
*Ekpe-WW, 1977	6,810	6	6	9,913	30,203,047	30.3
*Eku, 1966	5,420	1	6	1,608	14,861,191	30.8
*Enang, 1968	6,600	18	23	18,531	113,277,609	35.1
*Etim, 1968	6,200	7	9	18,594	99,114,888	32.9
*Idoho, 1966	9,020	3	4	2,030	27,976,695	30.8
Inim, 1966	5,850	8	10	17,726	133,519,784	37.8
Mfem, 1967	5,200	3	3	4,339	22,653,656	36.1
*Ubit, 1968	5,400	30	45	27,191	168,257,669	36.1
*Unam, 1968	5,180	6	9	6,733	38,167,314	33.5
*Utue, 1966	5,700	4	7	7,536	64,123,484	36.8
*Isobo, 1968	7,345	3	4	2,037	6,357,841	30.8
*Iyak	–	6	6	23,718	26,314,070	38.7
*Asabo 'D'	–	1	2	1,327	1,373,470	35.0
*Ata	–	–	–	–	433	–
*Oso	–	–	–	–	8,421	–
*Usarf	–	–	–	–	5,885	–
IMPEX						
Ogharefe, 1973	9,900	8	11	5,455	26,387,218	47.4
SHELL (MIDWEST)						
Ugh-Ogini, 1964	5,860	5	18	2,491	20,050,706	19.0
Ugh-Uzere-East, 1960	8,500	8	14	3,972	84,448,451	23.0
Ugh-Uzere-West, 1964	8,500	5	11	3,035	98,300,602	23.0
Ugh-Olomoro, 1963	7,000-10,000	14	33	15,258	269,882,416	22.0
Ugh-Oweh, 1964	12,300	4	11	2,331	91,616,216	28.0
Ugh-Kokori, 1960	8,000-9,800	17	27	13,809	304,530,524	42.0
Ugh-Afiesere, 1961	8,000-9,000	20	33	9,711	111,236,709	22.0
Ugh-Eriemu, 1961	12,500	14	16	5,539	39,559,309	26.0
Ugh-Ughelli-East, 1959	11,800	5	11	2,673	87,679,532	35.0
Ugh-Ughelli-West, 1963	7,400-10,200	5	10	2,880	30,963,842	21.0
Ugh-Utorogu, 1964	9,000	8	19	6,134	127,088,672	25.0

Table A.7a (cont.)

Name of field, discovery date	Depth, ft.	No. of wells Producing	No. of wells Total	Production 1986 average b/d	Production Cumulative to Dec 31, 1986 bbl	*API gravity
Ugh-Oroni, 1964	12,000	1	7	583	25,514,529	22.0
Ugh-Warri-River, 1961	12,264	1	3	990	14,521,505	31.0
Ugh-Evwreni, 1968	10,900	5	11	2,805	34,380,013	38.0
Ugh-Isoko, 1960	—	1	2	819	5,660,976	19.0
Forc-Odidi, 1967	10,980	14	25	17,480	196,223,250	37.0
Forc-Opukushi, 1963	7,823	4	15	16,307	104,736,336	29.0
Forc-Jones Creek, 1967	7,000-9,000	14	34	23,215	376,852,060	29.0
Rapele	—	1	3	1,499	22,052,181	44.4
Amukpe	—	1	2	978	11,211,014	38.9
Osioka	—	—	2	168	6,807,890	—
SHELL (EAST)						
Phl-Bomu, 1958	6,500-7,500	14	38	11,439	347,257,106	36.0
Phl-Imo River, 1959	5,800-10,000	29	45	33,564	445,753,287	32.0
Phl-Nkali, 1963	12,000	1	10	25	27,186,884	42.0
Phl-Elelenwa, 1959	11,000	3	11	2,011	29,671,024	39.0
Phl-Umuechem, 1969	5,800-10,700	8	18	6,646	145,124,471	36.0
Phl-Apara, 1960	9,000	5	7	4,404	23,171,605	36.0
Phl-Bodo-West, 1959	9,700	7	11	6,678	76,098,573	29.0
Phl-Afam, 1956	6,000	9	15	4,035	57,269,591	45.0
Phl-Yorla, 1970	11,917	7	13	4,704	57,022,633	44.0
Phs-Bonny, 1959	12,254	7	17	6,526	85,206,972	36.0
Phs-Cawthorne Channel, 1963	11,000	16	28	44,096	252,045,390	38.0
Phs-Ekulama, 1958	10,483	17	29	32,140	178,116,398	32.0
Phs-Soku, 1958	11,500	12	21	10,481	103,207,438	31.0
Phs-Orubiri, 1971	—	2	6	4,008	14,768,373	38.0
Egb-Oguta, 1965	10,300	9	24	9,738	126,067,988	46.0
Eade-Utapate South, 1974	—	5	11	6,940	32,946,680	44.0
Eade-Opobo South, 1974	—	4	6	6,889	14,183,795	44.0
Ibigwe	—	—	2	—	—	—

Name of field, discovery date	Depth, ft.	No. of wells		1986 average b/d	Production Cumulative to Dec 31, 1986 bbl	*API gravity
		Producing	Total			
Korokoro	—	6	8	4,121	18,137,585	34.3
Otamini	—	4	5	2,100	13,033,548	21.8
Ugada	—	1	1	69	994,393	—
Ahia	—	7	13	4,383	81,988,746	38.2
Akpor	—	1	3	138	1,795,146	27.5
Alakiri	—	5	15	4,331	60,674,129	38.2
Assa	—	—	2	—	—	20.7
Egbema West	—	5	17	6,185	75,057,068	42.2
Ebubu	—	3	8	218	18,606,369	22.2
Egbema	—	6	7	5,800	49,619,583	35.5
Cesw-Nun River, 1960	—	3	6	3,406	29,703,607	39.0
Cesw-Etelebou, 1971	12,000	5	9	11,011	114,374,821	33.0
Cesw-Kolo Creek, 1960	12,000	11	25	18,508	115,956,605	42.0
Cesw-Diebu Creek, 1966	—	10	12	12,176	98,597,774	43.0
Phl-Isimiri, 1964	5,900-11,000	3	6	1,798	36,562,113	28.8
Phl-Onne, 1965	10,384	3	3	872	8,680,261	29.0
Phl-Obigbo-North, 1963	6,500-10,000	25	41	14,884	165,400,569	22.0
Phl-Ajokpori, 1967	—	2	2	973	4,800,196	29.0
Phl-Agbada, 1960	8,000-12,000	22	45	19,233	165,277,346	32.1
Phl-Akuba, 1967	—	1	1	356	3,949,170	29.0
Cesw-Adibawa, 1967	11,950	5	23	8,501	66,782,991	26.0
Cesw-Adibawa NE, 1973	—	1	3	2,270	12,501,251	26.0
Cesw-Ubie, 1961	14,380	2	5	4,373	28,638,766	28.0
Phl-Obeakpu, 1975	—	2	4	3,504	14,602,796	45.0
Cosw-Nembe Creek, 1973	—	28	36	79,796	171,472,502	35.0
Phs-Akaso, 1979	—	1	1	1,540	2,327,374	30.0
Bugama Creek	—	1	6	226	12,654,206	43.0
Kalaekule	—	2	5	1,227	447,856	39.6

Table A.7a (cont.)

Name of field, discovery date	Depth, ft.	No. of wells Producing	Total	1986 average b/d	Production Cumulative to Dec 31, 1986 bbl	*API gravity
Krakama	–	1	10	632	16,737,788	23.8
Odeama Creek	–	3	4	13,036	9,987,094	33.3
Tai	–	2	2	573	4,471,587	37.4
TEXACO CHEVRON *Pennington, 1965	5,000-10,400	2	3	2,429	23,654,492	38.2
*Middleton, 1972	5,000-7,000	4	5	3,105	13,952,875	36.6
*North Apoi, 1973	4,000-8,100	23	36	36,023	139,244,734	35.8
*Funiwa, 1978	5,000-7,000	21	32	23,395	27,703,650	38.2
*Sengana, 1967	–	1	1	357	663,682	46.7
TOTAL		1,253	2,151	1,467,542	11,344,561,207	

Source: *International Petroleum Encyclopedia, vol. 21* (Tulsa, OK: Penwell, 1988).

Table A.7b

Single Point Mooring

Year	Port/Field	Owner	Contractor	Maximum Vessel Size	Hose Size System	Data Dept.
1976	Lagos	Nidogas	IMODCO	2,000	1-3" & 1-4"/CALM	13
1968	Escravos	Gulf	IMODCO	100,000	1-16"/CALM	70
1968	Forcados	Shell	SBM	210,000	1-20"/CALM	83
1968	Forcados	Shell	SBM	210,000	1-24"/CALM	83
1971	Qua Iboe	Mobil	IMODCO	255,000	2-24"/CALM	90
1971	Forcados	Shell	SBM	313,000	1-24"/CALM	91
1971	Bonny	Shell	SBM	313,000	1-24"/CALM	91
1971	Bonny	Shell	SBM	313,000	1-24"/CALM	91
1972	Brass River	Agip	IMODCO	200,000	2-20"/CALM	96
1974	North Apoi	Texaco	SBM	50,000	2-20" & 1-12"/CALM	87
1974	North Apoi	Texaco	SBM	250,000	2-20"/CALM	93
1976	Brass River	Agip	IMODCO	250,000	2-20"/CALM	95
1977	North Apoi	Texaco	SBM	250,000	2-20"/CALM	94
1977	Escravos	Gulf	SBM	300,000	2-24"/CALM	102
1984	OPL 98 Block	Ashland	SBM	285,000	S-Y Jacket	140
1985	Bonny	Shell	Bluewater	350,000	CALM	92
1987	Brass	NAOC	SBM	N/A	CALM	N/A

Source: *International Petroleum Encyclopedia*, vol. 21 (Tulsa, OK: Penwell, 1988).

Table A.8

Substantive Production Data, 1960–87

Year	thousand barrels/day	million tons/year
1960	17.3	0.9
1965	272.2	13.6
1970	1,083.3	56.9
1979	2,303.0	114.7
1980	2,057.0	102.4
1981	1,369.0	68.2
1982	1,324.0	65.9
1983	1,232.0	61.4
1984	1,414.0	70.4
1985	1,445.5	72.0
1986	1,464.0	72.9
1987	1,238.6	61.7

Source: *International Petroleum Encyclopedia,* vol. 21 (Tulsa, OK: Penwell, 1988).

Table A.9

Oil Reserve Data
(billion barrels)

Year	Reserve
1960	3.0
1965	9.3
1970	20.2
1975	16.7
1980	16.7
1985	16.6
1986	16.0
1987	16.6
1988	16.0

Source: *International Petroleum Encyclopedia,* vol. 21 (Tulsa, OK: Penwell, 1988).

Table A.10

Summary of State Governments' Programs, 1981–85

Sector (1)	Total All State Govts. (2)	Anambra (3)	Bauchi (4)	Bendel (5)	Benue (6)	Borno (7)	Cross River (8)	Gongola (9)	Imo (10)	Kaduna (11)	Kano (12)
ECONOMIC											
Agriculture	2,188.931	81.720	147.869	112.980	170.250	85.120	67.257	83.257	72.350	218.600	214.400
Irrigation	245.659	1.500	59.500	–	1.750	13.300	–	6.950	–	39.800	96.000
Livestock	312.548	30.698	11.600	16.500	22.100	19.650	17.404	10.750	30.000	15.880	36.500
Forestry	173.972	6.200	2.130	21.000	14.280	20.250	6.631	8.000	3.300	8.300	29.300
Fishery	63.047	3.380	0.950	6.000	7.850	2.450	3.850	1.190	3.850	0.600	4.500
Mining & Quarrying	–	–	–	–	–	–	–	–	–	–	–
Manufacturing	1,335.661	143.850	19.500	107.000	84.550	33.850	69.405	33.220	199.970	152.900	49.500
Power	706.259	10.000	45.000	100.000	20.000	50.000	40.500	24.750	30.710	16.350	26.000
Commerce & Finance	714.207	85.900	70.080	20.000	39.422	27.900	38.003	16.360	67.000	19.091	105.700
Cooperative	147.826	11.750	10.250	9.020	8.000	18.600	6.566	7.200	10.000	12.860	3.200
Transport	3,518.695	137.060	113.100	350.000	135.450	203.790	120.043	222.850	137.000	115.900	230.000
Communications	–	–	–	–	–	–	–	–	–	–	–
Science & Technology	–	–	–	–	–	–	–	–	–	–	–
Subtotal	9,426.805	512.058	479.979	742.500	503.652	474.910	369.659	415.120	554.180	600.281	796.100
SOCIAL											
Education	4,253.020	184.200	123.684	300.000	112.040	264.100	173.789	209.574	121.520	255.574	408.300
Health	1,573.576	92.861	100.695	107.000	52.750	97.000	64.816	112.818	121.000	49.215	90.500
Information	314.964	25.500	15.900	24.000	11.260	34.660	16.075	24.180	17.000	7.878	10.697
Labor	–	–	–	–	–	–	–	197	–	–	–
Social Development	586.882	36.730	39.600	46.999	34.600	46.902	37.740	27.300	24.780	32.520	26.840
Subtotal	6,728.442	339.291	279.879	477.999	210.650	439.390	301.582	384.312	286.820	337.427	542.017
ENVIRONMENTAL DEVELOPMENT											
Water Supply	2,805.026	126.728	123.231	260.585	60.000	150.000	102.300	84.590	120.000	217.850	180.000
Sewerage, Drainage, & Refuse Disposal	482.139	3.508	2.100	65.000	15.000	12.800	15.300	4.750	7.000	2.500	26.052
Housing	1,033.552	36.000	24.000	30.000	55.000	75.120	56.000	26.000	42.500	104.670	21.000
Town & Country Planning	2,014.078	107.260	59.000	90.196	40.000	117.900	36.975	67.600	52.000	59.980	139.600
Environmental Protection	–	–	–	–	–	–	–	–	–	–	–
Subtotal	6,334.795	273.496	208.331	445.781	170.000	355.820	210.575	182.940	221.500	385.000	366.652
ADMINISTRATION											
General Admin.	1,429.897	45.533	68.050	70.000	80.900	89.180	87.828	146.310	101.500	42.290	96.158
TOTAL	23,919.939	1,170.378	1,036.239	1,736.280	965.202	1,359.300	969.644	1,128.682	1,164.000	1,364.998	1,799.927

259

Table A.10 (cont.)

Sector	Kwara (13)	Lagos (14)	Niger (15)	Ogun (16)	Ondo (17)	Oyo (18)	Plateau (19)	RiversT (20)	Sokoto (21)
ECONOMIC									
Agriculture	62.410	121.061	65.240	51.553	133.930	70.656	100.065	62.800	266.820
Irrigation	–	–	14.000	0.750	–	1.469	4.680	–	5.960
Livestock	7.450	1.809	9.050	9.550	8.201	11.266	20.820	17.200	16.120
Forestry	5.510	0.500	6.360	7.170	11.950	2.931	6.140	6.800	7.220
Fishery	0.820	1.645	0.310	1.770	2.929	12.623	4.130	3.000	1.200
Mining & Quarrying	–	–	–	–	–	–	–	–	–
Manufacturing	104.210	26.239	35.800	72.620	78.471	38.876	15.700	29.000	61.000
Power	48.000	32.300	24.430	25.000	45.550	26.869	30.000	90.800	20.000
Commerce & Finance	28.850	4.711	34.050	27.100	15.840	2.800	17.200	56.700	37.500
Cooperative	3.250	–	7.250	5.500	3.500	4.000	6.530	7.600	12.750
Transport	163.600	171.653	116.500	74.640	282.880	162.987	165.632	219.000	196.600
Communications	–	–	–	–	–	–	–	–	–
Science & Technology	–	–	–	–	–	–	–	–	–
Subtotal	424.100	359.918	312.990	275.653	583.261	334.477	370.897	492.900	625.170
SOCIAL									
Education	205.750	97.724	193.650	289.820	241.117	476.683	191.245	226.600	198.000
Health	48.790	73.616	43.550	87.435	86.300	116.290	97.420	58.320	73.200
Information	14.635	17.447	10.180	14.680	26.234	13.768	20.950	4.950	4.970
Labor	–	–	–	–	–	–	–	–	–
Social Development	26.840	16.823	19.870	13.269	28.787	23.652	29.210	35.020	22.630
Subtotal	296.015	205.610	267.250	385.204	382.438	630.393	338.825	324.890	298.800
ENVIRONMENTAL DEVELOPMENT									
Water Supply	104.000	453.790	94.700	102.631	139.090	164.871	143.160	71.700	105.800
Sewerage, Drainage, & Refuse Disposal	–	168.359	1.500	6.000	14.000	100.000	4.390	12.000	21.880
Housing	45.000	64.000	45.100	72.050	32.162	80.000	23.750	131.200	70.000
Town & Country Planning	50.980	514.773	45.200	25.900	52.724	72.133	40.714	364.400	76.800
Environmental Protection	–	–	–	–	–	–	–	–	–
Subtotal	199.980	1,200.922	186.500	206.581	237.976	417.004	212.014	579.300	274.480
ADMINISTRATION									
General Admin.	77.165	123.383	72.870	59.293	57.600	31.727	54.560	55.300	70.250
TOTAL	997.280	1,889.833	839.610	926.731	1,261.275	1,413.601	976.296	1,452.390	1,268.700

Source: Ministry of Economic Development, Central Planning Office, Lagos, Nigeria

Table A.11

Public Finance (in million naira)

Description	1976	1977	1978	1979	1980	1981	1982	1983	1984	1985*	1986*
A. Revenue											
Federally collected revenue	6,765.9	8,039.0	7,371.1	10,912.4	15,813.1	11,978.9	11,748.8	10,947.4	11,738.5	11,237.0	13,200.0
Less statutory transfers to states	1,142.8	1,572.5	1,240.0	2,044.0	2,819.8	4,910.6	4,258.4	4,156.0	3,926.6	4,443.8	5,144.0
Federal retained revenue	5,263.1	6,466.5	6,131.1	8,868.4	12,993.3	7,068.3	7,490.4	6,791.4	7,811.9	6,793.2	8,056.0
Add Special Funds											2,400.0
											10,456.0
B. Expenditure											
Recurrent Expenditure	2,672.5	2,348.1	3,427.8	3,187.2	4,781.2	5,077.5	4,859.3	5,278.8	6,072.5	5,473.0	5,635.0
Capital Expenditure	4,018.8	5,019.9	5,092.3	4,219.5	10,163.3	5,699.3	7,519.0	6,385.8	4,270.1	5,796.4	5,300.0
Total Expenditure	6,691.3	7,368.0	8,520.1	7,406.7	14,944.5	10,776.8	12,378.3	11,664.6	10,342.6	11,269.4	10,935.0
C. Balance											
Recurrent surplus(+)/deficit(−)	+2,950.5	+4,118.4	+2,703.3	+5,681.2	+8,212.1	+1,990.8	+2,630.9	+1,512.6	+1,739.4	+1,299.0	+2,421.0
Overall Surplus(+)/deficit(−)	−1,068.2	−901.5	−2,389.0	+1,469.7	−1,951.0	−3,708.5	−4,888.1	−4,873.2	−2,530.7	−4,476.2	−479.0

Source: Ministry of Economic Development, Central Planning Office, Lagos, Nigeria; Central Bank of Nigeria.

Note: * Annual budget statements

Table A.12

Nigeria: External Trade (in million naira)

Description	1976	1977	1978	1979	1980	1981	1982	1983	1984	1985[1]	1986[2]
Exports											
Crude oil	6,321.6	7,072.8	5,653.6	10,166.8	13,523.0	10,280.3	8,929.6	7,201.2	8,840.6	10,449.6	8,145.0
Non-oil	429.5	557.8	662.8	670.0	554.0	189.8	266.8	536.2	290.6	300.0	1,437.0
	6,751.1	7,630.6	6,316.4	10,836.8	14,077.0	10,470.1	9,196.4	7,737.4	9,131.2	10,749.6	9,582.0
Imports											
Oil sector	95.0	102.2	110.0	230.0	241.5	71.0	225.5	171.6	125.7	—	—
Non-oil sector	5,053.5	7,014.4	8,101.7	7,242.5	9,416.6	11,942.2	9,874.7	6,384.1	7,052.6	—	—
	5,148.5	7,166.6	8,211.7	7,472.5	9,658.1	12,013.2	10,100.2	6,555.7	7,178.3	7,852.8	6,707.4

Sources: Ministry of Economic Development, Central Planning Office, Lagos, Nigeria; Central Bank of Nigeria, Federal Office of Statistics

Notes: [1] Estimates.
[2] Budget projections.

Table A.13

Growth of Nigeria's Oil Export, 1960–81

Year	Total Exports	Change in Total Exports (%)	Crude Petroleum Exports (Nm)	Change in Crude Petroleum Exports (%)	Non-Oil Exports (N)	Change in Non-Oil Exports (%)	Share of Oil Exports in Total Exports (%)	Share of Non-Oil Exports in Total Exports (%)
1960	330.4	2.9	8.8	63.0	321.2	1.8	2.7	97.3
1961	346.9	5.1	23.1	162.5	323.8	0.008	6.7	93.3
1962	334.2	-3.7	33.5	45.0	300.7	-7.1	10.0	90.0
1963	371.5	11.2	40.4	26.6	331.1	10.1	10.9	89.1
1964	429.2	15.5	64.1	58.7	365.1	10.3	14.9	85.1
1965	536.7	15.0	136.2	112.5	400.6	9.7	25.4	74.6
1966	568.2	5.8	183.9	35.0	384.3	-4.1	32.4	67.6
1967	483.6	-14.8	144.8	-21.3	338.8	-11.8	29.9	70.1
1968	422.2	-12.7	74.0	-48.9	348.2	2.8	17.5	82.5
1969	636.3	50.7	261.9	253.9	374.4	7.5	41.2	58.8
1970	885.4	39.1	510.0	94.7	375.4	0.003	57.6	42.4
1971	1,293.3	46.1	953.0	86.4	340.3	-9.3	73.7	26.3
1972	1,434.2	10.9	1,176.2	23.4	258.0	-24.2	82.0	18.0
1973	2,277.4	58.8	1,893.5	61.0	383.9	48.8	83.1	16.9
1974	5,794.8	154.4	5,365.7	183.4	429.1	11.8	92.6	7.4
1975	4,925.5	-15.0	4,563.1	-15.0	362.4	-15.5	92.6	7.4
1976	6,751.1	37.1	6,321.6	38.5	429.5	18.5	93.6	6.4
1977	7,976.6	18.2	7,453.6	17.9	523.0	21.8	93.4	6.6
1978	6,064.4	-16.8	5,401.6	-27.5	662.8	26.7	89.1	10.9
1979	10,836.8	63.4	10,166.8	88.2	670.0	1.1	93.8	6.2
1980	14,077.0	29.9	13,523.0	33.0	554.6	-17.0	96.1	3.9
1981	10,470.1	-52.6	10,280.3	-24.0	189.8	-65.7	98.2	1.8

Source: Central Bank of Nigeria, *Annual Reports, Economic and Financial Review,* various issues.

Note: Table illustrates the rise of oil as a major export commodity of Nigeria as well as the relative decline of other revenue sources between 1960 and 1981.

Table A.14

State Budgets (in million naira)

	Total Revenue 1986	Total Revenue 1987	Expenditure (Total) 1986	Expenditure (1987)			Expenditure (1988)		
				Recurrent	Capital	Total	Recurrent	Capital	Total
Akwa Ibom	—	—	—	—	—	—	242.5	195.8	438.3
Anambra	370.8	410.2	485.2	379.8	111.3	491.1	584.6	208.5	793.1
Bauchi	208.4	249.2	228.7	221.2	69.3	290.5	389.1	120.1	509.2
Bendel	442.6	469.8	473.6	387.1	97.4	484.5	423.0	315.6	738.6
Benue	251.7	288.0	321.7	222.6	164.7	387.3	246.0	318.9	564.9
Borno	238.7	284.7	252.4	213.3	114.4	327.7	287.3	285.2	572.5
Cross River	271.4	316.5	331.4	292.2	117.2	409.4	149.4	100.8	250.2
Federal Capital Territory (Abuja)	—	—	—	—	—	—	62.7	593.6	656.3
Gongola	239.3	250.0	310.0	215.4	67.6	283.0	272.2	144.4	416.6
Imo	391.5	461.1	476.9	407.0	102.0	509.0	520.3	279.0	799.3
Kaduna	384.2	447.2	462.7	353.3	164.5	517.8	243.4	209.3	452.7
Kano	400.6	505.7	455.9	393.5	153.4	546.9	547.8	243.2	791.0
Katsina	—	—	—	—	—	—	162.7	329.4	492.1
Kwara	199.9	225.8	303.9	216.6	73.7	290.3	249.8	95.8	345.6
Lagos	601.7	680.7	935.2	492.2	445.2	937.4	1,211.3	538.7	1,750.0
Niger	146.3	173.5	173.1	172.5	30.8	203.3	183.5	173.3	356.8
Ogun	252.1	253.9	276.6	253.9	28.8	282.7	228.7	194.8	423.5
Ondo	328.6	401.5	390.7	370.2	35.2	405.4	419.1	139.6	558.7
Oyo	500.9	555.8	531.0	425.5	191.5	617.0	479.4	359.3	838.7
Plateau	190.5	260.2	210.5	259.2	1.0	260.2	291.0	88.0	379.0
Rivers	358.5	387.9	368.4	333.4	69.5	402.9	432.9	190.0	622.9
Sokoto	315.5	357.7	408.5	309.3	125.2	434.5	418.1	353.8	771.9
Total	6,093.2	6,979.4	7,396.4	5,918.2	2,162.7	8,080.9	8,044.8	5,477.1	13,521.9

Sources: *Economic Intelligence Unit Country Report*, no. 4 (1987); *Newswave*, Feb. 13, 1989, 23.

Notes:
  * Estimate by *West Africa*.
  ** Estimate by *Africa Economic Digest*.

Table A.15

Federal Budget Estimates (in million naira)

Recurrent Expenditure	1986	1987	1988	Capital Expenditure	1986	1987	1988
Cabinet office	145.3	106.0	368.7	Rural development	491.5	70.5	98.3
General staff headquarters	45.8	34.5	124.0	Agriculture (crops)	215.4	170.0	213.2
Office of the head of service	24.8	20.0	36.0	Livestock	31.1	1.2	35.5
Police	382.1	375.6	521.0	Forestry	8.0	0.4	15.8
Police affairs department	6.8	6.0	9.0	Fisheries	5.5	4.4	13.9
Agriculture, water resources, and rural development	32.9	29.2	54.3	Agricultural co-operatives	1.8	2.6	6.0
Federal audit department	5.4	5.2	6.2	Water resources	141.1	99.9	213.0
Judiciary	13.2	14.8	24.0	Communications	97.8	52.2	156.1
Communications	82.8	68.1	80.8	Industries (manufacturing and craft)	336.2	191.2	260.3
Defense	742.4	717.6	830.0	Trade	185.9	4.0	223.9
National planning	31.6	27.7	60.6	Information and culture	—	2.6	80.1
Education	209.0	198.4	302.3	Social development, youth and sports	4.6	3.3	46.5
Federal capital territory	20.3	14.0	15.9	Health	81.2	69.5	188.2
External affairs	89.5	79.6	440.6	Mining and quarrying	88.1	52.2	107.6
Finance	199.0	364.4	877.8	Power (NEPA and rural electrification)	121.0	34.8	54.5
Industries	9.6	9.3	38.8	Steel	357.8	104.3	224.5
Information and culture	148.9	111.0	146.4	Petroleum and energy	400.0	104.3	402.0
Internal affairs	190.6	220.3	262.5	Land transport system	359.2	275.8	420.1
Justice	8.3	6.7	15.3	Water transport	22.6	16.0	63.1
Employment, labor, and productivity	16.4	113.9	134.7	Air transport	36.5	21.1	64.4
Mines, power and steel	14.0	12.2	14.2	Education	442.0	139.1	281.8
Science and technology	75.2	54.3	102.3	Defense	164.7	92.1	440.0
Social development, youth, and sports	139.1	96.7	162.8	Science and technology	7.0	6.9	32.2
Trade	10.8	12.1	31.2	Environment	1.0	0.9	37.5
Transport and aviation	51.9	46.1	62.0	Housing	50.2	63.6	84.4
Petroleum resources	1.0	3.9	58.3	Surveying and mapping	8.8	3.8	118.9
Health	239.2	166.9	259.9	Employment, labor and productivity	2.5	3.6	35.9
				Prisons	3.0	5.0	11.0

Table A. 15 (cont.)

Recurrent Expenditure	1986	1987	1988
Works and housing	329.6	259.1	432.9
Contingencies	80.0	80.0	100.0
National Universities Commission	443.8	316.0	500.0
National Electoral Commission	–	–	40.0
Other commissions	9.1	7.5	14.6
Subtotal	3,828.5	3,577.1	6,127.4
Consolidated Revenue Fund charges	1,807.3	7,197.9	7,579.3
Total	5,635.8	10,775.0	13,706.7

Capital Expenditure	1986	1987	1988
Police	206.0	13.5	260.3
Federal capital territory	206.0	34.8	155.0
General administration	191.9	157.7	479.2
Directorate of food and rural development	–	400.0	500.0
Special projects	–	730.0	2,500.0
Capital Repayment (external loans)	1,166.5	938.2	522.8
Other financial obligations	79.0	174.0	241.0
Outstanding liabilities	–	700.0	500.0
External loans	500.0	1,998.0	1,506.4
Total	5,946.0	6,741.9	10,593.4

Sources: Economic Intelligence Unit Country Report, no. 4 (1987); Newswatch, Feb. 13, 1989, 23.

Table A.16

OPEC Production Data (in thousands of barrels per day)

	Population (in millions)	Current quota	Relative share (%)	Quota change	Previous quota	Relative share (%)
Saudi Arabia	11.5	4,524	24.45	181	4,343	26.16
Iraq	16.0	2,640	14.27	1,100	1,540	9.28
Iran	46.6	2,640	14.27	271	2,369	14.27
United Arab Emirates	1.4	988	5.34	40	948	5.71
Kuwait	1.4	1,037	5.61	41	996	6.00
Qatar	0.3	312	1.69	13	299	1.80
Venezuela	17.9	1,636	8.84	65	1,571	9.46
Nigeria	105.4	1,355	7.32	54	1,301	7.84
Indonesia	168.4	1,240	6.70	50	1,190	7.17
Libya	3.9	1,037	5.61	41	996	6.00
Algeria	22.8	695	3.76	28	667	4.02
Gabon	1.3	166	0.90	7	159	0.96
Ecuador	9.6	230	1.24	9	221	1.33
Total	406.7	18,500	100.0	1,900	16,600	100.0

Sources: 1. *Futures: The Magazine of Commodities Options,* February 1989, p. 16. 2. *African World News,* July-August 1988, p. 22.

Table A.17

Primary Petroleum Products Consumption and Projections in OPEC Countries

	1975	1980	1985	1990	1995	2000
Algeria	79.30	164.45	270.92	446.33	735.31	1,210.16
Ecuador	38.40	59.17	85.44	123.39	178.18	257.30
Gabon	12.40	20.59	33.13	53.49	88.46	141.20
Indonesia	253.20	385.86	549.12	914.77	1,409.48	2,168.65
Iran	383.30	657.77	1,044.98	1,660.12	2,637.38	4,189.08
Iraq	140.00	218.29	340.36	530.68	827.44	1,289.93
Kuwait	23.90	37.76	59.66	94.27	148.94	235.54
Libya	48.50	91.29	168.94	312.64	578.57	1,071.08
Nigeria	106.00	173.07	268.44	416.37	645.81	1,001.71
Qatar	5.10	8.47	13.62	22.00	36.38	58.07
Saudi Arabia	136.80	250.38	458.25	838.71	1,535.03	2,808.00
U.A.E.	25.00	41.52	66.79	107.84	179.35	284.68
Venezuela	2,113.00	322.45	505.90	793.51	1,244.61	1,953.16
Total OPEC	—	2,431.07	3.910.55	6,314.11	10,442.95	1,668.56

Source: Development Outlook, Vol. 1 no. 3 (August 1986): 35.

Bibliography

Abghari, M. H. "A Property Rights Application in Utilization of Natural Resources: The Case of Iran's Natural Gas." Ph.D. dissertation, University of Georgia, 1982.

"Action Plan for Sustainable Development of Indonesia's Marine and Coastal Resources." *Canada/Indonesia Medium-Term Planning Support Project.* Vancouver, British Columbia: Canada Department of the Environment.

Adelu, Richard. "Nigeria's Oil Resources Could Be Upgraded." *OPEC Bulletin* (June 1989).

Adenijo, Kola. "State Participation in the Nigerian Petroleum Industry." *Journal of World Trade Law,* March 1977.

African Heritage magazine. September/October 1987.

Afrifa, A. A.. *Ghana Gold.* London: Peak Cass Press, 1966.

Alberta Heritage Savings Trust Fund. *Annual Report 1986-1987.* Edmonton, Alberta, 1986.

Al-Chalabi, Fadhil J. "Problems of World Energy Transition: A Producer's Point of View." Presentation at a seminar on development theory and cooperation sponsored by OAPEC, Rome, Italy, April 1981.

— — —. "The Third Oil Shock: Causes and Implications of the Oil Price Decline of 1986." *OPEC Review.* Autumn 1988.

— — —. *OPEC at the Crossroads: Past Critique and Future Vision.* Exeter, Great Britain: Pergamon Press, 1989.

Al-Fatti, Gaadalli. "Security of Oil Supply and Demand." *OPEC Bulletin.* February 1989.

Almark, Barry and S. S. Alvarado. "Dependent Development in the Third World in the Decade of Oil." *Radical Political Economy.* Vol. 15, no. 3 (Fall 1983).

Alnasrawi, Abbas. *Finalizing Economic Development in Iran: The Role of Oil in a Middle Eastern Economy.* New York: Praeger, 1967.

Anastasia, Shkilayk. *A Poison Stronger Than Love: The Destruction of the Ojibawa Community.* New Haven: Yale University Press, 1986.

Anders, G. et al. *The Economics of Mineral Extraction.* New York: Praeger, 1980.

Anusionwu, E. C. "Management of Industrial Location Through Infrastructural Development: Nigerian Experience." *Nigerian Journal of Economic and Social Science* 20, no. 5 (November 1978).

Atlanta Constitution (May 24, 1987).

Awobajo, S. A. "Oil Spillage in Nigeria: 1976–1980." *Proceedings of the 1981 International Seminar.* Lagos, Nigeria: NNPC, 1981.

Awolowo, Obafemi. *Autobiography of Chief Obafemi Awolowo.* Cambridge, MA: Cambridge University Press, 1960.

Ayodele, Sesan. "The Conflict of the Growth of the Nigerian Petroleum Industry and Environmental Quality." *Socioeconomic Planning Science,* vol. 19, no. 5 (1985).

Azikiwe, Nnamdi. *Renascent Africa.* New York: Negro Universities Press, 1969.

Azubuike, L. A. "The Role of the Mining Industry in the Economic Development of the Less Developed Countries: The Case of Zaire." Master's thesis, Atlanta University, 1985.

Babangida, Ibrahim. "Government Unfolds Budget of Development Sustenance." *The Guardian* (January 1, 1990).

Baker, J. M. *Impact of Petroleum Industry on Mangrove Ecology.* Lagos, Nigeria: NNPC Occasional Papers, 1979.

Balabkins, Nicholas. "Industrialization and Economic Development: Nigerian Experience in Contemporary Studies in Economic and Financial Analysis." *JAL Press* (London). Vol. 33, 1982.

– – –. "Factors Which Have Influenced Nigerian Industrial Development." *Rivisita Internationale Di Scienze Economiche e Commerciali.* Vol. 35 (January 1988): 34.

Barbone, L. M. "The Corporation's Liability in Criminal Law: Systematic and Procedural Policy Choices Constituting a Reckless Disregard for Human Life." *Criminal Justice Quarterly.* Vol. 9, no. 3 (Fall 1985).

Bar-El, Raphael et al. *Patterns of Change in Developing Rural Regions.* Boulder, CO: Westview Press, 1987.

Baril, Raymond G. "Community Impact Management: Models for Compensation." A paper presented at the Annual Conference of the Canadian Nuclear Society. Montreal, Quebec, June 1983.

Bauer, P. T. Industrialization and Development: The Nigerian Experience in Reality and Rhetoric. London: Weisen and Nicholson, 1984.

Benjamin, N., and S. Devarajan *Oil Revenues and Economic Policy in Cameroon: Results from Computable General Equilibrium Model.* Washington, DC: World Bank Staff Working Paper no. 745, 1985.

Bersteins, Henry. *Underdevelopment and Development of the Third World Today.* Middlesex, England: Penguin Books, 1973.

Biersteker, T. J. *Distortion or Development? Contending Perspective on the Multinational Corporation.* Cambridge, MA: MIT Press, 1981.

Bock, B. et al. *The Impact of Modern Corporations.* New York: Columbia University Press, 1984.

Bogart, Carrol. "Autarky: A New Challenge. A Special Report on the Soviet Union." *Newsweek* (June 4, 1990).

Bornschier, V. *Multinationals in the World Economy and National Development.* Butten no. 32. Zurich: Soziologisches Institut der Universtat, 1978.

Box, George P. and G. M. Jenkins. *Time Series Analysis: Forecasting Control.* Revised edn. San Francisco: Holden-Day, 1976.

Briggs, Comfort A. "Fiscal Federalism in Nigeria Through the Second Constitutional Government: A Study of Political Influence on Revenue Allocation." PhD dissertation, George Washington University, 1988.

Buckley, James L. "Ecology and the Economy: The Problem of Coexistence." *Adress Imprimis.* Vol. 9 (February 1980).

Buer, P. T. *Ecclesiastical Economics in Industrialization and Economic Development.* London: Warden and Nicholson, 1984.

Bunker, S. *Extractive Economies: The Underdevelopment of the Amazon.* Urbana, IL: University of Illinois Press, 1985.

Butt, Gerald. "Iraqi Invasion Sparks Troubled World Response." *The Chrisitan Science Monitor* (August 3, 1990).

Campbell, D., and T. D. Cook. *Quasi Experimentation and Design and Analysis Issues for Field Settings.* Chicago: Rand McNally, 1979.

Carpenter, R. A. *Natural Systems for Development.* New York: Macmillan Press, 1983.

Central Bank of Nigeria. *Report.* Central Bank Publications, Lagos, Nigeria, 1981.

Chike, Ezimora. "Human Factor: Main Cause of Oil Spillage?" *The Guardian.* November 5, 1983.

Chinweizu. "Western Economic Order: The Plunder of Africa." *First World Magazine* (Winter 1977).

– – –. "Rise and Fall of Lootocrazy." *Third World Magazine* (February 1984).

Chouri, Nazli. *International Politics of Energy Interdependence.* Lexington, MA: D. C. Heath, 1986.

Cochran, Stuart, and J. Struthers. "Nigerian Oil Policies: Some International Constraints." *Journal of Energy and Development*. Vol. 8 (Spring 1983).

Collier, P. *Oil and Inequalities in Rural Nigeria*. Geneva, Switzerland: International Labor Office, 1978.

— — —. "Oil Shocks and Food Security in Nigeria." *International Labor Review* (November/December 1988).

Congar, Richard. "Estimation of Production Lost by Small Scale Independent Fishing as a Result of the Amoco *Cadiz* Oil Spill." *The Cost of Oil Spills*. Studies presented to the Organization for Economic Cooperation and Development. Paris, 1982.

Cook, T. D. and Campbell. *Quasi Experimentation and Design and Analysis Issues for Field Settings*. Chicago: Rand McNally, 1979.

Copp, J. "Social Impacts of Oil and Gas Developments." Center for Energy and Mineral Resources. Texas A&M University, College Station, 1984.

Country Profile: Nigeria. Washington, DC: U.S. Government Press, 1982.

Cutler, Tom. "Oil's Essential Role in War and Strategic Planning for Energy Security." *Petroleum Economist* (1989)

Dell, Sidney. "Basic Needs or Comprehensive Development: Should the UNDP Have a Development Strategy?" *World Development*. Vol. 9.

Development Outlook. Vols. 1 and 3. (Lagos, Nigeria, August 1986).

Dorian, P. and D. Fridley. *China's Energy and Mineral Industry*. Boulder, CO: Westview Press, 1988.

Dumont, Rene. *Socialism and Development*. London: Andre Deutsch, 1983.

Dundley, B. *An Introduction to Nigerian Government and Politics*. Bloomington, IN: Indiana University Press, 1982.

Ebare, Simon. "Oil Spillage Areas Deserve More Aid." *Sunday Times* (Port Harcourt, Nigeria, July 27, 1980.

Economic and Social Bulletin. Lagos, Nigeria: Federal Office of Statistics , 1985.

Economic Development in the Third World. New York: Longman Publishers, 1985.

Edelstein, M. "A Framework for Examining the Psychosocial Impacts of Toxic Exposure in Less Developed Countries." Unpublished manuscript, School of Social Sciences and Human Services and the Institute for Environmental Studies, Ramapo College of New Jersey, 1987.

Egbogha, E. O. Oronsaye. *Nigerian Oil's Future Prospects Seen Keyed to Government Policies.* Nigeria: University of Benin, 1979.

Emembolu, Gregory. "Petroleum and the Development of a Dual Economy: The Nigerian Example." Unpublished Ph.D. dissertation, University of Colorado, 1975.

– – –. "Future Prospects and the Role of Oil in Nigeria's Development." *Journal of Energy and Development.* Vol. 1 (August 1975).

Employment Growth and Basic Needs: A One World Problem. Geneva, Switzerland: International Labor Office, 1976.

"Environment and Economics." International OECD Conference on Environment and Economics, Paris, June 1, 1984.

Environmental Policy and Technical Change. Paris: OECD, 1985.

Erc, Robertson. "Oil Prices to Reach $27 by 1994." *OPEC Bulletin* (March 1988).

Fair, T. J. D. "Nigerian Unbalanced Development: Urban Growth and Rural Stagnation." *Africa Insight.* Vol. 14, no. 4 (1984).

Fajani, Olufemi. "Trade and Growth: Nigerian Experience." *World Development* (January 1979).

Federal Ministry of Information, Lagos, Nigeria, 1982.

Federal Office of Statistics. *Social Indicators Report.* 1985.

Federal Republic of Nigeria. An Address to the Nation on the 1984 Budget by Major General M. Buhari, head of the Federal Military Government. Washington, DC: Nigeria Information Services, 1984.

———. *Nigeria 1983.* Lagos, Nigeria: Department of Information, Executive Office of the President.

Federal Views on the Political Bureau Report. *National Concord Newspaper.* Lagos, Nigeria: Concord Press, August 11, 1987.

Forje, John W. "Modernization, Development, and Alien Penetration." *Journal of African Studies.* Vol. 2, no. 3 (Fall 1984).

Frank, Lawrence P. "Two Responses to the Oil Boom: Iranian and Nigerian Politics After 1973." *Comparative Politics* (April 16, 1984).

Freeman, R. et al. "Measuring the Impact of the Ixtoc Oil Spill on the Visitation at Three Texas Public Coastal Parks." *Coastal Zone Management Journal.* Vol. 12, no. 2 (1985).

Fubara, B. "The Ethics of Nigeria's Proposed Withdrawal from OPEC." *Journal of Business Ethics.* Vol. 5, no. 4 (August 1986).

———. "Targeting Strategy for Technological Acquisition in Sub-Saharan Oil Exporting States of Africa: Nigerian Experience." *Journal of Business Ethics.* Vol. 5, no. 5 (1986).

Gelb, Alan. *Oil Windfalls: Blessing or Curse?* New York: Oxford University Press, 1988.

Girling, Robert. *West African Oil Bonanza Brings New Wind of Change.* London: South Publication, 1983.

Government of Nigeria. *Facts and Figures About Nigeria.* Lagos, Nigeria: Federal Office of Statistics, 1986.

———. *Handbook of Nigeria and Our Heritage.* Lagos, Nigeria: Department of Information, 1953.

Grigalunas, Thomas A. "The Geographic Distribution of Economic Costs of Oil Spills: A Case Study of Amoco *Cadiz* in Assessing the Risk of Accidental Oil Spills." *OECD Report.* Paris, 1982.

Haas, John. *Corporate Social Responsibilitiy in a Changing Society.* New York: Theo Gaus and Sons, 1973.

Haas, Siner. "Dualism Revisited." *Journal of Development Studies.* Vol. 7, no. 1. (1979).

Haberler, Gottfreid. "International Trade and Economic Growth" in *Economics of Trade and Development.* James Thebberge, ed. New York: John Wiley and Sons, 1958.

Hackett, Paul. "Nigeria: Economy." *Africa South of the Sahara, 1990.* 19th ed. London: Europa Publications, 1989.

Hakiman, Hassan. "The Impact of the 1970s Oil Boom on Iran Agriculture." *Journal of Peasant Studies.* Vol. 15 (January 1988).

Hay, John R. et al. *Sociology of National Development: Theories and Issues in Third World Urbanization.* New York: Methuen Press, 1977.

Hazards of Oil Exploration in Bendel State. Benin: Bendel State Ministry, Governors Office, 1981.

Hills, Peter, and Paddy Bowie. *China and Malaysia: Social and Economic Effects of Petroleum Development.* Geneva, Switzerland: International Labor Organization, 1987.

Hogsbon, Susan. "Oil Exploration: Problems for Developing Countries." *Petroleum Economist.* Vol. 52 (July 1985) 23-25.

Holy Bible. New York: Thomas Nelson, 1982.

Hoole, W. F. *Evaluation: Research and Development Activities.* Beverly Hills, CA: Sage Publication, 1978.

Horwich, George, and David Leo Weimer. *Responding to International Oil Crises.* Washington, DC: American Enterprise Institute for Policy Research, 1984.

Hurewitz, J. C. *Oil, the Arab-Israel Dispute and Industrial World.* Boulder, CO: Westview Special Studies on the Middle East, 1976.

Hyman, David. *Public Finance (Intergovernmental Fiscal Relations).* New York: Dryden Press, 1987.

Hymer, Stephen. "The Multinational Corporation and the Law of Uneven Development." In Jagdish N. Bhagvati, ed., *Economics and World Order: From 1970s to 1990s.* London: Macmillan, 1972.

Igbozurike, Martin. *Problem-Generating Structures in Nigeria's Rural Development.* Uppsala: Scandinavian Institute of African Studies, 1976.

Igweonwu, C. "A Theoretical Perspective on Negotiations with Reference to the International Oil Industry." *OPEC Review.* Vol. 11, no. 2 (Summer, 1988).

Ikein, A. "The Impact of Oil Industry on the Indigenous Population in the Oil Producing Areas of Nigeria As Measured by Ecological Factors." Ph.D dissertation, Atlanta University, Atlanta, Georgia, 1988.

Ikpah, A. "Oil and Gas Industry and Environmental Pollution: Application of Systems Reliability Analysis for the Evaluation of the Status of Environmental Pollution Control in Nigerian Petroleum Industry." Ph.D. dissertation, University of Texas at Dallas, 1981.

Ikporukpo, C. "Management of Oil Pollution of Natural Resources in Nigeria." *Journal of Environmental Management.* Vol. 20, no. 1 (1985).

Imevbore, A. M. A. et al. *Proceedings of the 1981 International Seminar.* Lagos, Nigeria: NNPC, 1981.

International Petroleum Encyclopedia. Tulsa, OK: Penwell, 1988.

Iwayemi, Akins. "Nigeria's Internal Petroleum Problems, Perspective and Choices." *Energy Journal.* Vol. 5 (October 1984).

Jenkins, Gilbert. *Oil Economists Handbook.* London: Applied Science Publishers, 1977.

Journal of Energy and Natural Resources Law. Vol. 5, no. 4 (1987).

Kadhim, Al-Eyd A. *Oil Revenues and Accelerated Growth: Absorptive Capacity in Iraq.* New York: Praeger, 1979.

Kassim-Momodu, Momodu. "Nigeria's Transfer of Technology." *Journal of World Trade Law.* Vol. 22, no. 4 (August 1988).

− − −. "The Duration of Oil Mining Leases in Nigeria." *Journal of Energy and Natural Resources Law.* Vol. 6, no. 2 (1988).

Kates, R. W. et al. *Perilous Progress: Managing the Hazards of Technology.* Boulder, CO: Westview Press, 1985.

Kemp, Alexander. *Petroleum Rent Collection Around the World.* Halifax, Canada: Institute of Research in Public Policy, 1987.

Koyonda, Johnson. "Oil Spillage Problems! Answer Lies in Building Permanent Settlements." *Sunday Tide,* July 27, 1980.

Kumar, Krishna. "Transnational Enterprises: Their Impact on the Third World Societies and Cultures." *Westview Studies in Social and Economic Development.* Krishna Kumar, ed. Boulder, CO: Westview Press, 1980.

Lax, Howard. *States and Companies: Political Risks in the International Oil Industry.* New York: Praeger, 1988.

Leistritz, L., and B. L. Ekstrom. *Social Impact Assessment and Management: An Annotated Bibliography.* New York: Garland Publishing, 1986.

Leistritz, L., and R. Chase. "Socioeconomic Impact Assessment of Onshore Petroleum Development: A Conceptual Consideration and Case Study." Paper presented at the Second International Conference on Oil and Environment, Halifax, Nova Scotia, August 16-19, 1982.

− − −. "Socioeconomic Impact Monitoring Systems: A Review and Evaluation." *Journal of Environmental Management.* Vol. 15 (1982).

Lewis, A. W. *Economic Development with Unlimited Supply of Labour.* Manchester, England: Manchester School, 1954.

Linden, Henry. "World Oil − An Essay on its Spectacular 120-Year Rise (1859–1979), Recent Decline, and Uncertain Future," *Journal of Energy Systems and Policy.* Vol. 11, no. 2 (1987–88).

Livingstone, A. *Social Policy in Developing Countries.* London: Humanities Press, 1969.

Lubeck, Paul. "Nigeria: A Political Economy." *Africa Today.* Vol. 24, no. 4 (October, 1977).

Lukman, Rilwanu. "The Energy Outlook: Possible Strategies for Oil Producers and Consumers." *OPEC Bulletin.* September 1988.

———. "Nigeria's Outlook on International Cooperation for a Stable Oil Market." *OPEC Bulletin.* October 1988.

———. "OPEC President Stresses Need to Restore Oil Market Certainty." *OPEC Bulletin.* November/December 1988.

Mabro, Robert. *OPEC and the World Oil Market: The Genesis of the 1986 Price Crisis.* New York: Oxford University Press, 1986.

Macpherson, Stewart et al. *Comparative Social Policy and the Third World.* New York: St. Martins Press, 1987.

Madunagu, Edwin. *Nigeria: The Economy and the People.* London: New Beacon Books, 1984.

Maitra, Priyatosh. *Population, Technology and Development.* London: Gower Publications, 1986.

Markandya, A. and M. Pemberton, "Economic Policy with Fluctuating Oil Revenues." *OPEC Review.* Spring 1988.

Mathews, William H. *Man's Impact on the Global Environment: Assessment and Recommendations for Action.* Cambridge: MIT Press, 1970.

McCann, Kevin. "OPEC Policy and the Future of Oil." *OPEC Bulletin.* October 1988.

McLin, Jon. "Petroleum Price Roller Coaster: Some Social and Economic Effects on Producing States." *International Labor Review.* Vol. 127, no. 4 (1988).

Midgley, James et al. *Community Participation: Social Development and the State.* New York: Methuen Publication, 1986.

Moore, R. R. "The Impact of Oil Industry in West Texas." Ph.D. dissertation, Texas Technological College, 1965.

Moore, Wiber. *The Impact of Industry.* Englewood Cliffs, NJ: Prentice Hall, 1965.

Munkirs, J. R. and J. T. Knoedler. "Petroleum Producing and Consuming Countries." *Journal of Economic Issues*. Volume 22, no. 1 (March 1988).

Murdock, S., and L. Leistritz. *Socioeconomic Impact of Resource Development: Methods of Assessment*. Boulder, CO: Westview Press, 1981.

Muruako, D. "OPEC Population vs. Oil Reserves." *African World News* (July/August 1988).

Myrdal, Gunnar. *The Challenge of Wealth and Poverty, Part I*. New York: Pantheon, 1979.

Nafziger, Wayne. *Inequality in Africa*. New York: Cambridge University Press, 1988.

Nash, A. E. K. *Oil Pollution and Public Interest*. Berkeley, CA: University of California, Institute of Governmental Studies, 1977.

Nazli, Chouri. *International Politics of Energy Interdependence*. Lexington, MA: D. C. Heath, 1976.

Nelson, D. *Country Profile: Nigeria*. Washington, DC: U.S. Government Press, 1982.

"Nigeria." OPEC Member Country Profile Report. May, 1983.

"Nigeria: Africa's Oil Giant Comes to Terms with Austerity." *Financial Times* (London), Section 3, November 29, 1982.

"Nigeria: NNPC Background and Role in Nigerian Oil Industry." *OPEC Bulletin*. Vol. 16. (July–August 1985).

"Nigeria Pushes Energy Plan." *New York Times*, September 17, 1979.

"Nigeria: The New Government is Clamping Down on Industry Corruption and Illegal Sales of Crude and Products." *Petroleum Intelligence Weekly*. Vol. 23, No. 9 (February 27, 1984).

"Nigeria: The Next Phase of Development." *Petroleum Economist*. Vol. 45 (November 1978).

"Nigeria Will Fully Enforce the Findings of Tribunal Investigation of the Country's Oil Industry." *Platts Oilgram News Service*. August 14, 1980.

Nigerian Standard newspaper. May 7, 1982.

"Nigeria's Economic Problems." *African Heritage Magazine.* (September–October 1987).

Nijkamp, Peter. *Theory and Application of Environmental Economics.* New York: North Holland Press, 1977.

Nkrumah, Kwame. *Neocolonialism: The Last Stage of Imperialism.* London: Thomas Nelson and Sons, Ltd., 1965.

Nnoli, O. *Path to Nigerian Development.* Dakar, Senegal: Codesria Book Series, 1981.

Nore, Petter. *Oil and Class Struggle.* London: Zed Press, 1981.

Nwogu, E. I. "Law and Environment in the Nigerian Oil Industry." *Earth Law Journal* (1985).

Nwokedi, J. "Nigeria's Oil Business." In *Nigerian Handbook.* Lagos, Nigeria: Patike Communications, 1985.

Obidake, Yeri. "The Impact of Nigerian Petroleum Industry on the Transportation Pattern." Unpublished manuscript, Syracuse University, New York, 1982.

Ochola, Samuel A. *Minerals in African Underdevelopment.* London: London Viller Press, 1975.

Odell, Peter R. *Oil and World Power: Background to Oil Crisis.* Middlesex, England: Penguin Books, 1970.

Odofin, Dare. "The Impact of Multinational Oil Corporations on Nigeria's Economic Growth: Theoretical and Empirical Explorations." Ph.D. dissertation, American University, Washington, DC, 1979.

Odogwu, E. C. "Focal Point Environmental Affairs: Shell Petroleum Development Company of Nigeria in Petroleum Industry and Nigerian Environment." *Proceedings of the 1981 International Seminar.* Lagos, Nigeria: NNPC, 1981.

Offomey, J. K. "The Oil Industry in Nigeria." Lecture given at the Nigerian Institute of International Affairs, July 13, 1973.

Ogbonna, O. "The Geographic Consequences of Petroleum in Nigeria with Special Reference to Rivers State." Ph.D. dissertation, University of California, 1979.

"Oil and Related Problems for Producing Regions." UNRISD Research Note no. 7. Geneva, 1985.

Oil Spill Bulletin. Aberdeen, United Kingdom (December 1983).

Ojo, Ade. "International Financing of Energy Resources." *OPEC Bulletin.* Vol. 11 (June 1980): 18–43.

Okogu, B. E. "The Outlook for Nigerian Oil: 1985–2000." *African Review* (December 1986).

Olayiwola, P. *Petroleum and Structural Change in a Developing Country: The Case of Nigeria.* New York: Praeger, 1984.

Olorunfemi, M.A. "Managing Nigeria's Petroleum Resources." *OPEC Bulletin.* (December–January, 1986).

Olusi, O. S. "Nigerian Oil Industry and the Environment." *Proceedings of the 1981 International Seminar.* Lagos, Nigeria: NNPC, 1981.

Omorogbe, Yinka. "The Legal Framework for Production of Petroleum in Nigeria." *Journal of Energy and Natural Resources Law.* Vol. 5, no. 4 (1987).

Onoh, J.K. *The Nigerian Oil Economy: From Prosperity to Glut.* New York: St. Martin's Press, 1983.

Onibokun, A.G. *Environmental Pollution in Nigeria: Guidelines for Action.* Ibadan, Nigeria: Nigerian Institute of Social and Economic Research, 1986.

"OPEC: A Bloom and Burst Saga." *Development Outlook.* Vol. 1, no. 3 (August 1986).

Organization for Economic Cooperation and Development. "Methodological Guidelines for Technology Assessment." *OECD Report.* Paris, 1975.

– – –. "Oil Spillage Incidents." *OECD Report.* Paris, 1977.

– – –. "Social Assessment of Technology: Review of Selected Studies." *OECD Report.* Paris, 1978.

– – –. "Assessing the Risk of Accidental Oil Spills in OECD Member Countries." *OECD Report.* Paris, 1982.

Osai Sai, Franklin E. "Environmental Implications of Toxic Wastes and Dumping in Underdeveloped Countries." Paper presented at the Institute of International Studies, Berkeley, California, October 19, 1988.

Ostheimer, J. M. *Nigerian Politics.* New York: Harper and Row, 1973.

Osuntokun, Jide. "Oil and Nigerian Development." *Development Outlook.* Vol. 1, no. 3 (August 1986).

Oteri, A. U. "A Study of the Effects of Oil Spills on Ground Water." *Proceedings of the 1981 International Seminar.* Lagos, Nigeria: NNPC, 1981.

Oyebanji, J. O. "Identifying the Distressed Areas: An Integrated Multivariate Approach." *Socioeconomic Planning Science.* Vol. 18, no. 1 (1984).

Palinkas, L. et al. *System Approach to Social Impact Assessment: Two Alaskan Case Studies.* Boulder, CO: Westview Press, 1985.

Parhizgari, Ali M. "Optimum Depletion of Oil Resources in a Developing Country." *Energy Journal.* Vol. 8, no. 3 (July 1987).

Pearson. C. *Multinational Corporations, Environment, and the Third World.* Durham, NC: Duke University Press, 1987.

Pearson, S. *Petroleum and the Nigerian Economy.* Stanford: Stanford University Press, 1970.

Petroleum Intelligence Weekly. July 7, 1980.

Pindyck, R. S. and Rubenfeld, D. L. *Econometric Models and Economic Forecast.* New York: McGraw Hill, 1981.

Prast, W. G. "The Role of Host Governments in International Petroleum Industry." Ph.D. dissertation, Pennsylvania University, 1964.

Proceedings of the 1983 International Seminar. Lagos, Nigeria: NNPC, 1983.

Public Affairs Information Systems. Vol. 75, no. 6 (March 1989).

Quinlan, Martin. "Nigeria: The Next Phase of Development." *Petroleum Economist.* Vol. 45, no. 11 (November 1978).

― ― ―. "Nigerian Oil Policy Under the Generals Since December 1983." *Petroleum Economist.* Vol. 51 (February 1984).

― ― ―. "Nigeria's Tough Policy Boosts Revenue." *Petroleum Economist.* Vol. 52 (March, 1985): 81-84.

Randell, Laura. *Political Economy of Venezuelan Oil.* New York: Praeger, 1987.

Rankine, Nigel. "Oil and Development: The Case of Africa." *Barclays Review* (May 1980).

Rawls, John. *A Theory of Justice.* Cambridge, MA: Harvard University Press, 1971.

Redcliff, M. "Sustainable Development: Exploring the Contradictions." *Journal of Development Studies.* Vol. 25, no. 1 (October 1988).

Redelfs, Manfred. "Citizens' Participation in Technology Assessment Practice at the Congressional Office of Technological Assessment." *Impact Assessment Bulletin.* Vol. 6, no. 1 (1988).

Report of the Presidential Commission on Revenue Allocation: *Main Report, Vol. 1.* Lagos, Nigeria: Federal Government Press, 1980.

Richard, Fred. "Nigeria Pours Trouble on Oil Waters." *African Business* (December 1984).

Roberto, S. "The Impact of Oil Industry in Mexico." *Third World Planning Review.* Vol. 5, no. 1 (February 1983).

Robinson, Colin and Eileen Marshall. "Oil's Contribution to U.K. Self-Sufficiency." London: Policy Studies Institute and the Royal Institute of International Affairs, 1984.

Rogers, E. M. et al. *Social Change in Rural Societies,* 3rd edn. Englewood Cliffs, NJ: Prentice Hall, 1988.

Saad, Jafar M. "OPEC Oil Production and Pricing Policies." *OPEC Bulletin* (April 1988).

Sanchez, Roberto. "The Impact of Oil Industry in Mexico." *Third World Planning Review*. Vol. 5, no. 1 (February 1983).

Schatzl, Lott. *Petroleum in the Nigerian Economy.* Ibadan, Nigeria: University of Ibadan, 1969.

Scott, David Clark. "Antarctic Oil Spill Adds Fresh Fuel to Anti-Mining Campaign." *Christian Science Monitor* (February 8, 1989).

Seers, Dudley. "The Meaning of Economic Development." *International Development Review.* Vol. 11, no. 4 (December 1969).

Shapiro, Dan. *Social Impact of Oil Industry in Scotland.* Hart, England: Gower Publication, 1980.

"Sheikhs of Black Africa: Nigerian Oil Industry and the Economy." *Economist.* Vol. 256 (August 1975).

Shkilayk, Anastasia M. *A Poison Stronger Than Love: The Destruction of the Ojibwa Community.* New Haven: Yale University Press, 1986.

Sierra, Sanchez G. "Latin American Energy Organization." *OPEC Bulletin.* September 1989.

Singh, Ram D. "The Multinational's Economic Penetration, Growth, Industrial Output, and Domestic Savings in Developing Countries: Another Look." *Journal of Developmental Studies.* Vol. 25, no. 1 (October 1988).

Siqqi, Mohammed. *Economic Security in Islam.* Lahore, Pakistan: Kazi Publications, 1939.

Sohn, Ira. "External Debt and Oil Prices: Some Prospects for Oil Exporting Developing Countries." *Energy Policy* (October 1987).

Southern Economic Journal. Vol. 48, no. 4 (1982).

Spash, O. L. and Ralph C. d'Arge. "Economic Strategies for Mitigating the Impacts of Climate Change on Future Generations." Paper presented at the 65th Annual WEA International Conference, San Diego, California, June 29-July 3, 1990.

Stevens, Christopher. "The Political Economy of Nigeria." *The Economist.* London: Cambridge University Press, 1984.

Stock, R. *Social Impact Analysis and Development of the Third World.* Boulder, CO: Westview Press, 1985.

Subroto. "Present Dynamics and Future Prospects for the Oil Market." *OPEC Bulletin.* February 1989.

Szala, Ginger. "Energy: Where the Players Stand." *Futures: The Magazine of Commodities and Options.* Vol. 15, no. 10 (October 1986).

Taher, A. H. "OPEC Developing Countries' Energy Situation." *Energy: A Global Outlook.* New York: Pergamon Press, 1982.

Tanzer, Michael. *Oil Exploration Strategies: Alternative for the Third World in Oil and Class Struggle.* P. Nore and T. Turner, eds. London: Zed Press, 1980.

"The Cost of Oil Spills: Expert Studies." OECD Seminar, November 1982, Paris.

"The Formation of the African Petroleum Producers Association." *OPEC Bulletin.* March 1989.

Third World magazine. December 1980.

Thompson, J., and A. Blevins. "Attitudes Toward Energy Development in the Northern Great Plains." *Rural Sociology.* Vol. 48, no. 1 (Spring 1983).

Tudaro, Michael. *The Meaning of Development: Economic Development of the Third World.* New York: Longman, 1981.

– – –. *The Struggle for Economic Development.* New York: Longman, 1983.

Turner, L. *Oil Companies in the International System.* London: Royal Institute of International Affairs, 1985.

Turner, Terisa. "Oil Workers and Oil Burst In Nigeria." *Africa Today.* Vol. 33, no. 4 (October, 1986).

Uduehi, Godwin. "Compensation for Ecological Disturbances and Personal Losses." *NAPETCOR Quarterly* (1986).

United Methodist Church. *The Book of Resolution of the United Methodist Church.* Nashville: United Methodist Publishing House, 1988.

United Nations. *Poverty and Self-Reliance: A Social Welfare Perspective.* Publication no. E921V-1, 1982. New York: United Nations.

United Nations Commission for Social Development. *Report on the 26th Session.* Publication no. E/CN/.5/582. New York: United Nations Economic and Social Council, 1979.

United Nations Committee for Development Planning. *Report on the 6th Session.* Publication no. /4776. New York: United Nations, 1970.

United Nations Department of Economic and Social Affairs. *Development Digest.* Vol. 12. January 1974.

United Nations Symposium. "Financing Oil Exploration in Developing Countries." April 22-27, 1985.

United Nations University Research, *Human Rights and Conflict Resolution Network Update.* Tokyo, Japan: United Nations University, June 1988.

U. S. Department of Agriculture. *Africa South of the Sahara, 1981–1982.* London: Europa Publications, 1981.

– – –. *Sub-Saharan Africa, 1982–1983.* London: Europa Publications, 1983.

Usman, Yusufu B. "Behind the Oil Smokescreen." *Nigeria Standard* newspaper (May 7, 1982).

– – –. "The 1990 Budget and Our Future." *Nigeria Homenews* (January 25-31, 1990).

Usoro, Eno. "Economic Transition from Colonial Dependency to National Development: The Nigerian Experience." *Nigerian Journal of Economic and Social Science.* (July 1982).

Uzoatu, Uzor. *This Week Newsmagazine.* Vol. 1, no. 11 (September 29, 1986).

Vernon, Raymond. *The Oil Crisis.* New York: W.W. Norton, 1976.

Voyer R., and M. Gibbons. *Technology Assessment: A Case Study of East Coast Offshore Petroleum Exploration.* Science Council of Canada. Background Study no. 30 (March 1974).

Walde, Thomas. "Third World Mineral Development in Crisis." *Journal of World Trade Law* 19, no. 1 (January/February 1985).

Walton, Richard J. *The Power of Oil.* New York: Seabury Press, 1977.

Wang, George. *The Unchanging Nature of Imperialism: Fundamentals of Political Economy.* New York: Sharpe, 1977.

Webster, David. "Impact of Oil Prices on Developing Countries." *Crown Agents Report.* Vol. 3 (1986).

West Africa. London, July 13, 1987.

West Africa. London, March 28, 1988.

West Africa. London, January 9-15, 1989.

West Africa . London, October 23-29, 1989.

Wilensky, H. L., and C. Lebeaux. *Industrial Society and Social Welfare.* New York: Free Press, 1967.

Wionzek, Muguel. *Measures of Strengthening the Negotiation Capacity of Governments in Relation with Transnational Corporations.* UN Technical Paper ST/CTC/U. New York: UN, 1979.

"Workshop Reviews Global 2000 Activities." *Ghana Today.* Vol. 1, no. 6 (1989).

World Bank staff. "Poverty, Growth, and Development." World Bank, June 1980.

— — —. "Tribal Peoples and Economic Development: Human Ecological Consideration." May 1982.

Wright, Jesse. "West Africa Learns that You Cannot Eat Oil." *Euromoney* magazine (June 1982).

Wright, Peter et al. "The Developing World to 1990: Trends and Implications for Multinational Business." *Long-Range Planning.* Vol. 15, no. 4 (1982).

Xiamin, Xia. "Energy and Mineral Development Planning Process in the People's Republic of China." *China Energy and Mineral Industries.* Boulder, CO: Westview Press, 1988.

Yamamoto, Y. "Interorganizational Coordination in Crisis: A Study of Disaster in Japan." Ph.D. dissertation, Ohio State University, 1985.

Youssef, Ibrahim. *The Future of OPEC.* Washington, DC: Middle East Institute, 1984.

Zakariya, Hassan. "Transfer of Technology Under Petroleum Development Contracts." *Journal of World Trade Law.* Vol. 16, no. 8 (1982).

— — —. "Insurance Against Political Risk of Petroleum Investment." *Energy and Natural Resources Law.* Vol. 4 (1986).

Zartman, W. *Political Economy of Nigeria.* New York: Praeger, 1983.

Index

About the Author

Augustine A. Ikein, Ph.D. (Atlanta University), also holds a Bsc. (economics) degree from the City University of New York and an MBA (finance/management) from Adelphi University, New York. He has been a professor of economics, finance, and policy studies in several U.S. institutions and is a recipient of the UNCF and Lily Foundation Fellowship Awards. He is the author of such articles as "Barriers to Balanced Growth in Developing Countries"; "Growth Models and Structural Inequalities in the Third World"; "The Impact of Petroleum on the Africans: The Case of Nigeria"; "Socioeconomic Outlook for the Year 2000: The Impact of Ideology on Minority Employment and Economic Viability"; "Should Human Reserves Take Precedence Over Oil Reserves? An Alternative to the OPEC Quota Allocation System"; "Still Oloibiri: A Profile of Nigeria's Pioneer Oil Community"; "The Differences and Similarities between the Civil Rights Movement in the United States and that in South Africa"; and "The Political and Economic Reforms in Eastern Europe and the Implications for Third World Development". Dr. Ikein is also a coauthor of *Moral Equivalent of War? A Study of Non-military Service in Nine Nations* (Greenwood Press, 1990), an international comparative study on national service policy and programs. The author has a special interest in energy development in the third world.